Interviewing and Counselling

GW00724563

To Margaret

Robert Bessell

INTERVIEWING
AND COUNSELLING

B. T. Batsford Ltd London

First published 1971
First paperback edition 1976
© Robert Bessell 1971

Printed and bound in Great Britain by
Billing & Sons Ltd,
London, Guildford & Worcester
for the publishers B. T. Batsford Ltd,
4 Fitzhardinge Street, London W1H 0AH

7134 0965 7

Contents

Preface   5

Preface to the Second Impression   9

1   The Conceptual Framework: I Range and Methods   11
*Types of Interviewing and Counselling 13, The
Purposes of Interviewing and Counselling 15, Learning
Theory 17, Methods of Counselling 17, Agency
Function 31, Roles 32*

2   The Conceptual Framework: II Principles   35
*Acceptance 36, Self-Determination 39,
Confidentiality 43*

3   Problems of Communication   50
*Distortion of Perception 55, Social Psychology and
Communication 64, Effects of Culture on
Communications 67, The Communication of Values 68*

4   Preparation for Interviewing and Counselling   70
*Reception 70, The Waiting Room 75, The Intake
Worker 77, Facilities for the Social Worker 79,
Home Visiting 82, Interviewing Away from the
Office and the Home 86, Preparation by the Social
Worker 87, Plan of the Interview 88*

5   The One-to-One Interview   92
*Advantages of the One-to-One Interview 93,
Disadvantages of the One-to-One Interview 98, Agency
Considerations 102, Beginning the Interview 104,
The Body of the Interview 107, Length and
Termination of the Interview 110*

6 Group Interviewing and Counselling   114
   Some Advantages of Group Interviewing and
   Counselling 116, Some Disadvantages of Group
   Interviewing and Counselling 121, General
   Considerations 125, Composition of the Counselling
   Group 127, The Analysis of the Group Interview 130,
   The Balance of Power in the Group 132, Interaction
   Between Groups 134

7 Matrimonial Interviewing and Counselling   136
   The Concept of Fit 137, The Conduct of the
   Marriage 139, Decision in Marriage Counselling 141,
   The Crucial Decision 145, The Task of the Social
   Worker 146, The Social Worker's Prejudices 148,
   Agency Function 149, Reconciliation 150

8 Interviewing and Counselling with Families   155
   The Sociology of the Family 167, Family Group
   Counselling and Interviewing 171

9 Case Records   177
   The Reasons for Recording 177, The Nature of
   Case Recording 182, Process Recording 192,
   Confidentiality 194

10 Teaching, Supervision and Consultation   199
    Class-room Teaching 199, Student Supervision in the
    Agency 209, Agency Supervision 214, Consultation 217

    Appendix I: Universal Declaration of Human Rights   221
    Appendix II   227
    Appendix III   232
    Appendix IV   242
    Bibliography   256
    Index   265

Preface

I have been concerned for some time about an apparently growing divergence between social work and counselling. The gap is now such that it is possible to find separate training courses in social work and counselling in different departments of the same university and practically no relationship between the two.

The best explanation I can find for this development lies in the .traditional pre-occupation of British social workers with the poorer sections of the community. Given that resources were limited and that the origins of almost all branches of social work lie in the Charity Organisation Society, this bias is not surprising. However, in recent years the urgent needs of other strata of society for non-material help with social problems and particularly problems of human relationships have brought about the growth of a number of counselling services, of which the best known are educational counselling and matrimonial counselling.

This picture of social workers dealing solely with the poor and the inadequate while counsellors mainly serve the middle class is not wholly accurate. Medical social workers in particular have always had a greater social range, which no doubt reflects the traditional social mix of the hospital, and most social workers have had experience of middle-class clients, some more than others. However, despite this blurring of the edges, the general idea is substantially true that poorer people with matrimonial problems go to the probation officer while members of the middle class go to the marriage-guidance counsellor.

All of this matters a great deal because it represents a serious misuse of scarce resources and, even more important, threatens to build into the structure of the helping agencies a divisive view of society which must be unacceptable.

It is for this reason, primarily, that I have tried to examine just what goes on between the helper and the person seeking help in a way which I hope will seem relevant both to those who call themselves social workers and those who call themselves counsellors. With these considerations in mind the terms 'social worker' and 'counsellor' are interchangeable throughout the book. I should add that there is no intention of limiting the book to professional social workers and counsellors. Like most of the other people I know who are strongly in favour of adequate professional training, I am well aware of the invaluable help which can be given by volunteers and I do not believe that their work is different in essence from that of the professional. It is rather that their range is more limited, so that, for instance, they find it more difficult to work with those with whom they are not in personal sympathy, and volunteers generally need more supervision. As I have tried to exclude social work jargon from this book altogether, as a check on my own thinking, I hope that some of the many thousands of volunteers currently engaged in social work and counselling will find the book useful to them.

I am sufficiently aware of my own limitations to know that one book is not an adequate theoretical basis on which to build a unitary approach, but I hope that it may at least be a beginning in which others will join to end a division which can only have the effect of harming those in need of help.

There is, however, a second purpose in writing this book which derives from the fact that social work theory and practice have become increasingly out of step. This problem centres around the terms social casework, social group work and community work. For the purpose of analysis, it is obviously necessary to consider social work under separate headings, but there is a pervasive idea that not only can these aspects of social work be separated in theory but that they can be practised exclusively. It is true that there is a place for specialists in the various methods, but there is, at the present time, a much more urgent need for social workers with a basic competence in all of these areas.

At a time when the influence of the family, the peer group and the community on individual behaviour is increasingly recognised, the social worker must consider the place of the individual, the family and other groups and the community as a whole in every case, if only to decide on the best way to tackle the problem.

This matter is referred to on several occasions in the book, but the overall purpose is to construct a unified approach to interviewing and counselling, whether it is with individuals, families or other groups, which will free the ordinary social worker from a total reliance on the social work method in which he happened to have been trained and instead do the best for his clients. For this reason the book has been conceived as a unity in which each chapter depends on what has gone before and it would, therefore, be unwise to pick out particular chapters. To take just one example, the reference to Kelman's theory on the nature of group influence which is given in Chapter 6 depends on the discussion of influence in the one-to-one situation in Chapter 3.

To turn to matters of detail, I have not followed the traditional practice in social work literature of referring to the social worker as 'she' and the client as 'he'. This is not, I trust, from any feelings of anti-feminism but rather because I believe that this would indicate a state of affairs which is no longer generally accurate. I have no means of knowing whether the majority of social workers are men or women, but I am sure that the profession is no longer dominated by women. On the other hand, the vast majority of medical social workers are women and for this reason it has seemed more correct to refer to the medical social worker as 'she', and the same is true for clerical assistants and receptionists.

I should perhaps explain where the material contained in appendices 2, 3 and 4 came from. The 'Mr Crawford' interview was made by Patricia Lister, one of the social work students at the University of Keele in 1969, when I was a lecturer there, as a role-playing exercise. I think it shows some of the potential of role-playing as an element in social work training. The 'client' was her fiancé, Martin Crawford, also a Keele student, in natural science, and I am glad to express my thanks to them for allowing me to use this material, particularly now that they are married.

Unlike the Mr Crawford interview, which was entirely a product of the imagination of the participants, the interviews reproduced in appendices 3 and 4 are almost entirely taken from life. It was in 1967 that I first became interested in collecting taped interviews and I wondered how I could obtain some examples of matrimonial counselling. My friend Malcolm Pearce told me of a married couple who were willing to be interviewed with a view to the material being used for teaching purposes. He also arranged for another friend, Frank Trew, who had just left the probation service, to conduct the interview. The dialogue which is reproduced is a transcript of the tape, except for minor alterations, almost all of which were made solely to obscure the identity of the participants and their families by the substitution of pronouns for proper names. The syntax is just as it was spoken and, again, I am most grateful to all the people who made these interviews possible, particularly the couple, who, for obvious reasons, have to be anonymous.

The notes at the end of most of the chapters are more a reflection of my own reading and interests than any attempt to provide a general guide to the authorities on the subjects which I discuss. The bibliography at the end is much fuller, but again it has no pretensions to being complete, as it is not possible to list all of the relevant publications without seriously disturbing the balance of the book. However, knowing the limited time which social workers and students have for reading, I think they will find plenty to occupy them.

This book would never have appeared without a lot of help from other people. I take this opportunity to acknowledge my debt to my teachers, Miss Deed at the University of Liverpool and Miss Waldron at the University of Birmingham. I hope both of them will see this book as an acknowledgment of all the trouble they took with an unruly student.

Most of the ideas were first tried out in raw form on my friends John and Jenny Dessauer, and I am grateful to them for their patience. Both Chris Andrews and Geoff Pearson undertook the thankless task of detailed criticism of the typescript, and without their assistance I would have fallen into many more errors. I should also mention the help and courtesy I have received from Patrick Connell in preparing the book for publication.

I am afraid that too many people were involved in typing the various drafts and re-writings for me to mention them all by name, but I am fully aware that without their work the book would not have been possible. In fact, my wife organised much of this between her friends and herself, and cheerfully submitted to discussions on functionalism and other recondite points at the most inopportune moments. I hope that she and all the other people who have contributed to this book will gain some pleasure from the result.

Preface to the Second Impression

Any author is obviously glad to know that there is sufficient demand for one of his books to justify a re-printing. I am particularly glad as a Director of a Social Services Department to know that the recent turmoil of the double re-organisation of the past five years has subsided sufficiently to allow social workers to concentrate again on acquiring the skills of counselling, the knowledge of which is indispensable for every social worker. It is a part of the price we have had to pay for the many advances which have been made since the Social Services Departments came into existence in 1971, that there has been an unmistakable decline in standards of counselling and until that is made good, then much of the potential of the Social Services Departments cannot be realised.

I would hope that no-one would be satisfied merely to regain lost ground and in the preface to the first printing, I expressed the hope that counselling would come to be seen as a unifying force in all the helping professions, social work is all its forms and welfare work in education, health care and the church.

In honesty, it is not possible to record much progress and one is particularly concerned to see a continuing divergence between counselling in social work and education. The administrative difficulties of unifying these services are only too apparent, but at a time of economic difficulty and great distress there is even more reason to establish the underlying unity and at least to attempt to minimise the unnecessary overlap which still persists despite all the efforts of the Seebohm Committee.

It is no contradiction to say that as well as looking forward to more evidence of the unity of counselling, one also looks forward to the development of specialist counselling skills. For a time, matrimonial counselling seemed to be making great strides, but in the last year or two, it seems to have lost its way and with a divorce rate now in excess of 120,000 a year, there could hardly be a more serious or urgent social problem.

Similarly, some of the group counselling techniques which were being so vigorously explored a decade ago are much needed now to re-inforce a faltering programme of Intermediate Treatment for youngsters in conflict with society and their own families. The development of the techniques of Family Therapy promised to shed new light on long established traditions of family casework, before they were engulfed in the tumult of the past five years. However, as well as showing the need to revive this earlier work, the experience of Social Services Departments has demonstrated the need to develop a whole series of new counselling specialities, with old people, with all types of handicapped people and with young children. It is an unacceptable anomaly that social workers have extensive responsibilities for young children and yet many social workers are incapable of communicating with them effectively. The development of a theory of counselling in community work method is also long overdue.

I suspect that whatever disruption the administrative demands of the Social Services Departments may have caused, that is not the main reason why counselling has failed to develop its range of practice despite the ever-growing demands. The more likely explanation is that so little progress has been made in developing the moral framework.

As I have pointed out in the text, counselling is a moral activity, even though it is not limited to any particular form of morality. Unfortunately, practically no work has been done in recent years in exploring the distinctive moral principles on which counselling theory is based and without strong foundations there is no prospect of erecting an edifice of any size or permanence.

I only regret my own limitations in this important area and although morality has not recently been a fashionable subject, I understand that there is a growing interest among students in moral philosophy which gives hope for the future.

For myself, all my experience since *Interviewing and Counselling* first appeared has confirmed my view of the importance of counselling in social work and I am glad to record that my wife, to whom this book is dedicated, continues to be the greatest stimulus to my thinking.

Stratford-on-Avon   May, 1976

1 The Conceptual Framework: I Range and Methods

Although the general art of interviewing and the specific techniques of counselling are the main tools of the social worker, even a cursory examination of the literature on interviewing and counselling will show that social workers have contributed comparatively only a small part of what has been written.

In most libraries, the bulk of this material is concerned with interviewing as a tool of management, particularly personnel management, and the social worker can soon become aware how much attention the business community has paid to the acquisition of interviewing skills. The inevitable conclusion is that many commercial firms are convinced that this investment is worth while, that interviewing pays, and that it is effective.

This is encouraging to the social worker who has no easy means of cost benefit analysis, but the probability is that the most expert interviewers have themselves contributed very little to the literature, although quite a lot has been written about those who practise brainwashing as a means of persuasion and whose own lives frequently depend on the success of their art. Our knowledge of these methods of interviewing comes almost entirely from the accounts of their victims, but a book such as Arthur Koestler's *Darkness at Noon*,[1] which takes a wider view, makes absorbing reading and should be sufficient to convince even the most sceptical observer of the powers for good or ill of interviewing.

It should also be acknowledged that counselling is not exclusively a social work method although, unlike interviewing, which can be used for good or ill, counselling is essentially a means of helping. Most of the work on this subject recently has been concerned with vocational guidance and school and student counselling. These developments have mostly been inspired from the United States where the school counselling system is widespread but there are now attempts to work along similar lines in Britain.

As a result, there is sometimes a confusion between counselling as a general term and its specific application in vocational guidance. In fact counselling is a very wide concept which I define as the process of helping someone to mobilise his own resources to cope with a problem which he had previously found insurmountable, which includes giving information. This is not to denigrate the work which has been done in vocational counselling, which has proved enlightening in many other fields, but it is necessary to distinguish the part from the whole and it may be that vocational counselling in schools would benefit from the wider recognition and development of other aspects of counselling.

It follows from the reference to management and brainwashing that interviewing is wider still again than counselling and in the social work context, I would define it as the interaction between people for the purpose of the interviewer obtaining information for a specific purpose to do with the person who is interviewed. In social work interviewing, the specific purpose would be the welfare of the client either directly or indirectly.

From this we can see that social work interviewing includes the processes of helping both within the interview, i.e. counselling, and externally by using the information gained in the interview for the purpose of mobilising other resources. Counselling is exclusively concerned with the helping process within the interview, the interaction of personalities for the benefit of the client. In the social work process, counselling and interviewing frequently take place together and it would be rare indeed for the social worker to attempt to arrange outside help for his client without simultaneously helping the client to sort out his problem by himself.

The indirect nature of the help given by the social worker as the result of an interview is not always immediately apparent and it is perhaps best discussed in terms of concrete examples. It is for instance, one of the duties of a probation officer to interview people who are to appear before the courts charged with serious offences, with a view to preparing a report which will guide the court as to the appropriate sentence. If the probation officer recommends custodial treatment, it may be very difficult to persuade the defendant that the interview which led to this report was for the purpose of his welfare.

Similarly, the social worker who advises that a child should be placed in care, or makes application for enforced hospital treatment, would both have the same problem, but the essence of the definition is not the immediate, or even long-term, opinion of the client, but what, in the professional opinion of the social worker, is in the interests of the client and the rest of society. Plainly, if such sweeping powers to interfere in the lives of others are claimed, it is of the greatest importance that the right to these powers should be soundly based and just as important that the medium in which the social worker interacts with his client in coming to his decision, the interview, should be clearly understood.

Happily it is only comparatively rarely that the social worker will need to act without his client's cooperation and invariably every effort should be made to reach an agreed decision, so that most social work interviewing proceeds on the basis of a partnership between client and worker. Even so, it needs to be remembered that the process is not altogether dependent on the client's consent and there are important instances when the social worker must act in contradiction to the plainly expressed wishes of his client. It hardly needs saying that with such a possibility in mind, the social worker must have clearly established in his mind the principles on which he is working and we shall need to examine these principles in some detail, as they affect every aspect of social work interviewing.

Types of Interviewing and Counselling

Until quite recently, there has been a tacit implication in many of the general texts on social casework that interviewing and counselling is almost entirely conducted in an office between a social worker and an individual client and, increasingly, this has become the dominant pattern of social casework. In the pioneering days of modern professional social work in the nineteenth century, the office interview was much less frequently used and hardly seems to fit in with what we know of Octavia Hill or Mary Richmond who did almost all their casework in the homes of their clients.

There are a number of reasons for the change of emphasis, of which perhaps the most important was the influence of the theories of dynamic psychology and particularly of psychoanalysis in which the classic model was the sequestered therapeutic session in the analyst's room between analyst and patient alone.

The nature of psychoanalytic therapy demanded these conditions so that patient and analyst could concentrate hard on their verbal and emotional interchange, undisturbed by passing events or the complications of a third person's presence. As social caseworkers learned from the dynamic psychologists about the nature of personality so they tended to copy their methods and the office interview came into vogue as a pale reflection of the psychoanalytic method.

At the same time, social workers also became aware of the amount of material which manifests itself even in the one-to-one interview and which increases quite disproportionately both to the number of people involved in the interview and their freedom to move about. If the social worker feels the need to be in control of proceedings he will obviously have more chance with one individual seated in the social worker's office than with a group of children or adolescents, or a family moving about in their own home.

Despite the attraction of the office interview for themselves, social workers have now become increasingly aware that other forms of interviewing are sometimes preferable and from time to time there has been so much enthusiasm for a particular method that its advocates have declared it to be the only form of working. Thus at different times, common interest groups and family counselling sessions have been held to have a monopoly of virtue, no doubt as a result of the extension of psychoanalytic theory to groups and the dramatic methods of some of the family therapists in the USA. However, there is now a general consensus that each method of interviewing has its advantages and disadvantages. These will be discussed in later chapters under the various headings of the one-to-one interview, groups, matrimonial work, and family group interviewing, with a view to helping social workers decide on the appropriate method for particular situations.

This decision should not be made to suit the worker's preference. It is a matter of regret that this point needs to be made about a profession one of whose basic tenets is that its work is client-centred, but both social work education and agency practice point the opposite way. It is exactly like treating the medical patient with one remedy whatever his complaint and it makes a mockery of concepts of differential diagnosis and treatment in social work. Even so, in the United States, social work education has been specifically and often exclusively in casework, or group work, or community organisation, whereas in England there has not even been that choice. It has, in recent years, generally been casework, the one-to-one interview, or nothing. This is not to argue against the value of specialisation, but specialisation must rest on the foundation of an appreciation of the range of methods available. To continue the medical analogy, a system of specialist consultants is feasible only if the general practitioners have sound all-round knowledge.

This argument should not be over-stated as, even in the ' purest ' days of social casework, most social workers were involved in quite a lot of home visiting, although too often instead of responding to the situation which they encountered in the home, they seem to have tried to force it somehow into the pattern of the office interview.

The Purposes of Interviewing and Counselling

In order to evaluate any process there needs to be an understanding of intended goals, of why one embarks on the process in the first place. In social work, although this problem has been posed often enough, it is rare to see it considered in terms of social work theory. It may be that this is because so little attention has been paid to the philosophy of social work. Instead, the problem of evaluation has almost always been seen, either overtly or by implication, in terms of the agency in which it is practised. Thus the work of the probation officer in dealing with delinquency is judged by his success in keeping his clients from breaking the law, although the crude measure of reconviction is gradually being dropped. The probation officer's matrimonial work is evaluated by the number of reconciliations he achieves, and the medical and psychiatric social workers are judged by their success in helping people to recover from physical or mental illness or, better still, preventing the illness altogether.

It is apparent that these standards are borrowed from the related professions and institutions of the law and the courts, medicine and the hospitals. To give another example, the child care officer was expected, amongst other things, to prevent families breaking up so that the children need not be received into care. The attraction of these goals is that they can, apparently, easily be represented numerically and often in money terms. At a time when statistics and cost benefit analysis are much in vogue, these are important considerations but a closer examination of the professional tasks involved reveals that these are generally false measures.

It is obvious that a probation officer who is working with a disturbed client whose family has had a criminal record for several generations cannot be said to have failed because of one further conviction. If that were the case, probation as it is now understood would be impossible if only because the law is not a fixed entity and the objectives of the probation officer are concerned with more basic, if less tangible, matters such as the harmonious relationship of the individual to the society in which he lives. Similarly metaphysical concepts of health bear only a limited relationship to hospital admission policies. It is obvious that the initiative of the individual social worker has a comparatively small effect on the percentage rate of admission to care and if the work of the medical social workers is evaluated in terms of physical health then their work with the dying is presumably pre-ordained to failure.

In practice the only satisfactory means of evaluating social work is to consider whether it is directed towards enabling the client to manage without the assistance of a social worker. This is not always an easy measure to apply and one has to recognise that there are many clients of a social worker who will need assistance all their lives. This is accepted, and in these cases the aim is for the client to achieve as much as possible by himself, again recognising that this may be very little and conversely that no one can be entirely self-sufficient, ' an island entire unto himself '. In family terms, the social worker may well be working towards the emancipation of the next generation from dependence on social work help, but always the work is client-centred and for the client's maximum self-realisation.

This general goal of the whole social work process may be applied to the individual interview. So far it has not been possible to quantify the concept numerically, although some ingenious attempts have been made. Even so, it is more helpful to the social worker seeking to improve his work to have a principle that he can apply but cannot state mathematically, than a numerical formula which is misleading.

Learning Theory

An alternative method of analysing what goes on in counselling sessions is provided by the language of learning theory in psychology. This derives largely from experimental work in animal behaviour as originated in the work of the American psychologist, J. B. Watson, and others. The great advantage of learning theory, or behaviourism as it is sometimes known, is that it distinguishes between techniques which in themselves have no moral values and the moral systems which govern their use.

Reduced to essentials, learning theory states that all behaviour, of humans as well as animals, may be considered in terms of response to stimuli and the modification of behaviour consists of the reinforcing of the desired response and the removal of responses which are judged to be undesirable.

As a tool of analysis this approach can be invaluable, as all too often the process of a counselling session becomes so complex and so involved in value judgements that there is a basic difficulty in knowing objectively what is going on. However, the great merit of learning theory, that it is independent of any value base, is also its major limitation. The social worker who undertakes counselling, constantly needs a means of making moral judgements and he has to look elsewhere than learning theory.

It is a pity that there is sometimes thought to be some fundamental opposition between learning theory and the various theories of dynamic psychology formulated by Freud and other therapists who have not been primarily concerned with the methods of natural science. It is quite often possible to analyse a sequence of events both in terms of learning theory and dynamic psychology without any inherent conflict. The difficulties of counselling are such that a social worker would be unwise to disregard any approach which contributed to his knowledge. He would also be foolish to assume that any approach contained a monopoly of truth.

Methods of Counselling

It is now becoming possible to distinguish some of the methods which have been evolved by social workers, and others who have had an instinctive talent for helping those in difficulty, although much more work needs to be done on the analysis of a process which is still imperfectly understood. It must be remembered, however, that the greatest theoretical understanding of the dynamics of counselling is no substitute for a wish to help people in trouble. Equally, the best natural helper can always increase his aptitude by understanding what he is doing more fully.

The completely mature personality is an ideal unknown to the social scientist, however interesting this concept may be in philosophical speculation. Because the interview should be concerned with the client's problems and free, so far as is possible, from those of the social worker, it is necessary that the social worker should at least be aware of his own areas of difficulty so that the bias which they cause in interviewing may be allowed for and compensatory steps taken. For example, the social worker who is having difficulties in his own marriage, or with his children, will inevitably be inclined to focus on the matrimonial or parent–child relationships of his clients whether or not they are relevant to the client's situation and to see these relationships from the bias of his position in his own family. Similarly, the social worker who is lonely will be likely to look for affection from his clients and, unless he is aware of all these tendencies, the focus of the interview may be seriously distorted.

The way in which the intending social worker is taught to recognise and discount how his own problems may interfere with his professional work of interviewing and counselling is dealt with throughout the book and particularly in Chapters 3 and 10. Our immediate concern is to stress that, in the interviewing and counselling session, the social worker is dependent upon his own personality, his professional knowledge and the aura which he has from the agency of which he is a representative. It is important that they should all be of maximum value when they are needed.

POSITIVE LISTENING

A tape-recording of many social work interviews would reveal that the worker's verbal contribution was minimal and on some occasions practically non-existent. Most social workers have had the experience of working with clients who have a sense of grievance, of being ill-used, which they need to express. For instance, in matrimonial counselling one or both of the partners may have pent-up complaints stretching over a period of years and, when the dam-wall is breached, the first requirement is to have someone to listen and understand. Simply to find someone willing to listen without wishing to criticise or change the subject is rare enough, but the social worker would always do more than this, he would always try to understand how these things had come about and what might be done to alleviate the problem.

If the client is able to tell his story coherently, then the social worker will have only to encourage him in order to maintain the flow of the interview and this is usually done by gestures such as nodding and smiling. Stated in cold print, the details of interviewing and counselling can seem artificial and mechanistic and there is indeed an element of calculation about the social worker's response but this can be justified so long as it is directed towards helping the client.

Even when the client talks freely and relevantly about his problems, the social worker still has the task of taking in and making sense of what is being conveyed to him. This is, in itself, a full-time and demanding task, but the social worker has to do much more than take in the nuances of speech. The client also conveys important messages by his facial expressions and body posture and, even though he may not say very much, the social worker needs to respond appropriately with his own facial expressions. An enlighting way to study the interaction is to watch an interview on television with the sound switched off. It is difficult to believe that all the eyebrow raising, frowning and smiling, nodding, toe-tapping, and shifting of position are the inevitable constituents of the most emotionally-neutral conversations and this activity increases markedly with a rise in tension.

Being aware of all of this, of the client's choice of subjects and the order in which he presents them, and all the problems of communication which we shall consider in detail in Chapter 3, is sometimes known as listening with the third ear, that is, listening hard not only to the words which the client is using but also to the overtones of what he is saying. It is this, combined with encouraging the client to formulate and express his worries, which is known as ' positive listening ' and constitutes the basis of interviewing and counselling. Although the social worker may not say very much, he is far from inactive, and the physical and emotional drain of listening is well known to anyone who meets a social worker socially after such a session, when at best he is likely to be mildly anti-social.

Positive listening is only one of a number of factors in counselling and interviewing, but there are situations in which it is all that is required. The fact that a social worker will take the time to listen carefully to a problem can be very comforting and may be sufficient to reassure the client so that he can again face up to difficulties which he had thought insurmountable. The client may not be aware of the process, but it is not uncommon for him to thank the social worker for his good advice when the worker has hardly said a word.

VERBALISATION

One of the ways in which the social worker will show that he has understood what the client is saying is by repeating it, possibly in a slightly different form, and this is an important difference between counselling and ordinary conversation. In a conversation, it can be extremely tiresome for one person to repeat the words of the other, as it detracts from the two-way flow. On the other hand, in the counselling situation, the client may be so anxious to make sure that his point is appreciated that he will go on repeating it until the social worker shows that he has understood by saying it himself. This is sometimes known technically as verbalising the client's emotions and can refer not only to statements which the client makes overtly but those which he makes unconsciously and by implication. For instance, one might have the situation in which the social worker is going at a faster pace than the client can cope with emotionally. In matrimonial counselling, the social worker may ask about the matrimonial relationship before the client feels happy about discussing this subject. The sequence of events might then be that the social worker asks his question and the client makes an apparently irrelevant remark, maybe commenting on the weather or some detail of the office furniture or even asking some personal question of the social worker, such as where he is going for his holidays. The social worker might briefly respond by acknowledging that it had stopped raining or that it was an attractive picture but he would probably also respond to the unspoken emotion that the interview was becoming uncomfortable by saying that it must be difficult to talk to a stranger about such matters.

REFLECTIVE COUNSELLING

The repetition of what the client says may also be used as a technique in its own right as a means of enabling the client to sort out his own problems, using the worker as a sounding-board. If the social worker comes to the conclusion that the client has sufficient resources to solve his own problem but needs help in mobilising these resources and clarifying the problem then he would probably use this technique of reflective counselling. This is also different from ordinary conversation and needs to be used with great circumspection by the social worker or else it can come across to the client as a means of evading a responsibility to help. Great care needs to be taken before this technique is employed to ensure that the client has indeed got the resources, both material and emotional, which he needs.

Carl Rogers has dealt with the subject at some length in his books and the following example from America is quoted by Joseph Perez[2] who has closely followed his teaching.

Counselor: The last time we talked you indicated that you 1
    were thinking seriously of dropping out of school. Have 2
    you given this thought any further consideration? 3
Counselee: Yes, I have, Dean . . . As it is now I still 4
    believe that I may drop out of school. 5
Counselor: You feel that as things are going now you still 6
    plan to drop out of school. 7
Counselee: I think I will because, I don't know, unless 8
    something changes so that I can more or less get into the 9
    groove of things, I think I will drop out because I'd 10
    rather drop out than flunk out. 11
Counselor: I see. You feel that you'd rather drop out than 12
    flunk out. Unless you, uh, you uh, get into the groove as it 13
    were. 14
Counselee: Yes. It seems as if the instructors are not putting 15
    anything in the course. I'm rather disappointed. They are 16
    just talking and if you don't want to go to class you don't 17
    have to because they are just going straight from the text. 18
    They are just going through the motions, as far as I'm con- 19
    cerned. 20
Counselor: You feel that in some of these classes the in- 21

structors are just going through the motions, as you say, 22
and when you get into a class you're rather disappointed. 23
Counselee: Yes, I am, because I figure that here's my chance. 24
I don't know too much about the subject outside of what 25
I read and I figure, gee, a professor will start to elaborate 26
on some aspect of the course and he just rattles on about 27
what the book had already mentioned – nothing outside. 28
He just goes by the book. 29
Counselor: And you feel that this is probably an influential 30
factor with regard to whatever grade you may receive in 31
this particular class? 32
Counselee: I think so, because it depends – well, if some- 33
body reads the book and commits it to memory he's going 34
to get a good grade, but if there are certain things in the 35
book that you don't understand and the teacher isn't 36
taking the time to explain in class or even outside of 37
class, it's going to hurt your grade. 38
Counselor: It's a rather cut-and-dried kind of thing. It's 39
going to hurt your grade. 40
Counselee: Yes, it is. It is very cut-and-dried. It gets 41
boring at times. You wish you could get up and walk out 42
of the class but you don't dare. 43
Counselor: You feel that you'd like to get up and walk out, 44
but you don't dare because the instructor has his eyes on 45
you. 46
Counselee: Right. 47

Most British social workers would probably agree that this really is taking reflective counselling too far, but it certainly illustrates how the counsellor is using the reflective method to enable the client to sort out this problem for himself. It is also worth noticing even in this brief example that the counsellor by no means restricts himself to repeating exactly what the client says. The re-phrasing and the introduction of new ideas are worth careful examination. For instance, the first mention of concern about grades (marks), in line 31 is made by the counsellor. It is taken up with obvious relief by the student and stimulates him to make his longest and most revealing speech in the dialogue.

RELATIONSHIP

The casework relationship is a phrase which has been given many different meanings and in his book, *The Casework Relationship,* Fr Biestek[3] widens it to include both the principles and methods of social casework. However, it is more common to restrict the term itself to the nature of the relationship between the social worker and the client and to consider its wider connotations under the heading ' use of relationship '.

The casework relationship in this limited sense is derived from the psychodynamic concept that emotional maturity is dependent upon making successful social relationships, particularly with one's parents, or parent-substitutes, and that if these relationships are faulty, it may be possible to repair the damage by means of a therapeutic relationship with another person.

The idea is that ordinary social relationships are two-way affairs, that there is a giving and taking by both parties, in material things if that arises, but more important, emotionally, that one gives and expects to receive affection. If this process is impaired in childhood so that the child does not receive and, therefore is not able to give, affection, it may be unable in later life to enter into mature marital, parental or any other relationships. If the damage is extreme, a psychopathic personality may result, but if there has not been a major impairment, the situation may be helped by a social worker offering a one-way therapeutic relationship, that is one in which the social worker offers affection and esteem without any expectation of emotional return. It is hoped that because no emotional demands are made, that the emotionally immature client will be able to derive from this artificial form of relationship the satisfaction which will enable him to go on to cope with the demands of ordinary social relationships.

The development of such a relationship may well form a major part of the social worker's overall treatment plan, in which case the interview and counselling session would be conducted with this in mind. The social worker would need to show that he understood the client's point of view, that he respected him as a person, and that he was anxious to help him solve his problems.

The casework relationship is, of course, only a means to an end and· illustrates well the idea that the most reliable measure of social work practice is that which enables the client to dispense with the social worker's assistance. Whereas most social relationships tend to develop in intensity and exist in their own right as a source of satisfaction to the participants, the offer by the social worker of an undemanding, understanding relationship often has the effect of quickly arousing intense emotions in a client who has been feeling isolated and overwhelmed. Within a very short time there can be great dependency, but the evidence of the value of the relationship may come, paradoxically, when it has terminated because the client no longer needs the social worker as he can get his emotional satisfaction elsewhere. Every social worker has had the experience of meeting clients with whom he has worked very closely and hardly being recognised by them and, at times, being pointedly avoided. Despite the intellectual understanding and the professional training of the social worker to see that this sort of incident may well be tangible evidence of the success of his work, it is still likely to cause some feelings of hurt and is an excellent reason why social workers themselves need to have fairly mature personalities so that they are not emotionally dependent on their clients.

This is not to say that social workers do not derive considerable emotional satisfaction from their work. The idea that social workers needed to be detached and uninvolved emotionally at all costs from their clients has now thankfully been abandoned. However, it is still just as true to say that social workers have no right to make emotional demands for friendship, support or even respect from their clients, as this will generally have the effect of increasing a burden which the client already finds unmanageable.

CATHARSIS

In his famous book *The Psychiatric Interview,* Harry Stack Sullivan[4] lays it down as a basic dictum that an interviewer should adopt the greatest caution before arousing anxiety in a client. One can agree with this in general terms but there are rare occasions when the social worker is justified in increasing the emotional tension in order to help the client concentrate all of his emotional resources on breaking out of a generally deteriorating situation.

In *Wayward Youth,* August Aichhorn,[5] who was in charge of a residential school for maladjusted and delinquent children, describes how he dealt with a boy who was a persistent thief. He had known the boy for long enough to establish a relationship which the boy could trust and one day he sent for him to come to his study. Aichhorn describes graphically the process of a long interview which began very quietly but in which Aichhorn gradually let the boy understand that he knew all about the stealing. The tension rose all the time as the boy began to realise how far Aichhorn was aware of the facts until eventually the boy exploded and began to smash things in the room. However, from that point on, Aichhorn was able to work with the boy on the problem of stealing.

This incident gives some idea of the strength of the forces involved and if only for this reason social workers need to adopt the greatest circumspection in deliberately bringing about a cathartic situation of this type. It is the most dramatic technique available in the counselling and interviewing situation and, like all the others, it may be used for good or ill. However, if the situation calls for it, the social worker should not be deterred from using what can be a powerful method of helping because of the danger that he might be involved in a difficult emotional situation.

Consider the following situation. A social worker has been working for some time with a nineteen-year-old boy who is illiterate and socially backward. He is a member of a family with multiple problems in that the mother is worn out before her time, the father is feckless and chronically unemployed and the other children are educationally retarded and emotionally maladjusted in one way or another. The mother comes to the social worker and tells him that she strongly suspects an incestuous relationship between the nineteen-year-old boy and his sister, aged seventeen, and fears that the girl might become pregnant.

To the social worker, knowing the family, the story seems distinctly possible, and it seems obvious to him that he must take urgent and decisive action if only to avoid the genetic dangers of an incestuous pregnancy in a family which already had such overwhelming problems, but he also had a concern that if possible his intervention should take place without harming his client, the nineteen-year-old boy, or his sister.

In the event, he arranged for the boy to call to see him the same day and, in an interview which lasted over an hour, he began by discussing the boy's current activities with his friends, his problem in finding work and the restrictions which an inadequate income placed on his social life. From this the interview proceeded to recent family rows and to the fact that the only member of the family who took his side was his younger sister. From there, the interview focused on the nature of this relationship and it was not until after this point that any increase in tension was apparent. From then on events moved at great speed until it suddenly dawned on the boy that the social worker was well aware of the nature of his relationship with his sister. This had obviously been the subject of feelings of guilt and apprehension, but his reaction certainly took the social worker by surprise. He began to saw at his throat with a nail-file and when the social worker attempted to stop him it became apparent that he was suffering from some form of epileptiform attack in which, despite his poor physique, he was more than a match for the social worker and was only restrained from seriously harming himself by the intervention of another social worker who happened to be nearby.

No doubt this was an unusually violent result, although the social worker who uses catharsis as a method of treatment needs to be prepared for all eventualities, and for this reason it is sometimes advocated that catharsis is best used in an institutional setting where it is easier to arrange safeguards at the time of the explosion of emotion which is its distinguishing feature.

The outcome of this particular incident was not that thereafter the family or the boy had no further problems, but that it was possible for the social worker to work with his client in an altogether new way with fewer restrictions in the way of mutual understanding and confidence and as it happens, the sister did not become pregnant before she was married.

It would seem that there are two main considerations if a social worker is to use catharsis for the benefit of his client. One is the sense of a crisis shared. In practice, this is well known to social workers. It frequently happens that a social work relationship gets nowhere despite the best of intentions on both sides until the client suffers a crisis such as an illness, a bereavement or a court appearance, the worry of which the worker shares with the client and, as a result, there is an understanding between them which derives from this shared experience. Generally this sharing does not arise within the interview or counselling situation, as it depends on external events in the client's life, although they may be talked over in interviews. However, catharsis in the way it has been described above occurs within the interview and so is a shared experience between worker and client in a very special sense.

The other consideration is that catharsis may be used therapeutically to build up emotional tension to overcome resistances which had previously been hampering the client's progress and happiness. Because of the dramatic nature of the occurrence many similes come to mind. Catharsis may be compared to blasting a new channel, to the building up of psychic energy to overcome a previously insurmountable emotional obstacle, the concentration of effort required to reverse a vicious circle of cause and effect. However, all of these images fail to make the point that however intense the cathartic experience may be, it rarely solves, on any long-term basis, the human problems with which the clients of social workers are faced. What it does is to give a new opportunity for constructive work with the client. This is extremely valuable and should not be underestimated, but too much should not be expected from a cathartic experience which depends for its main effect on careful follow-up work.

Despite these general comments, it should be admitted that we do not know much about the mechanism of catharsis and there is often an understandable reluctance by social workers to become involved with forces which are so powerful.

There are, however, a number of safeguards which may be invoked, all of which relate to the theme that everything in interviewing and counselling, as with social work generally, should be focused on the needs of the client. If that principle is accepted, social workers should be able to recognise situations in which the use of catharsis is indicated.

Social workers can be involved in cathartic situations without any wish or intention on their part. Because it is the job of social workers to be involved with problems of human relations, they may at any time be faced with a situation in which there is this explosion of emotion which is the hallmark of catharsis. The probation officer going to see his client in the cells immediately after he has been unexpectedly sentenced to imprisonment, the medical social worker visiting the patient who has just learned that he is dying, indeed any situation in which the social worker meets his client just after he has had a great emotional shock is potentially cathartic. While it is not always the best course to encourage the client to express his feelings at this point, there are many occasions when to prevent this happening would be to act against the best interests of the client and would mean losing an opportunity to help which would probably not soon recur.

This sort of situation is, in a sense, outside the control of the social worker, who has to respond to a state of affairs which he did not bring about and which may have taken him as much by surprise as the client. However, as we have shown, there may also be occasions when the social worker deliberately brings about a cathartic situation and it is necessary to consider the circumstances in which this would be justified.

First, there should be the basis of an existing relationship between worker and client. At best, catharsis is likely to prove extremely disturbing to the client and if he is to be enabled to make use of this experience to accept the social worker's help, it is an advantage if the client already sees the social worker as a helping person. Even more important, if the client is aware, even sub-consciously, that the social worker has brought about the cathartic situation, then, unless he already recognises the social worker as a helping person, there is a danger that the client will perceive the social worker as seeking to gain power over him.

Catharsis is so powerful by comparison with most other social work techniques and it is so imperfectly understood that, in our present state of knowledge, it could be a rule that it should not be employed if any other technique is likely to succeed. Thus if the matter is not urgent or the situation deteriorating then it is usually preferable to use a less dramatic but also less risky approach.

Since it is of such importance and since the question of motivation is so difficult to analyse for oneself, the decision to use catharsis should be reached only in consultation with another social worker.

Finally, in making his decision to use catharsis, the social worker must ensure that he will have opportunity to follow up the openings which it is hoped that this emotional shake-up will bring about. It is unlikely that the single occasion will be sufficient to resolve the difficulty which brought it about. If the social worker is not able to follow up the leads which the cathartic situation has given and deal with the anxieties which have been revealed, the client could be left worse off with the worry of a very disturbing experience to add to his other anxieties. Almost invariably, the use of catharsis should be as a short-term shock, emergency treatment which needs to be backed up by the longer-term technique of counselling which we have already considered.

It may seem odd to have devoted so much space to a technique which most social workers use only infrequently, but the probability is that as our knowledge of the psychology of individuals and groups increases, the techniques of interviewing and counselling will become more varied and effective. One has only to remember the techniques of brainwashing and of some of the group and family therapy techniques to be aware how much is already practised in related fields. For this reason, it is important to consider the conditions which should govern the use of new techniques.

ADVICE GIVING AND REASSURANCES

Neither of these methods of counselling needs elaboration as they are both so familiar in everyday life, but it is safe to say that, in general, they are both the hallmark of the unskilled in social work. Nothing is so easy or satisfying as prescribing solutions for other people's problems. It is one's own which tend to be intractable and one can usually be certain that anyone with a serious or chronic problem has been surfeited with good advice which a great many people are only too happy to give away.

This is not to say that a social worker does not have a responsibility to give information to his client, but it is the exact prescription of which course of action the client should adopt which is to be avoided. ' If I were you ' is really a most unhelpful phrase.

Similarly, easy reassurance, which often stems from a wish on the part of the counsellor to allay his own anxiety and helplessness in face of the client's problem, cannot be of any help and by inhibiting the client from expressing his fears, may be positively harmful. Again, this is not to say that reassurance has no part to play in counselling, but in general it will only be helpful if a relationship has already been established and if the social worker is expressing an opinion on a subject on which he is either acknowledged to be expert or to have access to expert information. Thus the probation officer may tell the client that he will certainly not be imprisoned for a first offence of speeding, or a medical social worker may tell a patient whom she knows well that the consultant has told her categorically that the patient is not suffering from a malignant tumour.

INTERVIEWING

So far in this section only those methods of helping which can be used within the counselling situation have been considered but, to follow the distinction between counselling and interviewing in social work, it is also necessary to consider how the interview may be used to make the most effective use of external resources.

This occurs in two ways. One is the collection of information to assess how external resources may best be mobilised and made use of, and the other is to help the client cooperate in this process so that he can benefit to the greatest extent. Neither of these tasks is either easy or straightforward.

One of the difficulties in discussing this subject is that it covers such a wide range of possibilities that to include them all it is necessary to use such vague terms as ' external resources '. In practice, this means money, which the client is generally free to spend as he chooses, or specific services which may range from convalescent facilities for the invalid, home-help for the incapacitated or residential provision either voluntary or involuntary where appropriate. It has already been said that one of the interview tasks of the probation officer is for the purpose of enabling a court to make a decision with regard to a defendant, which might be far from meeting the client's wishes if it involves imprisonment. However, this example serves to illustrate a general problem of the social work interviewer, that the information which he is seeking from the client may often be used to determine a result with which the client himself would not agree. Imprisonment is an obvious case, but it can apply with equal force to a refusal to arrange a home-help service or grant the amount of money which the client is requesting either on absolute grounds that the client's request is inappropriate or relatively that only so much is available and other applicants have prior claims.

The key to the matter is again to approach the subject from the point of view of the client. If the social worker is concerned with the welfare of the client rather than approaching the subject either from the point of view of his own prejudices or, more likely in this situation, from the point of view of the administrative procedures involved, he will gain a great deal more information, whether or not the client approves of the decisions which are made as a result. It also behoves the social worker to make every effort to understand what the client is trying to communicate by tone of voice, the choice of subject, facial and body gestures, that is all of the subjects which are included under the heading of ' positive listening '.

One method of interviewing is to follow a pre-arranged questionnaire, either actual or notional, which has the effect of forcing the client into a predetermined pattern. No matter how comprehensive the questions or flexible the possible responses, if it is used as the framework of the social work interview it is sure to fail to reflect the infinite variety of the human personality as well as convincing the client that his welfare is of less importance than administrative convenience. The interviewer may eventually have to complete a questionnaire or submit a report set out in a standard way, but he will almost certainly make a better job of it if he approaches the interview intent on understanding the client's attitudes and his point of view.

Agency Function

Quite apart from his own personality and professional skills, the social worker needs to remember constantly that he acts as a representative of his agency. He will be affected in many of his actions by the policy of his agency and is only free to act within the limits of his position in the agency and the expectations which the agency has of him. This applies with equal force to interviewing and counselling in social work. A social worker with the duty of compiling a report for the court about an adoption must raise certain topics in his interview with the prospective adopters. However much freedom the social worker may have in this situation to arrange the sequence of topics to be discussed and the way in which they are dealt with, he can only work within the framework allowed by his agency.

Generally this will not cause any serious difficulty because the social worker will probaby have chosen to work for a particular agency, at least partly because of the congruity of its ideas with his own and so the social worker is usually quite happy to be identified in the mind of his client with the agency which he represents. It is rare for a social worker to be entirely in agreement with every aspect of his agency's policy, but if the divergence becomes too great then the social worker should change his job because of the conflict which his clients would find between the worker's view and those of his agency.

The point at which this situation would come about has never been identified or even fully considered in the literature of social work despite its importance, and some degree of divergence is obviously acceptable as it can contribute to the professional development of the agency. Many people have a responsibility to help a social agency formulate its policy but the voices of the professional staff certainly need to be heard in this process, both because of what the workers themselves have to contribute and because they are usually the chief medium of communication with the clients of the agency whose needs and opinions have to be taken into account.

Differences between a worker and his agency can be a source of difficulty for the social worker, particularly in interviewing where external resources are concerned, as these are more likely to be the cause of differences with the agency than the treatment of clients in counselling. The social worker may take a view that resources should be allocated in a particular way, when the agency takes another view. There could also be disagreement about who were the appropriate clients for the agency and the amount of time which should be spent on different groups. The resolution of this sort of conflict should be a matter of constant concern to all social work agencies.

The need to represent an agency as well as oneself is by no means an entirely negative matter. There are few social workers who have such all-round abilities that they are not able to benefit from the expertise of their colleagues and many newly qualified social workers have been very glad to be identified with their agency and their more experienced colleagues as a means of being accepted by their clients.

Roles

Role theory is now an increasingly complex subdivision of general sociological theory and, as such it is outside the scope of this book to deal with it comprehensively, but there are some aspects of role theory closely related to agency function which need to be considered if the position of the social worker in counselling and interviewing is to be fully understood.

The perception by the client of the social worker as a primary family figure, usually a parent, will be dealt with in more detail under the subject of transference in Chapter 3. It is not unknown for quite young social workers to be called ' mum ' or ' dad ', even by clients older than themselves, and common for them to be treated as parent figures.

For many years, social work agencies reinforced this situation by employing mainly older people as social workers, either by imposing definite minimum age limits or else by the structure of salary scales. However, for a whole variety of reasons, most agencies have now radically modified their recruitment policies and the process has begun of exploring the use in social work of roles other than those of a parent figure. An obvious example, in view of the large number of younger women now practising as social workers, is the role of the helpful elder daughter who can be a tower of strength in a difficult family situation.

None of this has so far received much attention in the literature of social work, which may partly explain why so many social work students complain of the irrelevance of their training, but, as the present trend to use younger workers seems likely to continue, the way in which their age will affect their role in practice needs to be examined if they are not constantly to be placed in false positions and if their potential to be helpful is to be fully realised.

This sort of consideration is a factor of great importance in the interviewing and counselling situation, but is not always solely determined by the personal attributes of the particular social worker. It is now well established that the representative of a social work agency can be invested with a parental role whatever his age, sex or personality and if the social worker is to appreciate why his client is reacting in a particular way then he needs to give careful attention to his client's perception of the social worker.

The limitations of space mean that one can do little more than indicate some of the factors which contribute to this public image. One of these is certainly the historical development of the agency in a district and if for many years it was known for its harsh, inquisitorial methods then it will take more than a change of policy to alter things in the short term. As an example of a lingering image, one could cite the education welfare service whose officers are still occasionally known as ' the school-board man ' many years after school boards have ceased to exist.

The cumulative actions of the members of an agency and the policies which they implemented tend to live on in the memories of the community, and a social worker would be wise to understand what sort of reaction the announcement of his arrival is likely to arouse in his clients. A study of child care officers made in 1968[6] concluded that '. . . children's departments are often known and feared as the agency that takes children away ' when from the official point of view the child care officer ' feels free to give his advice and the client, to a considerable extent, is free to take it or leave it '. Role perception by the client is by no means always so negative, but every social worker would be well advised to think about the image of his agency both generally in the community and to particular clients.

1 Koestler, Arthur, *Darkness at Noon*, 1940
2 Perez, Joseph, *Counseling: Theory and Practice*, 1965
3 Biestek, Felix, *The Casework Relationship*, 1957
4 Sullivan, Harry Stack, *The Psychiatric Interview*, 1955
5 Aichhorn, August, *Wayward Youth*, 1936
6 Handler, Joel, 'The Coercive Children's Officer', *New Society*, 3 October 1968

2 The Conceptual Framework: II Principles

If what social workers did made no difference to the lives of their clients, or was generally ineffectual in society, then their activities would be a matter of general indifference, apart from concern at the misuse of resources. However, we have already seen that techniques such as catharsis may have very dramatic effects and although other traditional counselling and interviewing techniques may be less drastic, in the long run they have an equally great effect on the lives of individuals, groups and society as a whole.

Until quite recently, social workers have tended to concentrate their attention on the individual, or the individual family, rather than society as a whole and, in Britain, social workers have concentrated on the poorer members of the community. There are well-known exceptions to both these statements and indeed it is not possible fully to separate the individual from the society of which he is a member.

It is easy enough to see that this preoccupation with the poor has come about mainly because they were the section of the population in greatest need and, with limited skill and resources, some selection had to be made. This has sometimes given rise to the criticism that the purpose of social work was to prevent the poor upsetting the stability of a society which was organised for the benefit of its richer members. There are elements of truth in this which deserve examination, but what is more true is that by concerning themselves with the poor, social workers became of little account in society. Their work was generally considered by those who were influential to be either irrelevant or unimportant. Socialists, who were also preoccupied with the poorer sections of society, have tended to see the solution in political and economic terms and others who have held political power have seen the problems of the poor as a permanent feature of society which, although it might be regrettable, could at best be palliated.

This state of affairs now shows signs of altering in several ways. Social workers are increasingly concerned with all sections of society and are becoming aware of the needs of communities and of society as a whole instead of being almost solely preoccupied with the individual or the family, although it is still true that the main focus of social workers' attention is on the poorer members of society who are disadvantaged in some way, emotionally or physically. In line with these changes methods of helping with community problems are being evolved and there does seem to be recognition in society that no group can be treated as unimportant, that the welfare of society is indivisible as all groups are mutually dependent and that social problems are so intractable that there can be no quick solution. As a result, social work is gradually being allowed its place as a profession and, together with the other professions, is being recognised as having a special contribution to make to the welfare of society.

This combination of increasing technical competence and public recognition places a heavy responsibility on the profession of social work to define its basic principles and to ensure that its work is carried out for the benefit of the individual and of society. The task of defining the principles of social work has been attempted many times by many gifted minds, but while it is true that there are constant elements which reflect what is unchanging in society, the principles of social work also contain changing elements and it is only by re-definition that one can begin to see what is relatively permanent and what is true only for the time being. It is also necessary when one is dealing with methods as important in the practice of social work as counselling and interviewing to state the principles of which these methods are the expression.

Acceptance

One subject on which all the authorities seem to agree is that acceptance is the central principle of social work and that it is absolute. That is to say that, unlike other principles of social work, there are no exceptions, no special circumstances in which the principle of acceptance does not apply. The main difficulty with this principle is that it is so difficult to define and everyone who writes about it seems to have a different idea of its true meaning.

Thus the apparent unanimity that the principle of acceptance is absolute is to some extent misleading because the agreement only relates to the label.

In part this is due to the nature of social work, which relies heavily on the use by the social worker of his own personality to help others in trouble, and as every social worker is different, so every social worker needs to work out for himself how to apply the principles of social work.

Another difficulty is that the principle of acceptance seems to include a number of separate but related concepts and failure to distinguish between them has sometimes resulted in confusion. The most important of these concepts is an uncompromising belief in the infinite worth of the individual human being, that this is never a matter for compromise or negotiation.

This is usually understood to mean that the offer of social work help is solely dependent upon proof of need within the scope of agency function and does not depend on the personal preferences of the worker. It is foolish to pretend that the worker will not have feelings about his client, although with experience they may become less obtrusive, but the quality of help offered should be related to the client's needs and not to the worker's own emotions.

The usual corollary to this statement is that it is possible to distinguish between the individual and his acts and, while the social worker is bound to make moral judgements about the actions of others, this is essentially different from condemning the person. The most graphic statement of this paradox is in the New Testament, ' Hate the sin, but love the sinner '.

Whether it is possible to make a total distinction between a man and his actions in all circumstances is a philosophic question on which not all social workers are agreed. However, it can be used as a reliable working rule. The social worker who has helped his client extricate himself from one crisis, and is anxious that the client should not repeat the conduct which brought on the trouble, will certainly be tempted to use the social work relationship to add force to his persuasion. The temptation is either to state or imply that if the client acts in a way which the worker disapproves, the worker will withdraw his esteem for the client. This is stated in general terms because it applies to so many possible situations in which almost all social workers are constantly involved, but it is only by holding firmly to the statement that the offer of esteem is unconditional that the social worker is still credibly able to offer the help which the client is even more likely to need when he is in even more trouble.

A further element in the principle of acceptance is the offer, usually implicit and not always consciously understood by the social worker, to share the client's problems. This can be expressed in many different forms which range from the aphorism ' a trouble shared is a trouble halved ', to the theological doctrine of atonement, the ramifications of which go far beyond the boundaries of this discussion. Nevertheless, no matter how the concept is worked out, the core idea is of helping by sharing another's sufferings and it is no accident that words such as empathy and sympathy, which are part of the common usage of social work to express this concept, are derived from the Greek word for suffering and also convey the idea of a helping person sharing the pain and thereby lightening it.

Although this concept is widely recognised, the machinery for putting it into practice is not fully understood even though its value has long been appreciated by social workers, who have sometimes found tangible means of expressing this form of help. The word tangible is particularly appropriate because physical contact is often involved. The social worker may well put his arm around his client to express his willingness to share the client's distress. This would be more common with women social workers dealing with women clients or children, for reasons of norms of behaviour, but the very fact that it is so unusual can make a similar gesture by a man an even more powerful means of sharing in a sense of forlornness and desolation which might be felt, for example, by a client whose wife or child has died, or who has just been sentenced to a long period of imprisonment.

Simply because children are less used to expressing their emotions verbally, social workers have traditionally made more use of physical expressions of concern such as taking a child on their knee or holding his hand. These are means of demonstrating the sharing of trouble to the client, and the magistrates' court missionaries who were the pioneers of the probation service, often used to stand in the dock side by side with their clients and plead for them from that position. In a less dramatic way, social workers are often asked by their clients to be with them in difficult situations, and not always just to act as advocates but to give moral support, a phrase which expresses one aspect of this elusive concept as well as any.

Self-Determination

The principle of self-determination, the right of the client to take decisions for himself and to act as he thinks best, is usually derived from the political philosophy of democracy that society consists in the main of rational men who should be allowed the freedom to conduct their own affairs in their own way so long as this does not conflict with the common good. Self-determination is also a corollary of the principle of acceptance.

The relevance and importance of this principle in social work may be demonstrated both negatively and positively. Despite warnings, most social workers have burned their fingers in working out a neat solution to a client's pressing problems and then, in trying to impose the solution on the client, have succeeded only in worsening an already difficult position. Problems of chronic debt prove a common snare. The worker may learn that the client owes hundreds or thousands of pounds as the result of a maze of hire-purchase agreements, credit purchase and accumulated household debts. The social worker's first step is to get a clear picture of the financial position, which is usually possible with the co-operation of a grateful client who is suffering from the oppression of court hearings with possible imprisonment, debt collectors at the door and the threat of eviction with services, such as gas and electricity, cut off.

Having clarified the position, the social worker then often exerts himself to equate income and expenditure by writing to creditors, consolidating liabilities and generally tidying up his client's financial position so that the worker is eventually able to tell the client that all he needs to do is to put aside two pounds a week, which, with careful budgeting, he can afford, and in two years' time, he will be free from debt. The client will then usually express his appreciation for all that the worker has done and the chances are that in six months the client will be in more trouble than he was when the process started.

Conversely, if the worker is able to involve the client in formulating a solution to his own problem, what might have seemed a hopeless situation can be transformed by utilising one of the strongest forces known, the human will. This subject has been most fully explored by social workers following the lead of the psychotherapist, Otto Rank, an early associate of Freud, but who later differed from Freud, mainly on this subject of the use of the client's will as a helpful factor in the therapeutic situation. Rank's work was the original inspiration of the Functionalist school of social work theory, mainly centred at the University of Pennsylvania at Philadelphia and, while the theoretical position is seldom fully understood in Britain, the emphasis on the involvement of the client's will in his own treatment is becoming more widely appreciated.

In some circumstances, the mobilisation of the client's will-power can have the most dramatic consequences and a great deal more work needs to be done to help social workers understand how this powerful force can be best used. In terms of emotional energy it may be compared with catharsis, to which it is no doubt related, but, unlike catharsis, it may persist indefinitely, although it may also manifest itself in a short, tremendous burst of energy. It may, for instance, occur in the case of someone who is addicted to alcohol or drugs for whom the usual methods of therapy are unlikely to succeed, but who may be able to break himself of the habit as the result of a crisis either within himself or centred externally on another person, or an ideal.

The connection with religious conversion is also apparent and it is known that there are certain ages at which individuals are morely likely to be involved in this sort of situation, during the childhood period, during adolescence when life patterns become fixed, and on marriage. It occurs comparatively less frequently with older, mature people, although the phenomenon is by no means unknown to this group. However, when considering the principle of self-determination in social work, the main point is that without the client's active cooperation, very little help can be given, however resourceful and energetic the social worker may be. With the client truly involved in tackling his own problem then all sorts of obstacles and handicaps may be overcome, for proof of which one need look no farther than the achievements of many people suffering from severe physical handicaps.

Although there is so much power in the human will, its expression is not necessarily florid. Quiet determination may be a very accurate description and may have more force than a mere demonstrative expression of intention. However, although the effects of will-power alone may exceed all reasonable expectation, its effects may also be less easily discerned because the full power of the will has not been mobilised. It may also be that the energy generated by the will may be indistinguishable from other factors such as the worker-client relationship.

Another reason for understanding the principle of client self-determination is to appreciate its limitations. To admit that there are major limitations on the right of the client to make decisions for himself in the social work situation is not in any way to derogate from the importance of the principle. The child cannot decide many things for himself, a man must be restrained from hurting others, and the rules of any social work agency will constrain both client and worker.

Following the golden rule of social work to focus on the client, it is convenient to consider the limitations of the principle of self-determination in terms of the client with regard to himself, with regard to other members of society, and then in respect of the social work agency and the social worker.

The right of the rational man to make decisions in respect of himself even to his own detriment is that aspect of the principle of self-determination which is most nearly inviolate. It is, for instance, at the basis of the law of contract which has all manner of far-reaching implications for social work, and the fact that attempted suicide is no longer a criminal offence in Britain is a further extension of the same idea and may be seen as an expression of John Stuart Mill's notion of the ' self-regarding action ', that a man's private, that is non-social, actions are his own affair and not a matter for legislation.

The difficulty arises, of course, in the notion of the rational man. It would be generally agreed that the child and the mentally sick person should not be regarded as having adequate ability to ensure their own welfare, and this naturally means that there are all sorts of grey areas where a person is on the borderline of maturity or mental health. There are also some actions which would themselves be held to be evidence of irrationality which would justify interference. Self-mutilation and suicide are obvious examples in which one could justify interference, on the grounds that the client ought not to be committed to irreversible conduct at least without the benefit of further reflection.

These considerations apply to all members of society, but social workers have an additional responsibility for the welfare of their clients although this is not uniform. For instance, a court, on behalf of society, may declare implicitly that a person is not able to manage his own affairs and needs to be under the statutory supervision of a social worker. Although the social worker will still seek to involve the client in his own treatment, the responsibility of the social worker to the court is clearly laid down.

In other circumstances, a client may voluntarily surrender to another person some of his rights of self-determination. The voluntary patient in the mental hospital and even, to some extent, the old person who goes into a home, give up some of their right of choice. However, it needs to be stated that not all the clients of a social worker intend to surrender their freedom of action, and for this to be misunderstood can lead to anger and hostility, particularly if the client is not free to assert his independence. A misunderstanding on this point can do a lot to frustrate what the social worker is trying to do.

In the case of interfering with the individual's right to self-determination because of the harm he might do to others, there is the even more difficult task of weighing the welfare of one individual against another. The resolution of this problem depends upon whether one believes that the happiness of one individual can be increased at the expense of another, in which case there is the problem of deciding priorities or of quantifying happiness. If one believes that contrary to appearances, human happiness is indivisible, then the interests of all individuals and all groups are always compatible and may be identified from whichever viewpoint it is most convenient to take. This position may be derived from a belief in Natural Law, that there is a fundamental harmony and interdependence in society, that the good of the many is the sum of the happiness of individuals. This certainly makes the social worker's task easier in deciding when to impede his client's right to make his own decisions because it may be done either by reference to the client's own welfare or by reference to others whom his conduct would harm. The essential harmony of the interests of all members of society may, of course, also be derived from many sources other than Natural Law.

As we learn more about human conduct so it becomes more apparent that there is no such thing as a private action in any absolute sense. In so far as every individual is a member of society and his actions affect himself, so they affect society through him. Thus the social worker is never faced solely with the situation of interfering with a man's right to make his own decisions for himself, because the interference can always be considered in relation to its effect on others. While this makes the philosophic position easier, it does not make the task of the social worker any easier when faced with a particular problem, although it may be some consolation and incentive to know that there is a correct answer however difficult it may be to ascertain.

For the social worker's position to be tenable, he must believe that the interests of individuals are not fundamentally incompatible as it would hardly be possible to work to help a client knowing that at the same time one was acting to the detriment of another.

In considering apparent conflicts between agency policy and function and the client's right to self-determination, the idea of the need for a fundamental identity of interest between the agency and its clients allows the worker to consider the problem either from the point of view of the client or that of the agency. Otherwise there is no means of resolving conflicting claims and, in view of the dependence of the worker on his agency, in any solution by priorities the client would tend to be the loser. As it is, if the interests of the client and the agency are seen to be in harmony, far from having to reconcile discrepancies, usually at the expense of the client, the resolution of conflict may well involve an adjustment of agency policy.

Confidentiality

Confidentiality is probably the most difficult principle of social work to set out if only because almost any statement needs to have so many qualifications. Every social worker frequently finds himself in difficulty in trying to apply the principle of confidentiality to his work with any consistency and yet it is obvious that many clients rely on the social worker's discretion not to use the information which they give to him to their detriment. If this confidence were destroyed, the worker would be wasting his time, as he would be unable to enter into a working relationship with many of his clients.

One basis for the principle of confidentiality is that of a contract between the social worker and his client in which the worker undertakes not to divulge the confidences of the client to his detriment, and that the social worker will use his professional judgement to determine how he will make use of his knowledge. Some such implicit understanding is the foundation of all professional relationships, such as banking, the law and medicine, and it is one of the distinguishing features of a profession. It is fairly common for social workers to discuss with their clients what confidentiality implies and to obtain their agreement to a sharing of information, for instance in a family situation when the worker thinks it advisable that a parent or a matrimonial partner should be informed about a particular subject. However, this is not to be seen as a dispensation from a vow of secrecy as the need to ask permission to divulge a confidence is by no means invariable, but when it is used, it has the advantage of involving the client in the treatment of his problems.

By reference to the notion of confidence, the social worker may judge to whom he can impart information outside the range of those defined by agency policy as being entitled to know and it is significant that in this way the principle of confidentiality may be focused on the client's needs instead of having to be related to an ill-defined, abstract idea. However, although this makes the principle of confidentiality more manageable and also relates it to the practice of social work agencies, there is still the difficulty of defining the circumstances in which the social worker should disclose information against the wishes of the client.

The general answer to this problem, as with self-determination, is that the worker may breach confidentiality when the client is endangering the welfare of himself or of others, with particular reference to the social work agency and the worker. As with self-determination, it is easy enough to establish the truth of these propositions by some self-evident examples, but it must be admitted that there are just as many borderline situations in which these rules are anything but easy to apply.

If the social worker is told by a ten-year-old boy that he has several times been approached by an older man with suggestions of indecent behaviour, the social worker will generally have no alternative to informing the boy's parents however much the boy objects, but if a seventeen-year-old girl tells him that she is having an affair with a married man of nineteen then it is by no means clear that the social worker should break this confidence and inform her parents. The worker's decision in this case will depend on all sorts of other considerations, such as the client's emotional maturity and the nature of her relationship with her parents.

Similarly, if a client confided to the worker that he intended to poison the town's water supply or otherwise endanger life, no social worker could suppress that information, but if the worker were told by his client that he intended to seduce another man's wife, then again the social worker's conduct would have to be determined by such additional factors as the relative age, maturity and social position of all the parties involved, including such things as the children of the families concerned. If the client seriously endangers the welfare of the social worker or his agency, the worker is entitled to defend himself by disclosing confidential information, but this would not apply to every trivial complaint, which again leaves a whole area of difficult decisions between these two extremes.

Finally, there is the question of public policy, the importance of which is just beginning to be realised in social work practice but which is, as yet, far from being rationalised, so that the social worker is very much on his own in making very difficult decisions usually in the most trying circumstances. There would seem to be a number of reasons why this subject has not previously caused much difficulty but which suggest that social workers will in future need to give it a lot more thought.

The increasing efficacy and sophistication of counselling and interviewing techniques has already been commented upon and this will almost certainly mean that social workers will know more about the lives of their clients who will be drawn from a wider cross-section of society.

Side by side with this increase in the information in the possession of social workers is a growing realisation by other people of how useful this could be to them. To take just two examples which are far removed from each other, the debt collector would often be glad of information from a social worker in pursuing his enquiries and the divorce lawyer would often like to have access to a probation officer's records of attempts at matrimonial reconciliation, when presenting his case in court.

At present many social workers treat these matters more by reference to their own feelings than any more objective principle, although there would probably be a large measure of consensus on these two issues. With regard to debt collection, most social workers have had some experience of poorer families being taken advantage of by hire-purchase salesmen and so they would probably refuse to disclose a client's address to any private debt collector, although they might be willing to pass on a letter or a message. In matrimonial counselling, it has now been held in the English courts that the maintenance of family life is of such importance that probation officers, and no doubt other social workers, are entitled to refuse to answer questions in court relating to attempts at reconciliation unless both parties to the court proceedings agree that the information should be divulged.

This particular example may well give a clue as to how the problem may be resolved in the future, in that it has been expressly stated in the matrimonial courts that the privilege is that of the parties and not of the social worker.

There are, however, occasions when public policy and public opinion work against the confidential relationship. In a murder investigation, for instance, no court would allow a social worker to refuse to answer questions about his client, and indeed many social workers would feel that they had a positive duty to volunteer to the police any relevant information which they might have. In child care, the death of a child in care invariably means that the agency will have to make its knowledge known at least to the coroner and often much more widely than that and, indeed, in every agency there are occasional events of such gravity that many considerations of confidentiality are over-ridden.

Just because it is so difficult to establish priorities in a crisis and because such serious matters fall to be decided at these times, it is incumbent on social workers to have thought through the issue of the circumstances in which they will not reveal what they have learned professionally.

It may be objected that this is not the duty of the individual social worker but for the policy makers in the agency and that, in a public social work agency, a social worker must act within the law. The reply would be that the law is fallible, and that if it is unjust, then it is the duty of the social worker, like every other individual, to defy the law.

This was the principle of Nuremburg, which is now universally accepted, although the standard against which the law of a particular country is to be measured is known under such different headings as human rights, conscience, natural law, democracy, socialism and the public good.

One codification of this objective standard is the Universal Declaration of Human Rights proclaimed by the United Nations on 10 December 1948, the full text of which is set out in Appendix 1. The preamble begins ' Whereas recognition of the inherent dignity and of the equal and inalienable rights of all members of the human family is the foundation of freedom, justice and peace in the world.' The proclamation itself is more specific but it is a fair comment to say that even accepting this declaration of human rights as a measure of the law of a particular country, still leaves an immense task to the individual conscience in deciding whether the laws of his own country are unjust and to be disobeyed. The cynic could say that the United Nations declaration only gains widespread acceptance because it is written in such general terms and the social worker who sought to use these standards in his work would need to give a lot of thought to how it related to his own personal philosophy and his professional outlook.

A fair test of how well a social worker has thought out the question of confidentiality would be the way in which he communicated his conclusions to his clients, both in general terms and specifically when a crisis loomed. A skilled social worker will often know when a client is intending to impart a confidence, and indeed a client will often announce the fact directly or ask the worker if their conversation is confidential. If the worker has not clarified his own mind then the chances are that he will fail his client at a time of real need.

It is not possible at this stage in the development of social work to make a comprehensive statement of how social workers should apply the principle of confidentiality and their actions will largely be governed by their personal moral codes. This is also true of the other principles of social work.

Just because so many actions of a social worker are determined by his personal philosophy, it may be helpful to consider this subject briefly. Any survey of professional social workers will show that there is no agreement about their own philosophy or their view of social work. Many have a religious motivation but there are also many who are agnostics or atheists, and they may be inspired by political or humanist ideals, or simply believe that human rights are self-evidently worth working for and social work is a means to this end.

It is certain that motivation for social work is extremely varied and that no one group has a monopoly of ability to help people in trouble. Because the spread is so wide and it is apparent that equally competent social workers have such diverse sources of motivation, the temptation is to think that personal philosophy is unimportant, that it does not matter what a social worker believes and it does not matter how well it has been thought out.

Although the range of philosophies to which a social worker may subscribe is extremely varied, it is not all-embracing. A social worker must hold that all individuals have inalienable rights and that this ideal is compatible with the good of society. It follows that a strict application of many philosophies, from the Leninist who believes that in certain circumstances the individual should be sacrificed for the benefit of society, to the anarchist who feels that the freedom of the individual is incompatible with the welfare of the many, would cause serious difficulty for the professional social worker. Even religious beliefs, if interpreted too rigidly, can create problems.

Therefore, although it would not be a generally accepted point of view, it can be argued that it is possible to practise social work only in a society in which the rights of individuals are recognised as compatible with the welfare of society as a whole. For this reason social work, as we have defined it, was not possible in England in modern times before the middle of the nineteenth century because, for instance, the rights of the poor were not generally recognised.

It may be that, recognising a sympathetic social system, social workers have traditionally relied upon a general consensus in society of what constitutes justice, instead of formulating their own views. It may be significant that until recently moral philosophy has had a progressively decreasing part in social work education. Now that in Britain there are signs that on important ethical matters such as punishment, abortion, divorce and contraception there is an apparently increasing divergence of opinion and if social workers are to help their clients to deal with these and many other problems, then they must work out their own personal positions. This is not so that they can persuade their clients to adopt their solutions, which would hardly tie up with the principle of self-determination. It is for exactly the opposite reason that, by knowing their own opinions, social workers will be able to take steps to ensure that they do not impose them on their clients.

3 Problems of Communication

Communication is the essence of interviewing and counselling and a great deal of the training of a social worker is to enable him to recognise and deal with the problems involved in communication. The client has a problem which he cannot manage by himself and so he needs to communicate it to the social worker. In turn, the social worker has to understand the problem and demonstrate to the client that he has understood. They are then both involved in the problem-solving work, an interchange of values, ideas and emotions, so that the client may eventually regain his independence. All these processes are liable to distortion. Satisfactory communication will not itself solve the problems with which a social worker deals but it is a powerful therapeutic aid and any improvement in communication must be of value in the social work process.

Communication is the interchange of messages and the first problem is simply the overwhelming number of messages which are transmitted. Let us consider the following dialogue between a woman social worker and the client, Mr Crawford.

S.W. Mr Crawford?	1
Mr C. Yes.	2
S.W. Do come in.	3
Mr C. Thank you.	4
S.W. Won't you sit down?	5
Mr C. Thank you.	6
S.W. I understand that you made an appointment earlier this	7
morning.	8
Mr C. Yes, yes, I did.	9
S.W. Er, how can I help you?	10
Mr C. Well, I don't know whether you can. I went to this	11
day-nursery school today to see about putting my kids	12
there while I'm out at work. I have a nine-to-five job . . .	13

and er . . . and they wouldn't take them, they wouldn't   14
accept them, they said there was no room so . . . er . . . I   15
made a few calls and they said come and see you . . . you   16
seem to be the only person around who could . . . be   17
bothered to help so . . .   18
S.W. Well, what's happening during the day with them at   19
the moment?   20
Mr C. Well, at the moment they're with the neighbour next   21
door . . . and I don't think . . . er mm . . . she can really   22
cope, she's got three of her own and er I don't want to   23
impose on her any longer, you know . . . I want something   24
a bit better for them . . . they're in this kitchen all day   25
long you know . . . and er well . . . I'd rather get them in   26
something better.   27
S.W. I see, this must be very awkward for you.   28
Mr C. Well, yes, it is yes, and it's . . . it's the kids I'm really   29
worried about . . . they're not getting much of a life at the   30
moment, you know . . . so what can you do . . .?   31
S.W. How old are your children, Mr Crawford?   32
Mr C. Well . . . Robert is four and Debbie's three and er . . .   33
well this is the problem, you know, that they're at that age   34
where they need somebody with them all the time and er   35
. . . I'm just not there.   36
S.W. Well, it is a problem, isn't it, because it's quite a time   37
before they go to school?   38
Mr C. Yea, yea.   39
S.W. How long has your neighbour been looking after them?   40
Mr C. Well, you see my wife left me about eighteen months   41
ago and she's been looking after them since then.   42
S.W. Does your wife have any contact with the children at   43
all?   44
Mr C. No, she doesn't er . . . I saw her about twelve months   45
ago but she hasn't seen them since she left. The point is   46
. . . I went round yesterday to this place and er . . . and I   47
er saw the man in charge, whoever he was, and I said there   48
must be . . . surely you can fit in my two kids here, you   49
know. He said . . . no, no, no, we haven't got room, you   50
know, crowded already, can't get any money and all this   51
and that and that er . . . I thought well hell, you know   52
. . . what am I going to do with them . . . er . . . isn't there   53

anywhere in town where I can put them? . . . there must   54
be some sort of agency where they can spend the day   55
. . . I just can't have them with this woman all the time   56
and they're going to go on the streets at the age of three   57
or four.   58

The reader will remember from the preface that this dialogue is extracted from a role-playing exercise undertaken by the students at the University of Keele. For this reason it could be said to lack the authenticity of a live social work situation, but anyone familiar with the work of a local authority social work department would recognise much that was familiar in the situation and the interaction between the client and the social worker.

This interchange takes perhaps three or four minutes and yet in that brief period of time the client makes over a hundred statements of facts. The whole interview, which is given in full in Appendix 2, lasts about fifteen minutes, during which he makes perhaps four or five hundred individual statements and it immediately becomes obvious that nobody can fully digest this mountain of information at one hearing. It is equally true that nobody would want to, as so much of the information is trivial or irrelevent, but even in propitious circumstances with one reasonably coherent client, the social worker will have difficulty in comprehending what the client is saying, even on a basic factual level.

In practice the problem is much greater. Limiting our interest to verbal matters, the choice and arrangement of words, the tones of voice, hesitations, repetitions, silences, all convey their own meanings, some of which can be gleaned from a careful examination of the section of the interview given above. One could infer, for instance, that although the client has come to ask for help in coping with his children, he may also want help in his relationship with his wife. The basis for this hypothesis is the way the client answers the social worker's question in line 41 by gratuitously offering the information that his wife left him eighteen months ago. One would not place too much reliance on this deduction as there are other possible explanations, but it could be an interesting lead and certainly worth following up. Perhaps, also, some of the difficulties which the social worker gets into later in the interview arise because she concentrates so completely on the presenting problem of minding the children instead of considering other aspects of the situation.

Another mannerism of the client which a careful examination of this transcript reveals is his use of the phrase ' you know '. It is repeated seven times even in this brief extract and again, while one would not want to make too definite a point, it does seem from an examination of the client's sentence construction that he uses the phrase to underline points which he believes to be important. It is also interesting, if one examines the whole interview, to notice that he does not use the phrase when he is nervous, that is at the beginning when he is apprehensive or later in the interview when he becomes agitated about the possibility of adoption.

However, neither the factual statements nor the inference to be made from the words are the whole story which the social worker is expected to grasp. Tones of voice which are not apparent in the transcript can convey the most subtle messages. Quite apart from speech, there is the range of non-verbal communication. Facial expressions may convey a whole language of emotions and the perceptive social worker will register positive nervous mannerisms. Gestures and posture tell their own story and cleanliness and tidiness can give many clues and there is a growing appreciation of the messages to be conveyed by dress.

One could add to the list almost indefinitely so that the total number of separate items of information presented to the notice of the social worker in the interview which has been given as an example, may run into thousands, depending mainly upon the time available to analyse what occurred. However, the social worker has to digest the material on the spot and while there may be opportunities later to think about what occurred, generally the only source for this subsequent examination is the social worker's memory or a record which he made at the time.

It is easy to show that even social workers, psychiatrists, and other professional interviewers who spend a lot of their time in trying to take in the messages which other people are transmitting to them, in fact register only a small proportion and this goes some way to explain why interviewing and counselling is such hard work, as it needs so much concentrated attention. To some extent the omissions are compensated for by the experience and expertise of the social worker, and a selective concentration on certain salient features may serve to economise effort and maximise results. One obvious example would be in the case of anxiety which a client may manifest in six different ways – by hesitation in his speech, by over-complicated syntax, by raising his voice, by shifting in his seat, by fingering his tie and by glancing nervously around the room. The social worker need pick up only one of these signals to understand this particular message and there is a fortunate safeguard that if the social worker misses something which it is important to the client to convey, the message is likely to be repeated until it is acknowledged. In cases in which the worker is particularly unreceptive for some reason, the client may be unable to make any progress in the interview because he needs to be sure that his basic point has got home. The result can sound just like a record which is playing the same few notes over and over again.

The fact that it is impossible for the social worker to grasp everything which the client is conveying in the one-to-one situation in the social worker's office is even more true when the social worker is dealing with a group of clients or is working in an environment which he cannot regulate. In the first case, not only does he have to receive the messages which are intended for him by all the members of the group but he also has to take account of the messages passing between the members, so that with a group of four clients there may be something like twelve times the amount of material that an individual client would produce. When the social worker visits a client at home he may have to take into consideration not only the client's response to the social worker but also to the stimuli of the home, and this can also add greatly to the complications of the situation.

It is likely that it is this superabundance of information which deters many social workers from working with groups or out of the confines of their own office. They are aware of how much they have to contend with even in the one-to-one situation in an office and fear that any large increase will make the whole thing unmanageable. This is understandable although it is unprofessional as it means the work is based on the worker's fears rather than the client's needs. It may be some encouragement to realise that even in the one-to-one situation there has to be a process of editing and selection and while this goes on to a greater degree in group counselling, there is no difference in principle.

Messages may be perceived by any of the senses. Smell and taste are used comparatively rarely, although on occasion they may perceive information of great significance. Hearing and seeing are the principal means of reception, but the whole question of touch in social work is one which is only just beginning to be explored.

It may be paradoxical that just because physical contact is so important in human relations so its full significance has failed to be recognised in social work. Obviously some of the deepest human emotions are expressed physically, such as sexual intercourse between man and wife and the holding of the child by the parent. In order to safeguard these relationships, other touching has become restricted and hardly occurs in the formal social work interview. It may also be that physical contact was thought to contravene the goal of detachment by the worker which tended to characterise social work at one time. Touching is inevitably a two-way process which must involve both participants.

As this study is concerned with a wider range of counselling and interviewing methods than the one-to-one interview, so touching as a means of communication has to be considered. Indeed it is one of the main advantages of some forms of group interviewing that they allow many more opportunities for physical contact. Not all of these are beneficial. Aggression is frequently expressed by physical assault, but for the client who is limited verbally, touch may be both a means of expressing needs and of receiving comfort and for this reason cannot be ignored by the social worker.

Distortion of Perception

The sheer number of messages with which the social worker has to cope in interviewing and counselling is only one of the problems of communication. In addition, a whole series of things can go wrong both with the sender and the receiver of a message so that either the message which is transmitted is not what was intended to be sent or else it is distorted by the recipient.

We shall now look at some of these difficulties in more detail but it is worth saying by way of preface that, in view of the number of pitfalls, what is surprising is not how many distortions occur in communication but how much gets through. Ensuring that a message is sent off and received as intended may be com-

pared to the hazards of carrying a message between the headquarters of opposing armies when the messenger has to cross
minefields surrounding both positions. The fact that if the message
is important enough it stands a reasonable chance of getting
through is evidence both of the persistence of the senders and the
skill of the messengers.

TRANSFERENCE AND COUNTER-TRANSFERENCE

It may be helpful to examine these difficulties from several
points of view and the concepts of transference and counter-
transference are borrowed from the language of psychoanalysis.
Although they have a precise technical meaning when used by a
psychoanalyst, the main import of the terms is familiar enough
and may be described as the irrational elements which are inherent
in every relationship and which are carried over from other relationships. Thus when two people are first introduced to each other,
they may feel what is sometimes described as an instinctive liking
or antipathy. Similarly, if one hears the name of a stranger one
may develop an attitude towards him when the only information
that is known is his name. In itself this is irrational but it often
requires no great insight to see that the name or other attributes
of the stranger remind one of a person with the same name or
similar appearance or mannerisms and so the attitudes are transferred. As a result, one acts towards the stranger in a way which is
only appropriate to the person whom he represents.

While the general mechanism is easy enough to understand, its
implications for an individual are often infinitely subtle and to be
fully appreciated require an intimate knowledge of a person's
history from early childhood and how the important events of his
life and his close personal relationships have affected his personality. This is generally beyond the scope of the social worker but
the significance of the general concept in interviewing and counselling is clear. Unless the social worker is able to understand
that many of the attitudes and statements of his clients are not
a response to him personally, but to the person whom he represents for the client at that moment, then he will often not make
sense of what is being said. Occasionally clients will make the
point quite directly as when the small boy calls the social worker
'Dad' or 'Mum', or without using these words, older clients
will show that they are reacting to the social workers as to a parent,

or a personal friend or even, if the client and worker are opposite sexes, as a boy-friend or girl-friend.

The literature of psychoanalysis makes a number of relevant points such as the general division of transference phenomena into two categories. It may show itself as a displacement of specific attitudes to which it is confined so that, for example, an adolescent boy who is involved in a conflict of authority with his father is likely to see any older male in a position of authority as an extension of his father and react accordingly while in other situations he would behave quite rationally. This situation, which is quite familiar to social workers who spend a lot of time with adolescents, not only helps them to understand sullenness and aggression in some of their clients but also gives them an opportunity to resolve the problem by allowing a boy to express his aggression and work out a happier relationship with the social worker which can in time be transferred back to the father.

Transference may, however, distort a person's whole outlook and this generally means that a primary relationship has gone wrong to a pathological degree. For example, one sometimes meets people whose father was effectively absent from their childhood. Either he died or the parents were separated and the child may have been brought up by a mother and maternal grandmother and maybe a maiden aunt. In such cases it could be that the child's whole outlook would be distorted and, in an interview situation, the social worker would be able to understand what the client is saying only if he had knowledge of this early history.

Both of these examples have been taken from a disturbance of primary relationships at a formative period and this is in accordance with classical psychoanalytic theory that transference is ultimately rooted in the primary relationships between parents and child. However, social workers generally take a much wider view and would speak of transference when the transferred relationship is between brother and sister, husband and wife or close friends.

It is not that there is any conflict between the views of the social worker and the psychoanalyst. The fact that a woman client acts towards a man social worker as though he were her husband, derives ultimately from her early relationship with her father, but often the social worker would not find it appropriate to work back so far.

Another difference is that it is a prime task of the psychoanalyst to bring about a transference neurosis and help the patient to work through it. It is not possible here to give a full statement about the transference neurosis but in general it means that the patient is brought to see all his anxieties in terms of his relationship with the analyst. This is not the function of the social worker, who does not have the training to treat this degree of disturbance by the therapeutic use of his own personality. Instead, the social worker uses the methods of treatment described in Chapter 1.

To summarise the difference in approach by the social worker and the analyst to transference phenomena, the analyst seeks to bring it about so that he may use it as a means of treatment, whereas the social worker generally does not seek to bring it about, although he often has to deal with it. In the main, the social worker is interested in transference as a hazard to communication which must be taken into account. The analyst deals with transference as a psychoanalytic phenomenon while the social worker deals with it on a psycho-social basis.

One subject on which both social workers and psychoanalysts agree is the use of the words positive and negative with regard to transference. As one would expect, positive transference denotes a predisposition in favour of the worker on the basis of an earlier relationship while negative transference is the opposite. However, one needs to be careful not to equate 'positive' and 'negative' with 'good' and 'bad'. It may be that the girl who has had a happy, mature relationship with her father would be inclined to favour the social worker who reminded her of her father, but positive transference would also include the case in which a girl might have had a neurotic over-dependent relationship on her father which she was seeking to transfer to the social worker.

Counter-transference may be described as transference by the worker who perceives the client not as he is but in terms of some other relationship which may be a part of the worker's private life or another part of his professional work. Everything which has been said about transference applies equally to counter-transference, but it should be added that it is not generally within the power of any worker, however gifted or experienced, to understand the ramifications of counter-transference as it applies to himself. If this is not to cause an irrational bias in his work he will need the benefit of a consultant who has no direct concern

with the social worker–client relationship. The role of the consultant is more thoroughly explored in Chapter 10.

It should not be inferred that either transference or counter-
transference are something which in a perfect world would dis-
appear and that social work relationships would thereby be somehow purified. This line of thinking would betray an ignorance of
the process of emotional development, a vital element in which is
the transfer from one relationship to another of the lessons learned
in previous relationships. Social workers may indeed find transference and counter-transference to be complicating factors in
interviewing and counselling, but this is not because they are an
impediment but rather because they reflect the richness and endless
variety of human relationships. The task of the social worker is not
to eradicate transference and counter-transference but to understand it more. As with many other aspects of social work, a great
deal more work needs to be done on the subject of transference
and counter-transference to improve the very incomplete understanding which we have at present. It is also necessary that social
workers should do some of this work for themselves and cease to
depend so much on the psychoanalysts, as the two groups inevitably approach the subject from different standpoints.

PSYCHOLOGICAL DEFENCE MECHANISMS

It may be helpful to consider some of the basic psychological
mechanisms which can interfere with perception and communication in human relations and which can be constitutent factors in
trasference or may operate in their own right.

The general rationale for the distortion of perception seems to
be to defend the personality against anxiety and the usual tactics
are either to distort the potentially threatening message into an
acceptable form, or else to block the message so that it does not get
through. The ingenuity and inventiveness of the human personality in defending its integrity is a never-failing source of wonder
and it is not possible to make a comprehensive list of all the
stratagems which have ever been adopted. It is, however, necessary
for the social worker to be familiar with the main defence mechanisms or else he will fail to recognise some of the most important
signals in interviewing and counselling.

To use a simple classification in respect of these subtle and
complex phenomena means that there must be some overlapping

and in any case our knowledge of the nature of personality is not great enough to allow for complete differential definition. There is also the question of degree of intensity. Every personality makes constant use to some degree of defence mechanisms which, if forced to extremes, become pathological. For instance, withdrawal may be no more than a sense of retreating into comparative silence for a time because someone has made a mildly offensive remark, or it may refer to the social isolation of the recluse or the emotional isolation of some psychotic patients. The social worker usually works somewhere between these extremes but, as well as recognising the nature of the disturbance, he also needs to recognise its degree and relate this to what the client can tolerate.

Avoidance is closely related to withdrawal but involves the client in recognising the threat before it is implemented, though the resulting counter-measures are then identical. Isolation is perhaps an even more extreme expression of the desire not to be hurt and means giving up all relationships, whether potentially dangerous or not. By regression, the person who finds the present too uncomfortable may take refuge in an earlier happier period.

If these defensive manoeuvres do not work, a whole series of devices are available to take the sting out of the hurt to the self-esteem and if they are not recognised by the social worker they can be very misleading in interviewing and counselling. Denial enables a person to believe that the unpleasant event simply did not occur and having convinced himself he can often persuade other people of the same thing. If this will not work, displacement is a psychological means of deflecting the blow. Like a boxer with a weak chin who takes a blow on his arm, the psychological assault may be absorbed by the well-defended aspects of the personality.

All of these devices refer to the means whereby the personality protects itself against external attacks but there is also the danger of forces from within the personality threatening discomfort and there are a whole series of ways that are used to minimise this threat. This problem occurs when psychological needs cannot be gratified, as when important relationships are threatened and there is a lack of affection and no prospect of self-esteem. In these circumstances the individual will feel anxiety but it must be remembered that, although anxiety is a mental state, it is by no means only induced by psychological deprivation. Nor are the results purely psychological, and the perceptive social worker has to take into account physiological signs like twitching muscles, sweating palms, heavy breathing and a whole series of nervous mannerisms. Chronic anxiety can cause psychosomatic illness and even organic damage, such as stomach ulcers.

While the personality invariably seeks to diminish anxiety it may have positive consequences. Sublimation is one of the rarest psychological phenomena as it involves the transformation of one drive into another. In its highest form, it is the transformation by the mystic of his physical drives into his love for God, but at a more approachable level it is the mechanism whereby the childless woman gains full satisfaction from working with deprived children and it is an important element in motivation for social work.

A more common result of the same situation is substitution, which differs from sublimation in that the satisfaction gained from the alternative is regarded as second-best and only acceptable so long as the first object is unattainable, but in an imperfect world this mechanism can be of great value. There is, of course, no demarcation between sublimation and substitution as the one merges into the other.

Repression is a much cruder means of dealing with anxiety by unconsciously willing to stop whatever was causing the anxiety whereas suppression involves a conscious act of the will. In cases where a powerful drive is involved repression and suppression are both extremely difficult and gratification of the drive may be gained in all manner of devious ways. To take an obvious example, the compulsive smoker who stops smoking may find himself eating lots of sweets and biting his nails. The literature of psychopathology contains many instances of similar effects, some of which may be very unfortunate. On the other hand, repression can work quite well, particularly in the short term, and is frequently used by social workers as a first-aid procedure until a longer-term resolution of a problem may be achieved. No doubt in the perfectly integrated personality repression would have no place, but in practice it may prove quite effective and, properly reinforced, it can operate for long periods without breaking down. Without the mechanism of repression, society would have to contend with a lot more disturbing behaviour.

Whether these mechanisms are helpful or unhelpful, they all have the effect of confusing communication in interviewing and counselling and the social worker must be able to recognise them and allow for their effect if he is to understand what it is that the client is trying to convey to him. The fact that the social worker may be working to foster some of these psychological mechanisms as a means of helping the client deal with his problem, only underlines the worker's responsibility to understand what is happening.

As in transference and counter-transference, the operation is by no means one-sided. The social worker needs his own satisfactions and defences just as much as the client. Reliance on an academic knowledge of psychology may well result in sophisticated rationalisation and intellectualisation which are just two more of the psychological mechanisms by which spurious explanations, usually couched in the jargon of psychology, are used to disarm suspicion either by oneself or by others. The importance of a knowledge of dynamic psychology for social workers as a tool for understanding their clients should not be minimised, but as a means of dealing with their own personality difficulties they will need the services of a consultant who is not directly involved with the client.

The number of mechanisms to which the human personality may have recourse to avoid discomfort is almost infinite and although one may list the most important, this by no means exhausts the possibilities and even among those which are enumerated there are the most subtle variations and combinations. This is one good reason why the social worker should not be overhasty to make his interpretation known to his client. Even the most straightforward psychological mechanisms tend to have unforeseen complications. The question of sharing an interpretation with a client should depend on the client's needs rather than on the worker's technical skill.

Anxiety which cannot be resolved may be repressed but it may also be the cause of anger which may be generalised or specific. Although anger generally has the effect of making a person lose his judgement, this is not always the case, and it may be beneficial by enabling him to mobilise reserves of strength. Anger can also have a blinding effect and may be tied in with the mechanism of projection by which one sees in another the fault which one cannot admit in oneself. Thus a person with an undesirable character trait, such as greed or meanness, may well see this characteristic in all his friends and if it is causing him a lot of trouble, he may become angry with them. The significance of this in interviewing and counselling is readily apparent because, until he understands what is happening, the social worker is likely to have a very distorted view of what the client is saying to him.

Fantasy and phantasy are also, in part, defensive mechanisms. In essence, they denote different points on a continuum rather than separate concepts. Fantasy, which is the most common form, usually refers to the vague hopes and daydreams common to everyone whereas the alternative form, phantasy, is generally used to refer to a private world into which a person may withdraw, either temporarily or for the long term. The common element is wish-fulfilment which, if it is merely an idle, passing fancy, would be described in this terminology as fantasy, while at the other extreme, the locked-in, distorted world of some forms of psychosis would be known as phantasy. Although phantasy is always more extreme than fantasy, it is by no means always pathological. It is fairly common for healthy children to invent imaginary friends or animals who are obviously quite real to them.

While the treatment of an acute psychosis is outside the scope of a social worker, he is quite likely to have clients with psychotic traits, whose own private world must be taken into consideration if there is to be any possibility of effective communication in interviewing and counselling. In dealing with children, one can obviously get much farther if one knows about their imaginary friends and with all clients, to know about their wishes and daydreams will throw a light on aspects of their motivation of which they are not themselves fully aware.

The French proverb, ' to know all is to understand all and to understand all is to forgive all ', is appropriate in this context because lies and delinquency can prove a great obstacle to communication in interviewing and counselling. Obviously there is a danger that the worker will be misled and, of course, there are moral and legal considerations, but there is also the danger that when he discovers the lie or the delinquency the social worker could interpret the client's actions as an affront to his dignity. It is generally more helpful to take the view that the client lied or distorted the truth for some reason and that if the worker can discern the reason then it will help him to understand his client better. It is also wise to have regard to the nature of the untruth because, while the truth has a degree of objectivity, a lie is the creation of its fabricator and may give important clues about him. This is not to say that the worker would necessarily pretend that the lie or the delinquency did not occur, or even seek to minimise its culpability in court, or any other forum of society. However, it is important to remember that, whatever the client's obligations to society, he owes no special obligation to the social worker. If that is understood then at least one unnecessary obstacle to communication will be removed.

Social Psychology and Communication

The distortion of perception through the psychological mechanisms we have just described are reasonably familiar to most social workers as they are closely associated with the theories of dynamic psychology which have now constituted an important factor in social work education for the best part of fifty years.

Sociology has played its part in social work education even longer, but the middle ground of social psychology is comparatively unexplored. A great deal of attention is now being given to small group dynamics and the findings of research workers are gradually being incorporated into social work practice, but a subject which is perhaps of equal significance, the sociological analysis of communication in interviewing and counselling, has so far received very little consideration in the literature of social work.

The theoretical basis for this analysis has been known for over half a century since the early work of Georg Simmel on the nature of dyadic and triadic interaction as part of his larger study of the sociology of conflict. The sociology of the dyad, the one-to-one relationship, is considered further in Chapter 5 and the nature of triads, three-person groups, is discussed in Chapter 6, on group work, but it is also, to a large extent the sociological basis of Chapters 7 and 8, on matrimonial work and family group work.

Another way of looking at groups is in terms of leadership. In the group situation the social worker has to decide on his own role. It is common for him to seek to avoid the role of executive leader but rather to adopt the position of being able to help the group carry out their decisions as an enabler and, if necessary, as a resource figure suggesting a number of alternative courses of action from amongst which the group could make their own decision. The usual reasons for avoiding the executive leader position are to stimulate group responsibility and help the members to accept responsibility for their own actions and also to leave the social worker out of the divisive struggles which inevitably surround the leadership. This is not always possible and in many situations the social worker is forced into a central position. However, even when he is able to concentrate on the roles of enabler and resource figure these positions have aspects of leadership which affect his relationships with all the group members.

The result of all this is to complicate further the communications between social worker and client in the group. Those who are striving for leadership will resent the power of the social worker, while others will seek to ally with him to reinforce or improve their positions. Because he shares in the leadership he is likely to be implicated in the scapegoat role which is inseparable from the leadership.

Because they tend to be less inhibited and less sophisticated, it is usually easiest to see these forces at work in a group of children, and the social worker who goes camping with a group of children is likely to see all these concepts acted out in a very short space of time. With groups of adults, the same forces are at work even if they are sometimes less apparent on the surface. Just because he is an adult in a children's group, the social worker cannot disclaim responsibility however much he may wish the children to make their own decisions and carry them out. Similarly in the adult group, because he is a social worker and a representative of the social agency which sponsors the group or has convened it, so he will have responsibility.

When things go wrong, the social worker can expect to take at least some of the blame and when someone is sulking or acting badly to obtain more attention, it is likely to be the social worker's attention that he wants. He will be appealed to in disputes and ignored, threatened, bullied, cajoled, and treated affectionately, just to the extent that it suits the individual at that time. Adults may have greater skill in disguising their attitudes and may have a greater ability to tolerate frustration and postpone satisfaction but the same mechanisms still operate and it is not difficult to see how they affect communication. An individual may give a rational reply to a question but may just as easily ignore or give a surly or an affectionate response to fit in with his needs in the group. If he is trying to displace the social worker he may try to exclude him from the conversation and if he is seeking to enhance the position of the social worker he may try to make him the focus of attention.

Group interaction has also been analysed by the psychoanalysts as well as the social psychologists. W. R. Bion, an English psychiatrist, whose early papers are collected in his book *Experiences in Groups*[1] has propounded the view that whatever the programme of a group may be, there are certain basic processes which occur in every group situation and which must be considered together with the ostensible work tasks if the dynamics of the group are to be fully understood.

Briefly, Bion maintains that every group functions at two levels. On the surface, it is involved in a work-task which may be as different as a board of directors planning company policy or a group of children playing a game. Subconsciously, Bion maintains that what he describes as a 'basic assumption group' operates in a way which is similar to the id in individual personality. This 'basic assumption group' has as its aim an eternal, unsatisfied search for the perfect leader on whom the group may become dependent. The mechanism for this is known as 'pairing', whereby the group colludes in allowing two of its members to monopolise the proceedings in an irrelevant duologue.

So.long as the group is able to make progress and gain satisfaction in its work task, the basic assumption group will be held in check, but when the group is frustrated, for whatever reason, the basic assumption phenomena become evident. The group will either indulge in internal dissensions, usually about the leadership, or will be side-tracked by irrelevancies and Bion has named this 'fight-flight'. The implications of this concept of the basic assumption group for communications in group interviewing and counselling are legion and, without this tool of analysis, the social worker would often find it practically impossible to understand why the group members were acting towards each other as they do.

A means of exploring these basic processes has been developed in the United States and is known as the T-group, T for training. This is yet another example of social work borrowing from other disciplines, as the T-group was primarily developed as a training method for management and is widely used in that connection, although it has also been extensively used in psychotherapy. The T-group strives to examine the basic assumption processes by eliminating the usual work goals of a group. No programme is allowed and the only subject for discussion is an examination of the group processes of the present moment. It is usual for the group to have a non-participating consultant who confines himself to showing the members what is happening. No progress is expected in the group discussion as it is fundamental to the theory that the basic processes are immutable and ever-present. The aim is to make the participants aware of these basic processes and T-groups are sometimes called sensitivity groups.

There are obviously other ways in which social workers can become aware of these basic group processes, such as the differential analysis of several different groups in which no attempt has been made to eliminate the usual work task to see what factors they have in common. Whatever method of training is adopted, social workers who deal with groups, and that is all social workers, need some hypothesis for understanding the very puzzling conduct which occurs in all groups from time to time.

Effects of Culture on Communications

The list of subjects which the social worker should take into account if he is to have a perfect understanding of the communications between individuals and groups would be endless, and one of the aims of this chapter is to show how great a task it is to obtain even a fair understanding of what is happening.

However, one subject which cannot be ignored is the effect of the culture of the society in which an individual lives on every aspect of his personality. This will affect the words he chooses to use and all of his relationships in which the use of words is generally a key factor. It is possible for the social worker to learn the general facts of human development but this knowledge alone is not sufficient to help with a particular problem without a detailed knowledge of the neighbourhood in which a client lives. All the details of family structure and of role complementarity, both within the family and in the society groupings of which the client is a member, may differ considerably even from one district to another in the same town. If the social worker is asked to help with a child who is beyond the control of his parents, he must first have a knowledge of the expectations of parents and children in that district, or even in that particular road, so that if the parent complains that his twelve-year-old son did not go to bed until 10 pm it would be essential to know the bed-times of other local boys of a similar age before the worker could come to an opinion that the boy's behaviour was a cause for concern, or the parents were setting standards out of line with those of their neighbours.

Perhaps the best illustration of this need for local knowledge is the conclusion by J. B. Mays that, in certain areas of Liverpool, delinquency is so widespread that the boy who needs to see a psychiatrist is the one who has not been in trouble. Mays' book, *Growing up in the City*,[2] a vivid account of life in central Liverpool, is full of the sort of information which a social worker practising in that area would need to know. It is sometimes said that a social worker is not effective in a new job until he has been there six months and that he only reaches his maximum skill after five years. At best these can only be partial truths, but they are based on the solid fact that it would take at least six months to become sufficiently familiar with the nuances of local usage for the social worker to have any confidence that he understood what the client is trying to convey about such vital matters as his family, his work and his recreation, There is no short cut to this understanding, the importance of which is self-evident. The only course which the newly arrived social worker can take to free his work of this serious limitation of lack of local knowledge is to keep his eyes and ears open all the time and be prepared to learn from his colleagues and his clients.

The Communication of Values

A great deal has been made of the point that all social work should be client-focused and that it is not the task of the social worker to impose solutions on his clients but rather to help them find their own solutions even if these are apparently less efficacious than those which could be proposed by the social worker. One of the primary means of achieving this goal is the offer of a non-judgemental relationship by the social worker.

Even so, as we have already noted, self-determination is not absolute and in Chapter 2 a number of limitations have been noted which may be summarised as meaning that the solution which the social worker helps the client to find should be within the law and the general expectations of society. This frequently involves the social worker in the task of communicating these values to the client.

The early social workers had no difficulty in this area and saw it as one of their main tasks to impress conventional morality on the poor, usually by the most direct statements. The insights of dynamic psychology caused social workers to be less certain of the value of preaching as a means of communicating values, although this aim of helping clients to accept higher moral standards was never entirely lost sight of and, writing in 1952, at the height of the psychoanalytic influence on social work, Swithun Bowers can say no more than ' the client instinctively appreciates the values of the social worker which are communicated without conscious effort on the part of the worker '.[3] The way in which the values of the helper are accepted by the client has been more fully analysed by the American psychologist, Kelman,[4] who distinguishes three stages of influence – compliance, identification and internalisation.

By compliance Kelman means that the social worker can influence the client's conduct when they are together or even in specific situations which they have discussed and so long as there is no temptation to do otherwise. By identification the client is able to grasp the worker's reasoning and apply his principles in situations which have not been discussed but although the client is able to appreciate the worker's system as a reasonable entity, he has not adopted it for himself and although the worker's influence is not confined to his presence, it will need reinforcement from time to time. The final stage is when the client has reconciled his own values to those of the worker and so is able to determine his conduct without recourse to the worker.

This theory of the nature of influence is perhaps the most compelling reason why every social worker should think out a personal philosophy as the basis of his professional practice.

1 Bion, W. R., *Experiences in Groups,* 1961
2 Mays, J. B., *Growing up in the City,* 1954
3 Bowers, Swithun, ' The Nature and Definition of Social Casework.' *Journal of Social Casework,* USA, 1949
4 Kelman, Herbert C., ' The Role of the Goup in the Induction of Therapeutic Change.' *International Journal of Group Psychotherapy,* XII, No. 4, October 1963

4 Preparation for Interviewing and Counselling

Reception

Social workers frequently overlook the fact that the success or failure of their work may be largely determined by factors outside their immediate control. In the previous chapters we have looked at such things as the public image of the agency which defines the boundaries within which the worker is more or less confined, and transference situations and power struggles which all have their indirect effect on the interview.

Possibly the most important single factor which determines the public image is the way in which the agency receives its prospective clients and it is no exaggeration to say that, in many cases, what happens before the client sees the social worker will not only determine the outcome of the interview but whether the client will even be admitted to see the social worker and if he does, whether he will return. Agencies who find that a high proportion of their clients do not keep further appointments should consider not only their general policy and the skill of their social workers, but also the arrangements which they make for the reception of clients. It is not generally within the power of a social worker single-handed to alter reception procedure and anyone who tries is likely to meet very strong resistance, the analysis of which can prove quite enlightening, but it is the social worker's job to know how the arrangements for reception are affecting his work and, if the effects are undesirable, to work for change.

Even in agencies who employ an intake worker, it is still usual for the client to be seen first by a receptionist who is not a trained social worker but a member of the clerical staff, and there is plenty of evidence from many agencies that this arrangement can work quite satisfactorily. However, there is also far too much evidence that without adequate safeguards, it can be disastrous and much of the work of an agency can be vitiated by a bad receptionist.

The job of the receptionist is a key one in any agency, and while it is possible to consider general principles, the precise task ought to be considered very carefully by every social work agency in relation to its own circumstances.

The basic task of the receptionist is to demonstrate that the agency is anxious to help without invading the privacy of the client. For this purpose it will be necessary for the receptionist to make the client feel welcome and to ask him for just sufficient information to be sure that his call is appropriate. All of this is easier said than done but at least the arrangements for reception should be such as to make the task possible. For instance, the receptionist should be allowed to give her whole attention to the caller. If she is primarily a typist or a clerk and her work is seen in terms of her clerical duties, then it will not be surprising if she sees her duties as a receptionist as an additional burden on top of her real work. If this is the case, the client will very quickly get the impression that the agency, whose sole representative she is at that moment, sees him as an unwelcome intruder. If the receptionist is also the telephonist then, by definition, she will not be able to ensure her undivided attention to the caller and is likely to convey the impression that she has more important duties than dealing with his enquiry. If the size of agency justifies it, both receptionist and telephonist should be full-time jobs, so that an enquiry can be given immediate and undivided attention. It may be worth while noting that, in at least one joint-practice of three doctors, there is thought to be sufficient work for two receptionists, working shifts, and a full-time telephonist.

The physical arrangements for reception may literally create an obstacle, which may or may not be intended, but which the client will certainly perceive and which will have an inhibiting effect upon him. It is not unknown to have chairs bolted to the ground and for interviews to be conducted across very wide counters. The inevitable impression of this arrangement is that an agency is fearful of outbursts from its clients and determined to keep a distance between them and the staff. As a result, however helpful individual members of staff may be, if they are to gain the confidence of their clients, they have to overcome this problem of the physical and psychological barriers which the agency has placed between them and their clients.

A common obstacle is the grille, or hatch in a partition, which separates the caller from the receptionist. The effect of this is to limit communication between caller and receptionist to the two faces and, while the receptionist may become accustomed to this, it may be very disconcerting to the client who is used to expressing himself with his whole body. As people vary so much in size, many clients will have to stoop or stretch to present themselves at the hatch and this only adds to their discomfiture.

It is unlikely that the client will analyse his feelings. He may have been conditioned to believe that such a method of reception is appropriate, but he will still have feelings of discomfort, of being at a disadvantage, which can only be a handicap to the social worker who sees him later and who is wanting to involve him in the treatment of his problems. Except for the very articulate client, it is unlikely there will be any comment to the social worker about the vague feelings of unease which the manner of his reception arouses, but the feelings may colour the whole interview, for example by making a client far more aggressive than he would otherwise be, and may be the determining factor in deciding whether he will visit the agency again, or at best be a barrier to willing cooperation with the problem solving.

Reception in this way is generally a relic of the days when social workers were mainly concerned with the poor and the indigent and as they spent a lot of time refusing requests for material aid, they frequently needed to protect themselves against the attacks of incensed clients. This can still be the case today and the bank clerk is very wise to take refuge behind a glass partition at a time when armed robbery is becoming more prevalent. The banks accept the loss of personal contact with their customers as the price of increased security but, when social workers are seeking to convey to their clients their willingness to help and to increase their contacts with all sections of society, a more imaginative approach to the question of reception is necessary.

This is not to say that all clients will act reasonably. Probation officers have some tough customers from time to time, and in any agency a dissatisfied client may become violent. The probation office may decide that the problem merits the recruitment of a man to its reception staff, while in other agencies the risk of violence may be judged to be so slight that merely to ensure that there is always a man on the premises may be an adequate safeguard. On the other hand, a medical social work department set in the out-patient's department of a hospital may decide that no specific security steps need be taken, on the grounds that violence in such a setting is unlikely.

Another factor in the situation is the attitude of the staff to-wards the client and, while most cases of unruly behaviour are occasioned by the client, there are too many instances of a disturbed client being mishandled by the receptionist so that his conduct gets out of hand. Some receptionists seem to have no difficulty in handling the most troublesome clients while others seem to be regularly involved in hysterical scenes.

One of the reasons for this is likely to be personal insecurity by the receptionist which is communicated to the client and obviously this should be taken into account in the process of staff selection. However, it is also important that the receptionist should have a thorough appreciation of the aims and methods of the agency. It will not do to rely on the goodwill and common sense of the recep-tionist. If this is lacking, there are just too many opportunities for working out prejudices on the clients and, even if it is present, it may still result in attitudes which the agency would disclaim at once. For instance, in one probation office where the receptionist, who is also a typist and telephonist, sits behind a sliding window the stock question to any man over 21 who is not obviously a visit-ing social worker is ' Have you just come out of jail?' From her point of view the enquiry is eminently sensible. She has been in the office sufficiently long to know that ex-prisoners form a sub-stantial proportion of the clientele and it enables her to direct the enquirer with least possible fuss to the appropriate probation officer. However, the way in which almost every caller flinches when asked this question so bluntly is sufficient to demonstrate just how insensitive this particular receptionist has become.

There is an equal danger of erring in the opposite way and the receptionist who takes too much of an interest in the callers and identifies with the professional work of the agency will be liable to confuse her role with that of the social worker. The problems which bring clients to an agency are usually very interesting and it takes a real effort not to connive with the client who is often only too happy to pour out his troubles to a sympathetic ear. Here again, the solution must be to help the receptionist to see her role in relation to the agency as a whole and on this issue to show her that if the client is allowed to tell his story in detail to her it will increase the difficulties of the social worker who will want to hear it all over again.

Reception is not something which can be left to chance or instinct. The training of the receptionists should have high priority for every agency in its in-service training schemes. With the social workers, the agency may rely to some extent on professional training, but with the receptionists the responsibility belongs entirely to the agency to help them understand why people may be dirty, disagreeable and belligerent but are still entitled to the same rights as polite and well-spoken clients. They must also be shown how to deal with aggressive and excessively withdrawn clients and, above all, must be furnished with sufficient up-to-date and accurate information about the agency to enable them to fulfil their task of getting the client to the appropriate social worker with an impression of efficiency and willingness to help.

All of these considerations apply equally well to the client who makes contact by telephone. As anxiety is invariably a factor in approaching a social work agency it is not surprising that many people choose a method of approach from which they can escape with least difficulty. The result is that whoever is responsible for answering telephone enquiries is left to convey the helpfulness and efficiency of the agency solely by means of her voice.

Successful business firms rightly lay great stress on how their telephone calls are made and answered and social work agencies should not do less. All the considerations which apply to the receptionist apply with at least equal force to the telephone operator who, so far as a new client is concerned, is the agency, and who can in appropriate circumstances either create an impression on which a relationship can be built or else cause a client to break off an enquiry because of her manner.

While a great deal depends on the personality and training of the receptionist, she can function only within the limits provided by the agency, both administrative and physical.

Under the heading of administration we have already remarked that a receptionist can hardly give a client her full attention if she has other distracting tasks and however cheerful and friendly she may be, if the work of the office is so badly arranged that clients who call by appointment are regularly kept waiting unduly, it is more than likely that some of them will become exasperated.

The Waiting Room

The main physical aid of the receptionist is the waiting room, a subject to which agencies should give a lot more attention because the waiting room proclaims unmistakably to the client, and to the rest of the world, that this is what the agency thinks of its clients. It could prove salutary to some agencies to look at their waiting facilities with this in mind.

The excuse may be made that with limited funds nothing more can be afforded on an unimportant area where people spend a relatively short space of time. Nothing could be more misconceived. Most clients have some degree of apprehension when they first visit a social work agency and are anxious about their private affairs. To leave them alone in discomfort before they have seen a social worker is to ensure that only those who are compelled will repeat the experience and it will create the maximum difficulty for the social worker who wants to convey the idea that the agency wishes to further the welfare and comfort of its clients.

It is not possible to lay down model standards, as different agencies have different requirements, but nothing can excuse the entire lack of waiting accommodation or the uncomfortable seats in a bare, cheerless room, which is what too many agencies have to offer.

Some hospitals have in recent years given a great deal of thought to the question of waiting and have come up with some very imaginative ideas. The first essential is that a waiting room should be cheerful and comfortable. Even the waiting room of a downtown probation office can achieve this without sacrificing the durability which its fittings will need. It is likely that there will be less horseplay in a room which does not proclaim that it expects its occupants to behave like wild beasts.

Reading material is traditional in waiting rooms but it needs to be carefully related to the interests of the people for whom it is intended if it to be evidence that the agency cares about its clients. The right comics for children and even many adults may be appropriate but otherwise there should be just light reading matter which should be discarded the moment it becomes torn. In general, books and magazines are more items of decoration than a means of intellectual diversion in a waiting room.

The item of equipment which would probably be most useful in a waiting room is a television set, not so much for its entertainment value but for its hypnotic effect in making an uncomfortable period pass as painlessly as possible but it may be that the relatively high cost and fragile nature of the set would militate against its adoption. It would certainly ruin the whole idea to have the set specially barricaded against the clients.

Other alternatives which some hospitals have adopted are to have light music to cut out the silence, which can be one of the most nerve-wracking parts of waiting and tanks of tropical fish are known to have a soothing effect.

Waiting rooms are one of the most fruitful fields for volunteers and their activities can be extremely varied. The Women's Royal Voluntary Service have shown great understanding of the significance of food and drink at times of tension and their tea-bars are the brightest place in many hospital out-patient waiting rooms.

No doubt it is not practicable to provide refreshments in many waiting rooms but most people are aware of the soothing effect which a cup of tea can have on tense nerves and it would be foolish to rule this out altogether, even if it could only be produced in exceptional circumstances.

Allied to this is a need to think very carefully about toilet accommodation. It is amazing how many agencies fail to make any provision at all for their clients, when so much is known about the relationship between anxiety and the need to use a toilet, particularly as in many agencies the clients will include a high percentage of pregnant women and mothers with small children.

Because social work has been mainly concerned with the poor and the ill-educated, it seems to have been generally accepted that the staff of an agency could not be expected to share toilet facilities with their clients. In the long run it is likely that this will change and probably the best way to ensure adequate standards for the clients is for the staff to use the same accommodation. However, if that is unacceptable for the time being, then care must be taken to see that the provision for the clients is civilised and the discrimination between clients and staff must be as unobtrusive as possible. To have blatant notices 'For Staff Use Only' must create the impression among clients that the agency exists primarily for the benefit of the staff, who regard their clients as inferiors.

Some children's hospitals make excellent use of volunteers to organise playgroups for children in out-patient departments. To do this successfully requires considerable skill, as the group changes constantly when the children come and go for treatment and the activities have to be such that they can be very quickly learned but also prove absorbing enough to distract the child's mind from any apprehension he may feel. Although the specifications are exacting, the skills required are not necessarily those of a professional social worker and some volunteers have an amazing repertoire of suitable games, activities and toys which must ease the work of the hospital staff enormously by helping the children and their parents to become less tense and anxious.

Something similar has been tried at a probation office on the evening when all the young lads came to see the probation officer. One of the probation officers would preside at an endless game such as Monopoly, from which one player at a time would be detached for a private interview. This not only prevented rowdyism in the waiting room but had the additional merit that the lads were in a quieter frame of mind when they saw their own probation officer. Incidentally the conversation among the group of players was also frequently worth including in the case records.

Many variants of this theme are possible amongst professional social workers and voluntary helpers, depending upon their skills in drawing, painting, modelling, or some aspect of music. The activities need by no means be confined to children, although there is no doubt that having a few children present makes it much easier for adults to become involved on the basis of ' showing the children '.

The Intake Worker

Any large agency in which there are more than, say, six social workers in one building should give consideration to the provision of a social worker to see new clients who come without specific appointments. Every agency will have unexpected callers and it is placing too great a burden on a receptionist to decide if their enquiry is appropriate to the agency. Such a decision should invariably be made by a trained social worker and it is also important that they should be seen promptly on the grounds that they are convinced that they have a problem which needs immediate attention. The social workers have to plan their time and one solution is to arrange to have a worker available to deal with unexpected callers.

The arrangement is usually on a rota basis with all members of staff taking part, but it has been found to be an excellent way to use part-time professional help on a permanent basis and the result has often been that such workers develop an expertise in this specialised form of work. The disadvantage is that it adds an extra person to the helping process and there must be a danger that differences in the methods of the intake worker and the social worker, who is going to deal with the case on a long-term basis, may cause difficulties to the client. However, preventive measures can be taken against these hazards and the potential advantages are so great that every agency ought to consider whether this would not be a means of giving better service to its clients at the same time as using their resources of professional time more efficiently.

The great advantage to the client is that he is dealt with more promptly by a social worker to whom he is not an unexpected nuisance and if, for one reason or another, he has come to the wrong place the matter can be quickly rectified. It may be that he has come to an office which does not deal with his area or he may have mistaken the service he requires. Obviously some of this could be ascertained by the receptionist but transfer to another office is quite a skilled job if the client is not to feel that he is simply being shunted around. It is also possible for the intake worker who first meets the client to conduct an interview for another agency to whom the record will be forwarded, and to make a definite appointment with the appropriate worker so that the client may not have lost any ground by going to the wrong office in the first place.

Another advantage is that the social worker who is regularly on duty in this way increases his skill in one-interview social work. There are very few statistics to show the prevalence of this form of work and obviously it differs between one agency and another and between one office and another, but there are grounds for believing that it forms an important part of the work of most agencies. Possibly the reason that single interview cases have not received much attention is that the analogy with psychoanalysis has suggested a long-term model, extending at least over some months, as the ideal and anything shorter has been thought to indicate inadequacy on the part of the worker or the agency.

Whatever the explanation, single interview cases are an important and neglected feature of social work which can very well be dealt with by the special intake worker. Whether it is a problem which can be made manageable by the provision of an easily mobilised service, or there is a situation in which the client wishes to do nothing more than share his troubles or register his protest, the intake worker is in an excellent position to meet the need. He can also ensure, so far as it is possible, that the client is satisfied with this immediate service and leave the way open for reapplication for help if it is needed.

Facilities for the Social Worker

So far we have been concerned only with the general arrangements which a social work agency makes before a client meets the worker who will help with his problem on a longer-term basis. However, it is also important that certain preparations should have been made by the social worker, or on his behalf, to enable him to give more help when the client is with him. The busier the social worker, the more important it is to pay attention to these preliminaries. If the social worker has unlimited time at his disposal then he can afford delays and interruptions and the client may not suffer unduly but, if the social worker is hard pressed, he will need to use interviewing time efficiently if the client is to get a fair service.

When the work pattern of the agency demands that the social worker should spend a substantial amount of time interviewing in the agency, then there is everything to be said for providing him with his own office adequately furnished. Quite a lot is now known about the effect of environment on human interaction and an essential factor in the counselling process is the therapeutic use of the social worker's personality. Only if an agency wished to limit its social workers to a narrow, official line would it confine them to an impersonal interviewing room. If they are to be encouraged to utilise their whole personality to help, then it is essential to give them individual rooms in which their own personality might be revealed by the choice or absence of books, pictures and flowers, etc.

All of these details and a thousand more will convey the different facets of the worker's personality in a way which words will never achieve. This is not, of course, confined to the decorations and arrangement of the room. If the social worker's clothes are habitually dishevelled and untidy, no client is likely to place great reliance on that worker to help with disordered money matters. The worker's room rounds out the client's knowledge so that he can know with whom he is dealing.

The general character of the social worker's room also gives the client an indication of what the agency thinks about the worker. It will, for instance, give an idea of the worker's status in the organisation of his agency and the basic furnishings will serve to indicate the work which the agency expects to be carried out in the room. As with the waiting-room the provision for the client will carry a very real meaning of what the agency thinks of him. If, for example, the client is expected to sit on an uncomfortable wooden chair while the social worker has an upholstered armchair then the client may make inferences about who has first claim on the agency's resources. If the social worker reinforces this by requiring the client to sit on the other side of his desk then the social worker should not be surprised if the client concludes that their relationship is intended to be authoritarian, with the social worker giving orders which the client is expected to obey, and for which he will be held accountable.

The physical obstacle of a desk between worker and client will almost certainly be seen by the client as symbolising distance in their relationship. There are, of course, situations in which this sort of authority needs to be demonstrated, although they are not common. The point is, that all social workers should be sensitive to the effects of the physical configurations of an interview. Experts in brainwashing know a great deal about how to disquiet their victims by the use of lights and physical discomforts, and exactly the same considerations apply to putting a client at his ease. The social worker who is preparing to see a client in his office should give thought to the most propitious physical arrangements and his room should be designed and furnished to give him maximum assistance.

The minimum amount of furniture required for most social workers' rooms will be a desk and chair and two comfortable upright chairs, a bookcase, two easy chairs and a small low table. The rationale for all of this is that the social worker needs the desk for his own work and the two upright chairs for clients whom he decides to see at his desk. The easy chairs will be used when the social worker wishes to demonstrate the informality and relaxed Matrimonial counselling would provide many occasions when the social worker wishes to demonstrate the informality and relaxed nature of the occasion when the low table, possibly with flowers on it, would provide a convenient focus and would diminish the element of confrontation which occurs when people sit facing each other, however comfortable their chairs.

This amount of furniture could hardly be accommodated in less than 100 square feet if the social worker is to have any room for manoeuvre and this could be regarded as the basic minimum for agency planning purposes.

It is obvious that many social workers will have to manage with lower standards for some time to come, and for those social workers who spend little of their time in interviewing and counselling in their rooms the agency would not need to provide this sort of accommodation. It should, however, be recognised that if lower standards are adopted, the social worker will, to that extent, be limited in the scope of his work. The argument that in the past social workers have done sterling work in less favourable conditions is essentially Luddite. It is still possible to spin and weave by hand and much fine work has been produced in outrageous conditions but these are hardly arguments against providing workers with modern machinery in a healthy environment.

In group interviews, the room arrangements are, if anything, even more important. It has been argued that the whole character of the British House of Commons has been determined by its adaptation from a chapel, with insufficient seating for the members. To take some points at random, one can make a group feel very insecure by the provision of a superfluity of chairs, and the presence or absence of a conference table will alter the nature of the business transacted by a group. Lord Mayors and magistrates, and the chairmen of important committees, have long been aware that they can greatly add to their status by occupying an imposing chair around which there is a whole folklore of meaning.

As we shall see in Chapter 6, social work with groups can take many forms and it is possible to outline only the main considerations. If the social work of an agency makes much use of sedentary discussion groups then it may be possible to incorporate the necessary facilities in the worker's own room. A slightly cramped feeling can add to the intimacy of an occasion and will certainly be preferable to swallowing a small group in an over-sized conference room, the furnishings of which are likely to be conducive to anything but intimacy. However, in an agency which does a lot of work with groups and cannot afford to make individual provision for each worker, a number of specially designed and furnished rooms may be allocated for this purpose. Where the group intends to indulge in any activity other than talking, then specialist provision becomes essential.

Home Visiting

So far in this chapter we have entirely concentrated on the preparations which should be made in an agency before an interviewing or counselling session, but it is important to remember that a great deal of work often takes place outside the office, particularly in the client's home. Just because the social worker is less able to control the environment outside his office, so it is much more important to pay careful attention to his own actions and consider the effect which they may have on his clients.

LETTER WRITING

If a social worker has to make contact with someone for the first time by calling at their home then, almost invariably, he should announce his intention by letter, the contents of which, although brief, should be given careful thought. The reasons for writing instead of calling unannounced are quite compelling. For one thing it is common courtesy not to cause a disruption of family life, which is the usual effect of a social worker's first visit, without allowing the family an opportunity to make the arrangements which they think necessary. Even if the argument of courtesy is not accepted, the pragmatic argument, that the social worker's arrival may be embarrassing and arouse resentment which may seriously affect the willingness of the family to discuss the problem, should be convincing. For example, a probation officer who is calling to see about an adolescent's forthcoming appearance in court may well find the door answered by the father who knows nothing of the offence, or, more seriously, it may be a step-parent whose relationship with the boy is strained and the probation officer's ill-timed arrival could seriously threaten the stability of the family group. Similar situations are easy enough to postulate in other branches of social work and may so easily be averted by writing in advance. Finally, merely as an economy of effort, the social worker is more likely to find his client at home if he has given notice of his intention to call.

The main argument against writing in advance, apart from saving the effort of writing a letter, is an idea that by arriving un-expectedly the social worker will find out what the client is ' really like ', whereas if he knows that the worker is coming, the client will put on a show which will be misleading. The philosophy be-hind this is straight from the Victorian concept of charity visiting in which the visit was mainly for the purpose of deciding if the client was deserving or undeserving according to his conformity to the worker's standards. This approach will hardly square with the principles of social work as we understand them and, in any case, it is not true. An experienced social worker has very little difficulty in distinguishing between the permanent features of a home and those which are adopted to impress him. One also wonders how many middle-class homes which do not have paid domestic help would conform to the standards of the Victorian social worker, if visited at the wrong moment.

It is one thing to agree to send a letter but it is quite another to compose it, and most social workers have learned by bitter experi-ence that letters to their clients have to be composed with the greatest possible care. The golden rule is to look at it from the point of view of the recipient and to abandon all the preconcep-tions, including so-called correct usage if necessary. .

For instance, a decision needs to be made as to whether the envelope and the letter should be handwritten or typed and many factors may have to be taken into account in this elementary decision. It has been known that an adolescent living in lodgings was evicted because he received a typewritten, official letter. It aroused the suspicions of his landlady, who knew that he was not generally in receipt of official correspondence and, by judicious questioning, she learned that he had had a spell in a mental hos-pital, which she found unacceptable. On the other hand, a type-written, official letter may of itself ensure that the recipients take its contents seriously.

Addressing a teenager as esquire may boost a faint morale or may arouse the resentment of the parents or the institution where he is living, who may wish to emphasise his immaturity, and the social worker will have to decide on the correct course of action. Many social workers would themselves resent receiving a personal letter which was typewritten, but one knows of cases in which the recipient makes a point of thanking the social worker for sending a typewritten letter because it seemed more important and valuable.

Like so much else in social work, letter writing is not a subject about which it is possible to be definitive because there are so many factors to be considered, such as the attitudes of the client, the customs of the district and agency policy. Particularly with a first contact the most that one can hope to do is minimise misunderstanding because, like all other messages in social work, fear and anxiety can twist the most precise meaning and nothing can be done to prevent a client misreading a date and accidentally being away from home at the time of the suggested visit.

Even so, letter writing is a subject to which the social worker needs to give careful attention, to learn from his mistakes and integrate his developing knowledge of local customs. If he will do this, even though there may still be misunderstandings, it is likely that his intention to be helpful and to focus his work on the client will get through, and this is a very reasonable foundation for any interview.

ARRIVAL AT THE CLIENT'S HOME

In many districts the social worker's car, if he has one, will simply merge into the landscape, but there are still areas where a car is conspicuous and then the social worker will have to decide whether to park outside the house he is visiting or leave his car round the corner. It is fair to say that in these matters there is little danger in being over-sensitive as there is nothing to lose in that direction, while it is quite easy to ruin an interview because the family may be preoccupied with the effect that the social worker's car will have on the neighbours. One of the real dangers of increased experience in social work is a decline in sensitivity towards the feelings of the clients which should be a concern of the staff-development programme of the agency.

The client's greeting of the visiting social worker can be viewed in paradoxical terms. A hearty welcome is quite likely not to mean a recognition of the social worker's friendly personality but much more an indication that the client is faced with an unmanageable problem with which he is anxious to have the social worker's assistance. On the other hand, the fact that no one answers the door, when the social worker is sure they are at home, may indicate isolation and withdrawal but may also be an indication that the family can now manage without the social worker's help. The correct interpretation of this sort of evidence is one of the most difficult problems of social work. The basis for this reasoning is that the norm of society is that individuals and families can generally manage their affairs without the assistance of a social worker, whose presence indicates that they are in trouble. Indications of a desire to establish or discontinue contact with a social worker, however indirect or unorthodox these may be, are quite likely to be a measure of a client's need for help or his desire to re-establish his independence. This is yet another reason for focusing attention on the client's needs rather than the social worker's attitudes, because the natural temptation is to interpret the client's welcome as recognition of the worker's helpfulness when it is probably much more a measure of the client's helplessness.

Assuming that the door is answered, it is by no means a foregone conclusion that the social worker will be invited inside although the chances are much greater if he has written beforehand. Although some contact can be made standing at the door, the difficulties hardly need to be spelled out and the social worker has only himself to blame if he has arrived unannounced and so given the family no opportunity to ward off visiting friends and relations whom they may not wish to know about their difficulty.

If the social worker is invited into the house, he is at once faced with a number of problems which do not arise in his own office and which are probably the main reason why social workers have tended to decrease their home visiting. In the client's home, the social worker is a visitor and plainly he does not have the same freedom to arrange the environment as he has in his office. However, there are positive aspects to this state of affairs. For one thing, as the early social workers knew very well, simply to see a client in his own home is a great deal more revealing than seeing him in the office, and in Chapter 8, on the family group interview, we shall see how the opportunities which arise from this situation may be used.

It should also be remembered that the social worker is a visitor, not a guest who has a social obligation of falling in with his host's wishes. As a visitor, he must certainly respect the fact that it is the client's home but there is, for instance, no reason why he should not ask to see one of the members of the family alone or in whatever combination he thinks suitable. He would, however, be well advised to carry the family with him in his reasoning because, while they might comply with his request that he should see one member of the family alone, if they do not understand the reason, they can arrange to leave doors ajar or station the social worker in a room which people constantly have to cross. In this way the desired privacy can become a mockery and social worker and client are left knowing that every word is overheard.

Interviewing Away from the Office and the Home

Although the social worker's office or the client's home are the location for most interviewing and counselling, these activities can take place almost anywhere. The social worker's car is an obvious example and the results obtained from this apparently unpromising situation are sometimes so encouraging that it is surprising that more attention has not been paid to this medium. The explanation would seem to be that the element of confrontation which is one of the usual features of the one-to-one interview is eliminated because the participants are sitting side by side instead of face to face, and the client who is more at ease will feel free to talk more easily.

The social worker who has much to do with adolescents will soon learn that he can often obtain better results by consciously avoiding both home and office, as both may be too closely associated in the client's mind with the problems of authority which are bothering him. One would hardly recommend the social worker to engage in counselling or interviewing in the middle of a game of football or any other hectic activity, but a hike may provide invaluable opportunities and also avoid the element of confrontation, and every youth worker knows how much can be achieved in an informal discussion around a camp fire or over a meal. One of the advantages of residential social work is that potentially there are many more opportunities for these informal contacts. It is, of course, necessary to have sufficient staff to utilise these opportunities as they occur but an indication of this potential of residential work is given in Bruno Bettelheim's book *Love is Not Enough*.[1]

Preparation by the Social Worker

The aphorism ' time spent in reconnaissance is seldom wasted ' is particularly appropriate to the preparations which the social worker should make before he sees a client. However familiar the social worker may be with a particular case he still needs to prepare for every interview, or else many of them will almost certainly become aimless chats, or worse.

For the client who is well known to the social worker the immediate preparation may take no more than half a minute's thought of what it is hoped to achieve in the interview but, for the new client, the social worker should give as much time as he possibly can to preparation. We have already discussed the importance of training for all aspects of social work and this is certainly true of the preparation of the interview. The receptionist will probably have asked the client's name and address and a brief statement of the problem, that it is a matrimonial problem or the client believes he is being persecuted or whatever it may be.

From these bare bones, the alert social worker will already begin to formulate impressions and bring his training to bear on the problem. He will know right from the start that in matrimonial work the prime question that will have to be answered, however long it may take, will be whether the marriage is to be ended or mended and in any case which of the many techniques of matrimonial counselling should be employed. To all of this will be added the knowledge, from his professional experience, of marriage in the area where his client lives, such as the roles and expectations of the marriage partners in that district, so that he can formulate a norm to determine the pathology of the particular matrimonial problem he is about to hear.

In just the same way, with a story of persecution, the social worker will have to decide whether it is based on reality or delusion. In the former case, the social worker will have to know of the various agencies to protect the citizen and, in the latter, his knowledge of mental health and its psychological, sociological and cultural factors will be brought into play.

All of this may be summarised as a mobilisation of the worker's professional skill and knowledge and, at the same time, there must be a reference to the accumulated knowledge of the agency in the case records.

The case records, together with the professional expertise of the social workers, are the working capital of any social work agency and great care needs to be taken both by the social workers and the administrators of an agency to see that the records are informative, up-to-date and easily accessible. If these conditions are met then they are one of the most powerful means of support which an agency can give to its workers. In any agency which has been established for more than five years the chances are that a considerable number of the people who call will already be noted in the files.

The advantages to the social worker faced with a new client of having studied the records are obvious. The old record, which may refer to another member of the family, will give a picture of the family pattern, with its strengths and weaknesses, which will enable the social worker to make sense of the initial interview in a way which would be quite impossible without this aid. It may give a lead to enquire about problems which would not have been immediately apparent and in general it enables the social worker to add the dimension of time to a new case.

Now that the average length of service of a social worker with an agency seems to become increasingly shorter, the importance of the accumulated case records as the main element of continuity in the agency becomes relatively greater.

Plan of the Interview

The final, but perhaps the most important, task of the social worker who is preparing to see a client is to decide on his plan for the interview. This applies equally with new and old clients, despite the objections that with old clients the social worker has the advantage of familiarity and with new ones he is unlikely to have sufficient information with which to formulate a plan. If a plan is not made, the initiative will be left to the client, and the social worker will not be able to give the help which would be possible if the time available for the interview is to be used most effectively.

Even so, full account is to be taken of the client's priorities if the interview is not to be forced into a pattern solely determined by the social worker. Almost every plan should have as its first item to give the client an opportunity to express any pressing anxieties and we shall look further at this point in the next chapter on the process of the one-to-one interview. It is worth noting that the client has a greater opportunity to participate fully in the interview when this has been allowed for in the plan. Otherwise there is a danger, particularly in interviewing, as distinct from counselling, that the worker may be so anxious to obtain the information necessary for a report that the client's point of view may be overlooked.

Even with the new client, who has called out of the blue and whose name does not appear in the records, there may be a surprising amount of information available. There will certainly be the receptionist's account of the client's enquiry which should be more than a bare statement of fact and may include such information as to whether the client seemed agitated, or aggressive, or reluctant to give his name, how he was dressed, and any other details which seem appropriate. This is not to say that the social worker is asking the receptionist to do part of his job for him. It is not unknown for a client to tell a partial or misleading story to the receptionist for a whole series of reasons all of which are potentially very revealing. The client may be ashamed of his problem and will not wish to discuss it with anyone but a social worker or he may fear the receptionist would say that the case was not appropriate to the agency and would prevent access to the social worker. It is also by no means unknown for a client to tell his story in different ways to a man and a woman, or to a younger or older person and so, if the receptionist is a different age or sex to the worker, this can all have its effect.

Most social work agencies have non-social work affiliations and these can be a useful source of information, although great caution has to be exercised in this area because of the problems of confidentiality. It can be very enlightening to a probation officer to hear the comments of the policeman who arrested his client, but the probation officer has to be careful that he does not, in return, find himself under an obligation to provide information to the police about his client's general behaviour. Similarly, in hospital, the medical or psychiatric social worker would be foolish to refuse information from the nurse who is with the patient all day. In the local authority setting there are many potential sources of information, such as the comments of residential staff if the client has been in some form of institution, of health visitors and district nurses who often have their ears very close to the ground, and from all the other services such as housing and education and many more.

It is when one enumerates this sort of list that some of the less well-known skills of the social worker become apparent, because in every case when faced with a new client these are the possible sources of information which have to be reviewed, unless the worker is to be content with the biased and incomplete story which is the most he can hope to gain from his own interview. Even so, there is no chance of using all the possible sources of information in every case. The choice of what is appropriate often calls for the greatest skill.

As well as making the most effective use of the time available in the interview, adequate preparation also helps with the difficult task of aligning the short-term considerations of the individual interview with long-term treatment plans and with agency policy. It may be easier to understand these concepts if they are specifically related to fixed-period social work. The care order, in the case of a young person, generally ends at the age of eighteen years and so the social worker who has a sixteen-year-old client in care will have the general long-term aim of helping him to live independently, without social work support, in two years' time. Working backwards, the social worker would need to identify specifically what would have to be done to accomplish this aim. Managing money would be one item to be considered and if this was a difficulty then it would form the subject of one or more counselling sessions and in this way, the generalised problem of independence would be factorised and tackled in this differentiated manner. To take another example, it may be decided in a particular case that the core of the trouble lies in the relationship between the client and his father. However, instead of spending every counselling session on this subject, the social worker may decide that it is more fruitful to approach the painful area gradually. As a result of this sort of planning, one or two sessions may be devoted to the client's spare time activities, followed by a discussion of his work and then to personal relationships, such as those with his workmates, and so gradually leading on to his relationship with his father.

It has sometimes been objected, notably by Barbara Wootton in a famous passage in *Social Science and Social Pathology*,[2] that this method of working is underhand and indefensible, in that it seeks to circumvent the client's declared wish not to discuss a particular subject. On the other hand it may be argued that such an approach demonstrates the worker's method of working and allows the client to make up his own mind whether the worker is a person to be trusted and able to help with personal problems. If the worker has not conveyed this impression in his early interviews then clients have all manner of defences, both conscious and unconscious, to prevent an intrusion of which they disapprove.

1 Bettelheim, Bruno, *Love is Not Enough*, 1950
2 Wootton, Barbara, *Social Science and Social Pathology*, 1959

5 The One-to-One Interview

One of the problems with which the new social work student is faced is the definition of the subdivisions of social work. On the surface it all seems plain-sailing, that social work is divided into casework, group work and community work. The obvious implication is that casework deals with individuals, group work with what goes on in groups and community work in the relationships between the groups which make up a community. However, it will not be long before the student learns that this model differs from the practice of social work in a number of ways.

The explanation is partly historical. Social work in the nineteenth century developed primarily to deal with the growing problem of poverty, and social casework, as envisaged by the Charity Organisation Society both in England and the USA, was mainly concerned to help the poor to make the best of their situation, to be complementary to schemes for social reform. It was natural that the caseworkers should be interested in both individuals and families and given the circumstances of the late nineteenth and early twentieth centuries, these two interests were inseparable.

In the period after 1920, social casework increasingly came under the influence of dynamic psychology and, particularly, psychoanalysis. As the basic method of psychoanalysis at the time was the therapeutic session between analyst and patient in the analyst's consulting-room, it was natural that social casework concentrated mainly on the one-to-one interview, between caseworker and client in the caseworker's office.

On the other hand, social group work originated mainly from the organisation of recreational and leisure activities and the group workers did not become professionally organised until much later than the caseworkers. In addition, in the fields of social psychology and psychoanalysis, there were a number of important discoveries about group dynamics as a result of which group work came to have psychotherapeutic connotations.

The family is an obvious field of application for group therapy and so one now has a confused situation in terms of the classic divisions of social casework and social group work. The social worker who wishes to help the individual in his family setting obviously needs a whole range of skills which overlap the traditional divisions. This is not to say that there is no room for specialisation. Indeed, increasing knowledge in all areas of social work makes specialisation more and more inevitable, but at the basic level there is a growing appreciation of the need for all-round competence and this must have major implications for social work education.

Advantages of the One-to-One Interview

The social worker who is faced with the problem of which method of social work to employ in a particular situation needs to draw up an actual or notional balance sheet evaluating the different alternatives which are open to him. He will then decide upon an individual, group or community approach or some combination of these three, depending upon the client's interest and to a lesser extent, agency policy. It is worth remembering, however, that as every human situation is constantly evolving, so this decision must always be able to be modified in the light of new developments.

The great advantage of the one-to-one interview in the social worker's own office is that it is the most economical way to use the social worker's time. One interview can follow another in succession so that up to one-third of the time of a social worker may be spent in interviewing.

This figure is necessarily approximate as practice varies so much between agencies, and between individual social workers, and it may appear that working with groups would be more productive, at least in terms of client contact. However, in practice, group work has so many problems, such as changing membership and arranging mutually convenient times, that it is almost certain that over an extended period working with individuals is more productive, based solely on the criterion of the number of contact hours with clients.

It is also more economical of the social worker's time to see people at his office rather than visit them at their homes. He would then have no travelling time to allow for, the agency records are at hand together with secretarial services and, because he is in familiar surroundings, he does not have to spend time becoming adjusted to his environment. From this it could be deduced that where there is no inherent advantage between one method of tackling a particular problem and another, then the balance of economy and convenience would favour the office interview. An even more important consideration is that where there is a shortage of social workers, it might be necessary to weigh the individual office interview against another method of social work which was marginally preferable in a particular situation but would take more of the worker's time.

We have already seen, in the chapter on communications, that the one-to-one situation is the method of social work which is most dependent on verbal facility on the part of the client. Although there are other ways of conveying a meaning, it is important to the worker and the client that they choose the right words. There are many situations in social work where this reliance on verbal facility is a handicap and we shall consider these in due course, but it is perhaps less widely realised that there are also many situations in which a reliance on verbal facility may be a real strength. For instance, social workers frequently have as their clients people who are lacking in social skills, who cannot hold their own in a group of their peers. This applies particularly to children and adolescents whose peer-groups may have little sympathy with an inadequate member. However, it also applies to adults, particularly those who do not have a secure place in a family group.

The reason that social workers meet so many socially inadequate people is that the concern of these clients at their isolation often manifests itself in disturbed behaviour which can range over the whole field of social problems, such as delinquency, or physical or mental illness, with which social workers are primarily concerned. The measure of success in such cases is that the person is able to function satisfactorily in the group, but the treatment, at least in the initial stages, is often best done in individual interviews to build up confidence and help develop social skills. The deep-end treatment of trying to involve the person straight-off in a group situation would often have the effect of paralysing him altogether and reinforcing his inadequacy.

The indications for the use of individual interviews as the preferred method of treatment are that the client has shown himself
seriously handicapped in group situations and the social worker
relies on his own verbal facility to communicate his help to the
client. The one-to-one interview allows the client to enjoy the
whole attention of the social worker, and it then becomes a vehicle
for the casework relationship, the establishment of which is the
most important reason for the individual interview. Its purpose
is to demonstrate that the social worker thinks the client is worth
caring about, without expecting any emotional returns and in this
way helps the clients to mature so that he can enter into other
relationships in which demands are made on him.

From this one can deduce that the method of the one-to-one
interview is of use with emotionally deprived clients and may be
a preliminary to introducing them to a group established by the
social worker or to helping them directly to cope with the groups
which they meet in their ordinary lives.

This use of the one-to-one interview does not depend to any
great extent on the verbal facility of the client. The onus is mainly
on the social worker to maintain the flow of the interview, which
works provided a certain minimal response can be obtained. However, when the client is maladroit in the group but fluent in the
one-to-one situation, then the indications for individual interviewing become even stronger.

It is probably true that, among the poorer sections of the community, verbal fluency is regarded as synonymous with general
social competence but there are many exceptions. Among the
middle class it is not uncommon to find clients who are well able
to use words to communicate their feelings but who still feel inadequate about their group relations. This sort of situation is perhaps more evident in the United States where members of the
middle class are used to paying for the services of social workers
and psychological terms tend to be in everyday use. No doubt as
more British social workers are able to spare time for middle-class
clients they will see the need to have one-to-one sessions with
those who have serious problems in taking their part in groups.

It may be that the client who is having serious social difficulties
is inhibited by shame about his problem but, whether this is the
case or not, a desire for privacy is an indication for an individual
interview. Confidentiality is by no means incompatible with social

group work, but there are many clients who would feel themselves so inhibited at having to discuss their problem in a group that there is no alternative to an individual interview if they are to be taken on as clients. They may feel they would go down in the esteem of their family or their neighbours if their problem became public knowledge or even if it were known that they could not manage their affairs without help.

For instance, with an hysterical wife who comes to complain about her husband's treatment of her or with the patient who has become excited that he may have an incurable condition, it is a pre-requisite of help that the social worker helps the client to get over this out-pouring of emotion before he can progress to the next stage. In some cases, giving this help may be all that is required as it allows the client's own potential for problem solving to be mobilised.

The reason for deciding on a one-to-one interview in this situation is so that the client may have the unrestricted attention of the social worker whose professional training should enable the client to express all of his anxiety and thereby reduce the emotional pressure. The group situation is best avoided in these cases because of the danger of group hysteria, of a number of clients reinforcing each other's fears.

Most social workers are familiar with cases of adolescent boys and girls at war with their parents, who come to visit the social worker full of hostility and only too ready to see the social worker as a parent-figure. The treatment of such a case is almost invariably to help the client to express his negative feelings about his parents' authority and his frustration at his own indeterminate status. Thereafter the treatment would depend upon the facts of the particular case and it may be that no further help would be needed, or that participation in a group was what was needed, but if the adolescent was seen first in a group then it would be more difficult for him to perceive that the social worker was more willing to listen to him than his parents were. Furthermore, the presence of others with the same problem might cause him to believe that the problem must be caused exclusively by unreasonable parents, making it more difficult for him to take responsibility for finding a solution.

The fact that in all of these examples initial individual interviews might well be followed up by group work illustrates the point that the individual interview has a major role to play in the study and diagnostic phases of a case and there are in fact very few instances when a social worker would invite a client to join a group before he had had at least one and probably several individual interviews. However, the use of the one-to-one interview is not solely confined to the preliminary stages of social work. We have already seen that some clients would feel inadequate or inhibited with others present but the presence of a group would also introduce too great an element of uncertainty in those cases where the build-up of emotional tension has to be controlled carefully to prevent damage to an individual.

Where the social worker is functioning without the safeguards of a residential institution, he should not bring about a cathartic situation in a group. The case referred to in Chapter 2, of the incestuous relationship reported to the probation officer, is an obvious example. The consequences of the cathartic outburst were dramatic enough without the further complications of group reaction.

In another case involving catharsis, a young man aged about nineteen had, for some time, been taking drugs. He was seen individually from time to time, as he would not keep regular appointments, and it eventually became obvious that his health was deteriorating so badly as the result of his addiction that he would be dead in a few months if there were no major change.

The case was discussed fully with his doctor and the gravity and near-hopelessness of the situation was held to justify dangerous tactics. Although all the individual interviews were sporadic and irregular, they generally related to his relationship with his adoptive parents which had more or less broken down and his consequent isolation and lack of support. As well as accepting these feelings, the social worker made largely ineffectual efforts to help him find a permanent base either with his adoptive parents or in lodgings and gave him some financial support.

The boy consistently refused to be admitted for in-patient treatment as a drug addict and, as the result of a case conference, it was decided that this was his only hope. When he next called to see the social worker he made his usual request for financial help. This was refused on the grounds that he must be admitted to hospital if his life was to be saved. The social worker relied on the relationship which had been built up in previous interviews and tried to convey by his tone of voice and his words that his refusal of money was out of concern for the client.

Not surprisingly this explanation was rejected by the boy, who gradually became increasingly hysterical as he realised that the social worker was not to be persuaded to give him money. Eventually the boy announced that he would not leave the office until he had money and sat tight-lipped, refusing to speak or to leave. Eventually, the social worker told him that he would have to send for the police to remove him from the office. First, the boy said the social worker was bluffing and would not dare and when the social worker did telephone the police he said he would wait for them to take him away. There was then a period of about five minutes during which no words were spoken but the tension in the room became almost unbearable. They boy began to sweat and the social worker felt uncomfortable, to say the least. Finally, the boy could bear it no longer and standing up he began to swear incoherently and then picked up a chair which he waved around. Fortunately his physical condition was such that it was easy enough to take the chair off him and he ran out swearing and crying.

There was no miraculous change as the result of this drama, although he did turn up again at the office two days later to propose a compromise that he should go for out-patient treatment. The social worker felt that at least he could now communicate with the boy about the relationship between his drug-taking and his other problems, with a greater possibility of influencing his conduct and that this justified his conduct of the interview.

Such cases are still quite rare for most social workers, although it would be unusual to find a social worker who had no experience of this sort of emotional intensity, which illustrates the potential of the individual interview. It may be that as social workers achieve greater mastery of the techniques and methods of social work they will develop more confidence to use them to help with the more difficult problems of individual and social pathology.

Disadvantages of the One-to-One Interview

Although the disadvantages of the one-to-one interview are largely the converse of the advantages, the choice or rejection of a

particular method is not always made strictly as the result of a consideration of its relative merits or demerits. Too
often a social worker will declare that he is a caseworker and so
he only works individually, or else he likes using groups. It may
therefore be helpful to spell out some of the limitations of the individual interview independent of the preferences of the social
worker.

The most serious criticism is that it is so limited. By isolating
an individual in the controlled environment of a social worker's
office the worker is limited in his perception of the client by the
distorting lens of the artificial client-worker relationship. The extent of this distortion is very often brought home to social workers
and their clients if they have a chance to meet each other away
from the one-to-one interview. For instance, probation officers who
go camping with their clients will have an entirely different view
of them after they have been together all day long for a few days.
It is commonly remarked in such situations that it entirely alters
the whole basis of their relationship as the result of having a more
rounded picture of each other.

The social worker who has no direct contact with his client's
family would be foolish to assume that the client's description of
them could be relied upon as an objective statement of fact and
the same is true of other groups of which he is a member, such as
friends, neighbours and workmates. The limitations of the individual interview are such that, as a general rule, the social
worker is not justified in taking any important action on the sole
basis of information gained from this source. It would, for instance, be rash to mobilise social services, except on an emergency
basis, solely on the basis of what took place in an individual interview in the social worker's office, without any corroboration, and
even emergency action in these circumstances would be exceptional.
Unwary probation officers who have taken their client's story as an
objective statement of truth have often been made to look very
gullible in court, and no doubt the same is true for other social
workers who have to compile reports for outside bodies which
have other sources of information.

In counselling situations, it is sometimes less important that the
social worker should immediately relate the client's story to his
environment and so the one-to-one session would have greater
validity in its own right, but there is still no means of the social

worker knowing that he is giving the most effective help to the client.

It is inherent in the one-to-one interview in the office that there is a confrontation between social worker and client. They will generally sit opposite each other in order to communicate most effectively and, whatever may be done to put the client at his ease and to minimise the effect of such authority symbols as the desk, an element of ' opposition ' cannot be avoided. This is not necessarily to be regretted and there are many situations in which social workers need to make use of this element of confrontation, particularly in the resolution of crises which forms so important a part of their work, but the degree of tension it engenders can act as obstruction to the building up of a long-term supportive relationship and must be taken into account if long-term work is envisaged.

It may, however, be possible to avoid this difficulty in the one-to-one method of working by avoiding the necessity for worker and client to be opposite to each other. Many social workers have had the experience of going for a long car-ride with a client, maybe lasting several hours and finding that their relationship has taken on a new dimension. To some exent this is because the contact is so much longer than the average time of an office interview, but there is more to it than that. As we observed in Chapter 4, because the worker and client are seated side by side instead of opposite to each other, there is a relaxation of tension which makes it easier for the client to express his feelings.

The fact that such a journey is often for the purpose of taking a client to some form of institution may also have the effect of concentrating his mind, but the same effect is to be noticed even when there is no such critical purpose for the journey and, indeed, some social workers, when they have to make a journey, will invite a client along for the ride with this purpose in mind.

Another way in which the confrontation can be avoided is for social worker and client to be involved in some activity which allows naturally for movement. This state of affairs is more usual in the group situation and will also be considered under that heading, but there are many possibilities when the social worker is working with just one client. It may be that the activity is patently a device just to avoid confrontation, as when a social worker might suggest to a child that they should draw or paint together, not so that the child's drawings may be interpreted, but to take the anxiety out of the situation by focusing on the art-work rather than the verbal exchange.

At the other extreme, the shared activity may be deemed by the social worker to be a more effective way of building a relationship than any amount of conversation. Thus a social worker could go for a day's hiking or fishing with a client, when the amount of conversation would be minimal. This concept of the positive value of companionship is well known to close friends who derive great satisfaction from being together, even though there is little or no conversation, and has great potential in social work relationships.

Associated with the idea of a confrontation in the one-to-one interview is the problem of silence. Except with clients whom the social worker has known for a long time, it is practically impossible to have any sort of comfortable silence during an individual interview in an office. Each person is dependent upon the other to maintain the flow of conversation if there is not to be a great increase in tension. The onus for this mainly falls on the social worker and this task of avoiding embarrassing silences, which would further inhibit a reticent client, may seriously interfere with the other tasks of the social worker, to analyse and assess just what the client is meaning to convey and responding appropriately. Although the social worker accepts the major responsibility he still needs minimum cooperation from his client and, if this is not forthcoming, the individual interview may simply not be practicable.

Some of the most extreme examples of this problem can occur with children, and many social workers have had the traumatic experience of interviewing a shy nine- or ten-year-old child who fails to realise his social obligation to make a contribution to the interview. Every question, however carefully planned, will be answered by a monosyllable or a shake of the head and within five minutes the social worker can be at his wits' end. However sympathetic the social worker, the child is obviously ill at ease and the interview is ended as soon as possible to the evident relief of both worker and client. One or two cases of this sort are usually sufficient to convince the most traditional caseworker that some alternative has to be found to the individual office interview. Obviously this is an extreme example, but social workers ought to remember more often that many clients do not share their own verbal facility, and the strain of keeping up a conversation with a stranger of whom they are in awe can be a source of anxiety to some clients.

The last major disadvantage of the individual interview is that the social worker cannot see for himself the consequences of his intervention in the case. As the client lives almost the whole of his life in groups of one sort or another, so the measure of the social work is the client's increase of happiness in his social life. The casework relationship is only a means to an end and, however successfully it may be fostered, the social worker needs to know the effect which it is having on the client's life. For instance the timid, withdrawn client may gain sufficient confidence to stand up to a bullying parent, but if this is going to result in an adolescent being turned out of the house then the social worker will want to take steps to see that the consequences of his work are not more harmful than beneficial.

There are so many aspects of this problem that it is quite rare to find a social worker who relies solely on the one-to-one interview as a method of working. The usual concomitant is home visiting or other group situations in which the social worker can see for himself how the client is making out in his relations with others. Less satisfactory, but sometimes unavoidable, the social worker may have to rely on reports of colleagues. Social workers in specialist institutions, for instance, are often precluded by distance from having contact with the families of their clients and will depend upon reports from local social workers. However, even in these cases it is helpful if at least one visit can be paid so that the subsequent reports may build upon the social workers's own experience.

Agency Considerations

It would be naïve to suppose that a social worker had only to take account of the needs of the client in deciding on the method of interviewing or any other factor in treatment. There are all manner of pressures from the family, from other social groups, and potentially from every grouping in society, the neighbourhood, the community, pressure-groups and the state. This may seem to be an over-dramatic approach to a subject which is traditionally outside the sphere of political controversy, even in local authority circles, but as social workers begin to work out their part in the solution of community problems, then they are likely to become the subject of much greater political interest which already makes itself felt from time to time.

For the present, any difficulty about the choice of social work method in a particular case is likely to arise in conflict between the worker and agency policy and it can be represented simply as a struggle between the present, represented by the worker, and the past, represented by the agency, which in its turn represents the collected experience from by-gone years. This is only a part of the truth, because agency policy also represents the meeting place between the expectations of the social worker and society. So long as these are more or less in harmony there is no great problem, but the indications for the future are that social workers will see themselves as having a much wider scope than might be agreed by other forces in society.

In the local authority social work department, in which the authority of the councillors has to be taken into account, there is an obvious conflict as to whether the political views of the councillors or the professional principles of the social work staff shall determine the methods used by the social workers. It is perhaps surprising that with such a fertile ground for disputes there have been so few major rows, but, with the range of social work techniques constantly increasing, the present general tranquillity may be upset.

Translated into immediate practical terms, it is possible that some important forces in society see social work solely as a form of social control and, whatever the rights and wrongs of the situation, helping those who are discontented to accept things as they are. It is when social workers come to the conclusion that it is the situation that needs to be adjusted that the trouble starts. Thus the social worker who has as a client a housewife who cannot manage her money, has to take into account the possibilities that she is personally inadequate, that the family as a whole is malfunctioning, or that the family income is insufficient for their needs. In the latter case, for the social worker to help the family to adjust to an inadequate income without at the same time taking steps for the income to be increased is to use social work techniques as an instrument of oppression, but this is not how it might be seen by an agency.

The provision of inadequate facilities for the social worker to carry out his work are also subjects on which there may be conflict with the agency. We have discussed the effects of dismal waiting rooms and impersonal interviewing rooms on the content of an interview and, just because resources are always limited, so these things would indicate the attitude of the agency towards the work of its professional social work staff. It would be the responsibility of the staff to attempt to bring about a change and if, because the social workers were not allowed motor-cars, it was not possible to do sufficient work with families in their own homes, then again the staff should try to have this situation altered.

Beginning the Interview

Most individual interviews begin by an exchange of greetings and then a brief period of what may be described as social chat. In *The Psychiatric Interview*[1] Harry Stack Sullivan describes his customary procedure and explains the reasons for his conduct. In fact, if his behaviour was as stereotyped as this account suggests then he was failing in one of the usual purposes of these introductory moments, which is to show the client that the worker is a friendly and approachable person who wants to help. One of the serious problems of continuing as a social worker for a period of years is to maintain a freshness of approach which does more than anything else to convince the client that he is not just another, and probably unwelcome, burden. For everyone who does a lot of interviewing it is salutary to consider, from time to time, just how often he does repeat the same introductory phrases and what effect this must have on the client.

The other purpose of the social chat is to enable the client to collect himself and settle down in the strange environment of the social worker's office, and it is the the amount of time necessary to achieve these aims which will govern the length of this period. Thus the familiar client with whom the worker is engaged in working on an urgent problem may need no more than a brief greeting, while an apprehensive new client may need a few minutes before the interview can proceed.

The rule is the familiar one of focusing on the client's needs and, however much the worker may be pressed, when faced with a client who is worried about being in the agency, the worker has to take time over the preliminaries and, however much he may feel like chatting to a client whom he knows well, this should be governed solely by the dictates of the social work.

The decision about when the client is ready to proceed with the interview is not an easy one and, with the client who is feeling overwhelmed by the agency, it may be postponed for some time, particularly if there is no other pressing problem. However, the social worker should also remember that tangible evidence of his ability and willingness to help is certain to be reassuring to any client and he should not collude with the client in continuing to chat indefinitely because he does not want to take the first step of getting down to business.

If the client does not take the initiative of announcing his problems it is almost invariably correct for the social worker to begin an interview with an open-ended question. This is a technical description of a question which does not suggest a particular answer and thereby allows the interview to be centred on the declared problem of the client rather than any preconception of the social worker, however well informed.

It would be quite wrong to suggest any model for a preliminary open-ended question because the choice of words should be a reflection of the social worker's personality and to use a phrase suggested by another person, however apt, can seem mechanical. However, the sort of open-ended question which some social workers use is ' How can I help you?', ' Would you like to tell me your problem?' ' How are you?' is an ambiguous phrase which can be very useful if the social worker is not sure if the client has come to consult him about a pressing problem, because the client can pass it off as a social remark and answer ' Very well, thank you ', or if he is worried then he can give a more specific reply. On the other hand, ' How do you do?' has no such ambiguity and according to common usage can properly only be answered by a repetition of the same phrase, which tells the social worker nothing.

The reason for beginning almost every interview with an open-ended question is to allow the client an opportunity to express any immediate worry he may have on his mind. However familiar the social worker may be with his client's circumstances, he would not know, for instance, of a row that has just occurred between the client and his wife and yet until this was dealt with, the client might not be able to give his mind to any other subject.

It is not, of course, certain even with the opportunity presented by an open-ended question that the client will feel able to discuss a subject which is worrying him and so the worker needs constantly to be aware if the client is preoccupied, to allow him an opportunity to discuss what is on his mind.

It is fairly common for a client not to disclose the true reason for his visit at the beginning of an interview, either because he wishes to test out the social worker before admitting him to his confidence, or it may be that the client himself is not aware of the nature of his problem. In many cases there is no mystery at all about this phenomenon of the presenting problem and the underlying problem. It is a matter of common sense that a client will want to know the sort of person he is dealing with before disclosing what may be intensely personal matters and the easy way to do this is to pose a relatively unimportant problem and see how the social worker deals with that.

Just because this practice is so common, some social workers have come to the conclusion that it is inevitable and may spend a lot of time searching for underlying motivation. In fact, so long as the social worker can keep an open, receptive mind, there is no reason to be unduly concerned about detecting underlying motivation, because if it is important enough to the client he will eventually draw it to the worker's attention. Over-emphasis on the subject of underlying motivation is associated with a lack of attention to the presenting problem and social workers have sometimes been accused, for instance, of trying to adjust obscure psychological maladjustments while ignoring the fact that the client and his family are having to manage on an entirely inadequate income.

The beginning of an interview is primarily a period of study. The social worker wants to know as many as possible of the facts of a situation and it is obviously important to get the client's view and so the client is generally encouraged to tell his story in his own way. However, the client's viewpoint is not sufficient because by definition he is in a situation which he cannot handle by himself. Accordingly, the social worker has a responsibility to obtain an all-round view of the problem and one of the ways to achieve this is by suggesting alternative approaches to the problem. This has the advantage of rounding out the client's point of view for the worker's information but in addition, by re-directing the client's attention to aspects of the situation which he had not previously considered, the worker may engage the client in the problem-solving work. We have also seen how the careful attention which the worker pays to the client may be some of the best help the worker can give, and so, although the beginning of the interview is primarily for study, it also has important elements of diagnosis and of treatment.

The Body of the Interview

The relationship of the beginning of an interview with the main part may be compared to a game of chess. In the literature of chess there is more written about the openings than about any other subject and the same is true about interviewing and counselling. The reason, which is common to both, is that although many variations are possible in the opening moves, there is a tendency for certain openings to be used with greater frequency and these can be studied in detail. Thus in considering the beginning of the interview we can think of actual words which a social worker may use in framing an open-ended question and the precise length of the social chat which may precede the statement of the problem.

Once these initial stages are completed, the number of possible variations quickly becomes infinite and, as in chess, it is only possible to enunciate general principles to guide the social worker through what is, on every occasion, unexplored territory. It may be that from time to time he may recognise familiar situations with which he has had previous experience but even here their setting within the interview as a whole will always be new. The variety of human experience is so rich that the social worker would be well advised to examine carefully the most familiar incidents in an interview, not only to look for what is already known but to detect what is new. There will never be an exact duplication of an interview situation, if only because the social worker who is a factor in the matrix is a constantly changing person. As well as proving its greatest challenge, the freshness of every interview is its greatest attraction.

It has already been stated on several occasions that a guiding principle of social work is to make the client the focus of the work. By concentrating on the client's problems the social worker will ensure the impetus to get on with the problem-solving work and may well save himself from being diverted down blind-alleys. The best known of these is when the client ostensibly wishes to make the social worker the subject of the discussion. Social workers, like all other people, like recognition and there is a danger that they will believe the client has recognised their worth.

The fact that an interview is to be client-centred affects its whole structure, particularly in relation to time sequence. For instance, if the social worker's task in the interview is to gain the information necessary to compile a social history of the client, the inexperienced interviewer might think that the obvious way to set about the task is to enquire first about the client's childhood and proceed on to maturity. It is almost certain that to adopt such a procedure would produce much less information than by enquiring about the client's present situation, which is what he is most interested in and then asking him what particular incidents in the past had led up to the present state of affairs. This may seem to the client to be much more relevant. As well as being more informative, it has the additional advantage of involving the client naturally in the diagnostic work of relating past events to present problems.

For similiar reasons, although there may be strong indications that a client's problems derive from a defective relationship with his mother, it would generally be ill-advised to go to what the worker perceives as the heart of the trouble at a first interview. Just occasionally, and usually as the result of overwhelming distress, a client will be willing to talk of such matters even with a complete stranger and the social worker could follow up this opening, but even in these cases, when the anxiety of the moment has worn off, the client's reticence is likely to re-assert itself and it may even be that if he feels that he said too much, he might take pains to avoid the social worker in future. It is generally better for the social worker to show that he is willing to help at least at the client's pace if not always on the client's terms and in this way the social worker will concentrate on helping with the problem which the client presents to him, knowing that the client needs to feel confidence before he can expose an area which is of greater concern.

The social worker who has to compile a report in a predetermined way, or even complete a form which is not simply factual, is naturally tempted to shape the interview in the same pattern as the report or the form. Even trained social workers occasionally either reel off a stereotyped list of questions and note the replies or complete a form in the client's presence, asking for details of family relationships and the history of difficulties in the family without any attempt to help the client see the relevance of the questions that are being asked.

The objections to this manner of proceeding are that the information which is elicited in this way will be less accurate than if the social worker takes the trouble to help the client understand why the information is needed and what use is made of it. Secondly, if on the basis of a report compiled in this way the social worker is asked to help the client to resolve his problems, it will be difficult for the client to change his perception of the social worker from bureaucrat to enabler.

The other important principle of the individual interview is that it should be directed towards the elucidation and what is sometimes called the partialisation of the client's problem. This means that the social worker has a responsibility for understanding as fully as possible the true nature of the problem. The obvious first step is to listen carefully to the client's account and, if he is able to tell a coherent and lucid story, it is the social worker's duty to hear him out, limiting his own interventions to expressions of encouragement and interest. However, many clients need help in telling their story and then the social worker may help them to avoid undue repetition by repeating the point which the client feels it is so important to make. The social worker may also seek to round-out the client's possibly incomplete account by asking questions suggested by the tentative hypotheses which the social worker begins to formulate as soon as he makes contact with a client.

As well as seeking to know the details of the problem, the worker is generally also seeking to divide it up into manageable proportions, to partialise the problem in the knowledge that in many cases it is the accumulation of a number of problems which has defeated the client even though he could have dealt with any of them with relative ease. By disentangling the separate strands the social worker aims to help the client gradually to undo the knot which may have tied up his whole life.

It often happens that after a preliminary survey of a case the social worker and client will settle down and concentrate on one aspect of it in detail. This is a natural sequel to the process of partialisation, that, having identified the constituent parts of the problem, worker and client will go on to deal with them one at a time. Thus several interviews may be devoted to a troublesome relationship, exploring what is the cause of the problem, but it is just as likely that the focus of attention would be on a particular behaviour pattern. If the client had lost his confidence and was becoming more and more isolated at home, assuming that psychiatric illness had been ruled out, a number of interviews could be used to chart the client's progress in going out just for a short time with a companion, to making longer expeditions by himself. The content of these interviews could be used for a discussion of the client's anxieties and feelings of triumph when he makes progress.

Described in this way, such an interview may seem to be trivial and insubstantial, but it is by the aggregation of achievements which are, in themselves, relatively trifling that the clients of a social worker may be enabled to live happier lives.

Length and Termination of the Interview

There is no normative, correct length for an interview. It may be possible to do some useful work in five minutes and most social workers have also had experience of interviews lasting for several hours which have allowed the client to express very strong feelings and then to work through these feelings in one long session. It is sometimes possible to plan for these marathons so that the psychiatric social worker who wants to compile a comprehensive social history would be unwise to allot less than one hour as a minimum. On the other hand, the situation in which a very long interview is necessary can occur without warning and the social worker may feel that the needs of the client are such that he should respond even if this means cancelling other engagements. However, this should be quite a rare occurrence if the job of the social worker is to be carried on with any semblance of order.

Although the interviewing and counselling situation in the abstract does not postulate a definite period of time, it often happens that both the social worker and the client would consider that nothing more can usefully be achieved in a particular session. This could occur in many situations but frequently a first interview will be confined to an exposition of the problem as the client sees it, with the worker showing that he has understood what it is that the client is worried about. Apart from discussing any first-aid measures which might be necessary, the client and the social worker agree that it would be better to end the interview at that point. The worker would often be glad to have an opportunity to think about the problem while the client might feel satisfied that at least somebody now appreciated what was worrying him.

The interview set out in Appendix 2 is a case in point. The client has the problem of children for whom he is unable to make adequate provision and has the added frustrations of his encounters with unsympathetic officials. The social worker in this interview generally confines herself to allowing him to express his anxiety and suggests a possible, stop-gap solution whereupon the interview naturally comes to an end because there is nothing more to say.

Although it would be easy enough to produce many more examples of homogeneous interviews, there are also many interviews in which there is no such natural ending. In any case, even the natural ending is acceptable only if it falls within the limits set by the agency. In fact these limits are hardly ever explicit although they are none the less real and it can be very instructive to explore the reasons for their formulation. In the last analysis the limitations on the time allowed, or maybe insisted upon, for an interview are a reflection of the expectations which society has of the social worker.

This is an inevitable state of affairs and, while it may cause a social worker to try to alter these expectations even though he may be very successful in gaining extra resources, there will always be limitations of resources. The experienced social worker can use these limitations as a basis for answering what would otherwise be impossible questions, such as the desirable size of a caseload or the average amount of time to spend on an interview. The reasoning behind this statement involves consideration of the functionalist approach to social work. The allocation of resources between different social needs is a question for social and political philosophy, but the best use of the resources which are allocated is what primarily interests the functionalists, who have shown that the recognition of limitation can be a source of strength. For instance, if an interview has no limitation of time, it is very difficult to prevent it wandering aimlessly, whereas if it becomes progressively more difficult to justify after about half an hour, there is pressure on both social worker and client to make the best use of the available time. It is the hallmark of the skilful social worker to use such limitations to help the client increase his understanding of the realities of his situation.

When considering the termination of the individual interview, it may be profitable to return to the analogy of the literature of chess in which the end-game is dealt with neither in the specific terms of the opening nor the general principles of the middle-game. The end-game comes somewhere in between, with the main emphasis on situation and relative position. The analogy is not perfect because chess is concerned only with seeking advantage over one's opponents and ends with one side being vanquished, but even so, certain situations do frequently recur at the end of interviews with which the social worker should be prepared to deal.

It is, for instance, advisable to leave a little time in hand when drawing the interview to a close as it so frequently happens at that stage that the client summons up courage to say something of great significance, possibly because it seems the safest moment or else because he realises that it cannot be longer postponed. It is as well for the worker to be able to respond to such situations on the spot, however briefly.

If possible the interview should end on a positive note, although this must follow naturally from what has gone before. Nothing can create despondency more effectively than false reassurance, because then the client is convinced that the social worker does not understand the gravity of the situation or is, himself, unable to face up to it. However, if the interview ends after the client and social worker have been looking at what can be done about the problem, then at least the client will have something on which to build during the period between interviews.

It follows from this that the social worker would try to avoid the situation of beginning the discussion of a new aspect of a problem towards the end of an interview, particularly if the interview might have to end at a point at which the client was describing the overwhelming nature of his problem. As social work is so much concerned with helping people to manage more effectively, then the natural finishing point of an interview is when the social worker and client have discussed how the client may reorganise himself or receive outside help. In theory, the close of the case is when a social worker and client agree that the client can now manage without the social worker's further help. In practice, this ideal state is rarely attained, either because social worker and client do not agree, or the worker fails to realise the client's ability to be independent. What is even more likely is that the end of the relationship will be determined by such extraneous factors as a client's discharge from hospital, the end of a court order or the client's attainment of the age of majority. In these circumstances, the social worker would again be well advised to consult the literature of functionalism.

1 Sullivan, Harry Stack, *The Psychiatric Interview*, 1955

6 Group Interviewing and Counselling

Social group work has now come to have almost as many meanings as social casework and so a first essential is to define our terms. In this book, the terms ' group interviewing and counselling ' include all work with more than one client simultaneously. This covers a multitude of possibilities which need to be examined, but first it may be helpful to look at the antecedents of social group work in the forms in which we know it today. Essentially there are two main streams, recreational activities and group psycho-therapy, and it is the various offshoots and combinations of these major sources of inspiration which make up what is now generally described as social group work.

The development of recreational and leisure activities mainly with young people developed in the United States largely from the Settlement movement. It was encouraged by the propensity of American parents to send their children camping in the summer on a scale that has been unparalleled in Britain.

Although courses in social group work have been taught at American universities for over half a century, for most of that time there was quite a strict demarcation between group work and case-work, which was sometimes regarded as a superior pursuit. Social casework and social group work students were meant to know something of each other's activities but they were expected not to trespass on each other's territory and caseworkers cherished a stereotype of a group worker as dressed in gym shoes, with a whistle and a dogged enthusiasm for togetherness.

Group psycho-therapy was quite a different matter. Sigmund Freud did not extend the theory of psycho-analysis to groups in any detail although he touched on the subject on a number of occasions, but he prophesied that it would be one of the major developments of analytic theory after his death. This has certainly been the case and, in the field of mental illness, particularly the neuroses, the psycho-therapeutic group is now one of the most important forms of treatment.

As with the classical model of psycho-analytic treatment of the individual, social workers borrowed heavily from the findings of group psycho-therapy, of which there are now many forms, and many psychiatric social workers have had experience of working with psycho-therapeutic groups.

The present position is that the recreational and psycho-therapeutic strands of social group work are now inseparable. For the past twenty-five years in the United States social group workers have been associated with social caseworkers in the same professional association. In Britain, social group workers have only just begun to establish their professional specialism and current developments in social work education would seem to indicate that in future all social workers will be expected to have a basic competence in all methods of social work, with perhaps specialist knowledge in one area. Associated with the development of group psycho-therapy is the growing interest of social scientists, particularly psychologists, social psychologists and sociologists in such aspects of the nature of groups as leadership, composition, structure, communications and many other issues, all of which have been the subject of much research.

From all of this it may be gathered that the range of group counselling and interviewing is enormous. It includes the transitory waiting-room group described in Chapter 4, or it can be described as the way of life of some hospitals and psychiatric prisons, which are sometimes described as therapeutic communities. Therapeutic groups may meet in or out of a social work agency, they may consist of few or many members, with rigid or flexible rules of membership, and the sessions may last for any period from a few minutes to several hours and continue over a period of weeks in a social work camp, and months and years in a therapeutic community. Even so, despite these very wide limits, it is possible to distinguish different types of groups and to suggest a number of considerations to help the social worker decide if group counselling is appropriate in a particular case.

In terms of the most notable characteristic of the work of a social group, there are three types: activity groups, therapeutic discussion groups and participant groups. These three main types are themselves very broad and any particular group situation may have elements of all three, but one would usually predominate. The names are largely self-explanatory. The activity group would have a common activity for all its members, but this might range from a group hike in which the conversation would probably be stimulated rather than inhibited by the activity and the group structure would be fluid in the extreme, to a situation such as a social drama in which the activity was all-absorbing, when the members would enact a play which they make up as they go along, or a painting group in which conversation and art activity would co-exist.

The therapeutic discussion group would not have extraneous activities but would usually concentrate on a discussion of the problems of the members in order to alleviate their condition. This may be done most often in a psychiatric setting with a psychiatrist or psychiatric social worker as consultant to the group but, in recent years, it has often been tried in other settings, for example, prisons and borstals with basic grade prison officers as chairmen of the discussion group. A very frank account of some of these experiments is contained in the Home Office publication *Group Work in Prisons and Bostals*.[1] As a result of the work of Howard Jones at the University of Leicester, there was quite a lot of experimentation with therapeutic discussion groups in the probation service which is summarised by Hugh Barr in his study *Group Work in the Probation Service*.[2]

Participant group work is so called because it involves the social workers and the group members sharing some sort of life experience rather than merely the restricted contact of the counselling session. Thus the child care officer camping with a group of children may share the experience of cooking and eating and relaxing with the group, instead of just seeing them in the formal interview situation. Technically, all residential social work should be included under this heading, which gives some idea both of the potential of this form of work and its strain.

Some Advantages of Group Interviewing and Counselling

One of the basic hypotheses of social work is that man is a gregarious animal who needs to be able to function adequately in group situations. Obviously solitude plays an important part in the development of the individual, but prolonged isolation is generally a sign of serious emotional difficulty. It follows, therefore, that the social worker concerned with his client must always take into consideration how the client functions in groups. Although man is gregarious at all ages, this seems to be of special significance at certain points near the extremities of life. Any such suggestion that adolescents and old people are more gregarious than the rest of the population needs some qualification. However, it does seem to be true that the older child and the young adolescent seem to be happy only in a herd-like involvement with their group and direct their attention away from the family. The explanation for this lies in the need of the adolescent to change his role from that of a child to that of an adult. Anyone who wishes to specialise in social work with young people must take account of their predilection for peer-group activities and it is no accident that the recreational tradition of social group work is mainly concerned with youth, although other obvious factors influencing this are physical capacity and leisure.

The position is not quite the same with the old person. Certainly old age often involves a change of role which requires adjustment, for example the death of one of the partners. Since, in our society, it is becoming more uncommon for grandparents to live with their married children, this could force the remaining partner to seek the companionship of others in a similar position The difficulties with the old arise because there is no inherent reason for withdrawal from the family group, as there is with adolescents, but the social worker is presented with a ready-made problem which indicates the use of group counselling for dealing with a number of people in similar circumstances at the same time. Total identification with the peer-group is not so marked with old people, but any social worker specialising in this field will need to take these affiliations into account.

. It frequently happens that a social worker in his diagnosis will realise that a problem is essentially long-term. The multi-problem family who have been clients of the social agency for twenty years are not going to be able to manage independently as the result of a few one-to-one interviews, however talented the social worker, and the delinquent boy who lives in a delinquent sub-culture and who has no major disturbance in his family life is likely to be very little affected in his conduct by individual interviews. Similar examples can easily be found in every field of social work, and in many of them it will be necessary for the social worker to provide long-term support for his clients. The use of groups is an obvious choice for such clients if only because it avoids the dependence upon crisis which tends to be a feature of the one-to-one situation.

This truth was well known to the pioneer social workers in the days when social workers were almost exclusively concerned with poverty, which was obviously not going to be altered fundamentally on any short time-scale. Instead of seeing individuals at the agency, they relied on home visiting and this use of the family group will be considered in detail in Chapter 8. For their younger clients their one prescription was to persuade them to enrol in some group organisation. This reliance on clubs and uniformed organisations has sometimes been criticised as an abdication of the social workers' responsibilities, even though they sponsored and helped in running them, but it may be that in the circumstances they were taking the most effective course.

At the present time most social workers are often compelled to have clients with whom there is no pressing problem. It may be as the result of a statutory order or an administrative regulation which is fundamentally well conceived. For instance, no one would quarrel with the regulation that social workers regularly have to visit every child who is in foster care and, provided there is no special problem, the social workers very sensibly usually choose to visit when most of the family is at home. There are a number of reasons for this but, if the social worker visits when only one of the foster-parents is present, then it is practically impossible to eliminate all traces of confrontation from the interview.

The probation officer who has a client who is the subject of a probation order which extends beyond the period of crisis very often takes the line of spacing the interviews at longer and longer intervals, which tends to emphasise the stilted and unhelpful nature of the interviews when they do take place, when it might be much more constructive to see such a client in a group situation. This phenomenon may also explain why so many ex-prisoners who have opted for after-care help from the probation service fail to keep more than one appointment. It could be that a group meeting would be a more acceptable medium of help.

Clients who have no urgent, pressing problem are not confined to social workers who are mainly concerned with statutory orders.

The medical social worker with the long-term geriatric patient may find either that individual interviews are a great strain or else they are nothing more than social chats. In fact, there are a number of accounts which describe just how lively a group session of even apparently feeble old people can be.

One of the reasons why social workers choose to see their clients either in groups in the agency, or with the rest of the family in their own homes, is that it enables the social worker to see his clients' social conduct at first hand. It is often a revelation for social workers when they live with their clients for a time to realise how much of their personality was not revealed in individual interviews in the office. In the one-to-one static situation there is so much emphasis on verbal facility that the potential client who is not good with words just cannot be assessed and the social worker's knowledge is restricted by the inevitable distortions of the client's account of his own activities. In a participant group situation the social worker can see the client in a whole series of life situations and his knowledge of the client must be rapidly increased, as must be the client's knowledge of the worker. To a lesser degree this is also true of any group situation, even within the restrictions of a discussion group,' that it is still open to the social worker to observe the client's behaviour towards others directly.

The use of the group to bring together clients with similar problems is deeply rooted in social work practice. In the history of medical social work, for instance, at the beginning of the twentieth century, the problem of helping patients suffering from tuberculosis to persist with the unpleasant regimen which was then the prescribed method of treatment, was most effectively tackled by bringing them together as a group so that they could encourage each other. It is precisely the same technique which has been adopted successfully by Alcoholics Anonymous, which places so much stress on the community of problem that no one is allowed to attend the meetings who has not suffered from alcoholism. This example has now been copied by sufferers from neuroses and gambling and there is a basic similarity in some of the communities of former drug addicts who live together in order to solve their problem.

The main factor involved is mutual encouragement. Knowing all aspects of the problem, the group members can warn each other of unexpected difficulties, support each other at specially difficult moments about which they can sympathise, and, perhaps most important, because each one of them has at some time been personally overwhelmed by the problem, there is no destruction of self-respect which can come from the feeling of shame at being the only member of the group to suffer from the problem.

The role of the social worker in such circumstances is that of an enabler, to be as unobtrusive as possible but to bring about the circumstances in which these forces in the group can operate freely. Thus the social worker might take the initiative in bringing the group together and help them find a suitable meeting place. However, it would always be necessary to remember that the help would come from within the group and any over-active role on the part of the social worker could well have an inhibiting and, therefore, anti-therapeutic effect. As one of the aims of social work is to work towards a situation in which the client does not need the assistance of the social worker, so the natural progression is for such a group to function without the presence of the social worker.

A more sophisticated explanation of the uses which the social worker can make of the group situation in helping to modify the client's conduct has been outlined by Kelman in a very important paper in the *International Journal of Group Psychotherapy*.[3] In Chapter 3 we looked at the three stages of influence in the one-to-one interview defined by Kelman as compliance, identification and internalisation. In his study of groups, Kelman builds on this basic model and deduces that the corresponding stage to compliance in the one-to-one situation is compliance with the anticipated audience of the group. Identification with the social worker becomes identification with the group, which, to use the technical language of the social psychologist, becomes the normative reference group, the source of standards against which the individual can measure his conduct. Finally, the internalisation of the worker's standards is replaced by the acceptance of the group as representative of the values of society.

Here again, the emphasis is on the social worker as the enabler whose task is to set up the circumstances in which therapeutic forces in the group may be brought to bear on the individual. This reliance on the group instead of the social worker's own personality as the therapeutic agent is one of the major distinctions between work with individuals and work with groups. It is also an excellent illustration why work with families should be generally classed with groups rather than individuals, because working with the family as a whole involves the social worker working with the forces within the family rather than relying on his own personality as the major resource.

Some Disadvantages of Group Interviewing and Counselling

Some of the disadvantages of working with groups may be deduced from the discussion of the one-to-one interview in the last chapter. For instance, the client who is very immature may simply not be able to stand the competition for attention which is implied by the group situation. As such clients form a part of all social workers' clientele, it is important to remember that the method of treatment should be related to the client's needs rather than the worker's preferred method. It is well known that many forms of pathological behaviour may be caused by attention seeking. The young child who begins bed-wetting soon after the new baby is born, the child in the impersonal institution who begins stealing, may both be manifesting a lack of attention and to attempt treatment in a group, at least in the initial stages, is illogical. It may well be that a test of the effectiveness of treatment will eventually be how the client can function in a group, either his own family or some other form of group, but in the initial stages the social worker would be well advised to treat such a client individually.

This situation is not confined to clients who are children. The immature adult may present very similar problems and, because there is a greater expectancy of maturity in the adult, so there are fewer natural sources of help and it is all the more important that the social worker should make a correct diagnosis. A well-known attribute of serious physical illness is that it causes the patient to lose interest in what is going on around him. It is as if he needs to concentrate all his energy on overcoming his illness and it frequently happens that he regresses emotionally. The patient who is ordinarily able to tolerate frustration may become selfish and demanding and the experienced medical social worker would use individual treatment .

The obvious reason is that such a patient can have the undivided attention of the social worker and while this does not mean that his unreasonable demands would be literally gratified, he would have satisfaction for his emotional demands. All of this follows naturally from our consideration of the one-to-one interview but there is another important reason why a social worker would not attempt to deal with such a patient in a group situation. To continue with the illustration of the hospital patient, it sometimes happens that because of the architecture of our hospitals, a group of such patients may be housed together and may reinforce each others' fears to such an extent that there is a state of group hysteria. This is a very complex phenomenon which does not necessarily manifest itself in overt over-emotional behaviour but may be internalised in such a way that each individual is having to cope with the combined fears of all the members of the group. This is obviously an impediment to recovery which can best be removed by breaking up the group. The social worker should be wary of bringing such a group together and careful watch needs to be kept on all social work groups for any signs of this phenomenon. If this situation occurs then it is almost certainly advisable to break up the group.

This has particular relevance to residential institutions which, from one point of view, may be described as participant group work. In a specialist children's home, for instance, or in a probation hostel, there must be a danger of collecting together a group of immature clients who may make life more difficult for each other. At a time when there is a general shortage of residential accommodation it may not be possible to avoid this altogether but it should always be taken into consideration by anyone who has responsibility for selection. At least there should be an attempt to provide the immature members of the group with sufficient individual attention so that they do not feel compelled to upset their fellow-residents.

Quite apart from the immaturity which makes an individual unable to cope with the group situation, it is important for a social worker who has established a group or is working with one, to ensure that the group dynamics are positively therapeutic. This is a very general statement and to comply with it the social worker would have to pay attention to many features of the group. However, to neglect it can have serious consequences because the extremely strong pressures which a group can exert may be used to inculcate values which would not be approved by society. To take a well-known example, quite apart from all their merits, it is sometimes the effect of badly run scout camps or army cadet camps that boys are inculcated in the habit of smoking, even though this is contrary to the ideals of the camp leaders. Similarly, it sometimes happens at camps run by probation officers, who become preoccupied with the administration of the camp, that delinquent activities are planned in which there is pressure for all the campers to become involved.

This problem may be considered in terms of leadership, in which there is a struggle between the social workers and members of the group who will use delinquency as a means of subverting the support of the group members and so using a situation set up for one purpose, such as a probation camp, for quite different ends, the organisation of a delinquent gang.

It is by an extension of this mechanism that borstal and prison can become colleges and universities of crime and the probation officer who neglects his waiting-room should not be surprised if it becomes a centre where law-breaking is planned. This situation is not confined to delinquency. Anti-social activity can take many forms and may just as easily be expressed in physical and mental illness as in crime.

Social workers who do not take their clients camping, or who do not live with them in a residential institution, may not see this problem in such stark terms but what is known about group dynamics may give indications for or against the use of a group in a particular situation.

One of the factors which has to be considered is group transference and counter-transference. The importance of group membership to the individual is such that everyone has a whole store of experience which comes into play in regard to group situations in the same sort of way that ordinary transference affects individual relationships.

The client who has a lengthy history of being rejected by groups may feel what appears to be unreasonable diffidence about offering himself for membership of the most accepting social work group and may need special help to get over this difficulty. As with individual counter-transference, the social worker will be irrationally affected towards groups by his own personal experience and will tend to view social work groups in terms of this experience.

One can also look for help with this problem to the work of

Bion.[4] This has already been referred to in Chapter 3 with regard to problems of communication but it is also of significance in deciding the question of whether the social worker should use group methods of treatment in a particular situation.

As we have already seen, Bion's thesis is that any group operates at two levels, the task performance and the basic assumption group. The work group involves using the resources of the group to perform whatever task has been set, but if for any reason this is not possible, that the task is beyond the capability of the group, or that it is ill-defined or that there is a lack of unanimity in the group, then the basic assumption group takes over.

The basic assumption group is related to the id of the individual personality and might almost be described as a group id as it is potentially always present in the group situation and its most salient factor is that there is no learning or progress in the basic assumption group.

The significance of this analysis for the social worker considering the use of a group is that unless the purpose of the treatment is to give the client insight into the nature of group dynamics as in sensitivity group training, then it is vital to have an attainable group aim.

Stated in this condensed, abstracted form the meaning may not be clear, but many social workers who have, for instance, experimented with forming a discussion group from amongst their clients without any clearly defined purpose in mind may well have found the project becoming more and more diffuse, like a river losing itself in a marsh until eventually the main stream is entirely lost sight of. Similarly, if there is no agreement as to leadership or the execution of decisions, there may be all manner of irrelevant side-tracking and bickering between the members which is of no assistance to them in the solution of their problems and may be positively detrimental.

Consideration of this problem will be of assistance in helping to decide the form which a group should take. In the one-to-one situation we saw how an office interview without the distraction of any other activity tends towards confrontation and crisis. In the group situation, unless the group has a definite problem which may be solved by discussion, then the social worker ought to take steps to involve the group in some form of activity or else the attributes of the basic assumption group will come to the fore. In

Alcoholics Anonymous there is a deliberate attempt to foster a sense of continuing crisis in order to prevent the activity of the group being hindered in this way and it is an important characteristic of every successful group that it works in unity towards an attainable goal. The social worker who sponsors a group of foster-parents will have no problem in keeping the group interested in the solution of the many problems which face foster-parents, but if the aim is to keep a group of youths off the street then something much more active than a programme of discussions is called for.

General Considerations

BREAKING UP A GROUP

As well as using his knowledge about groups to decide whether or not to introduce a client into a social work group, a social worker may also act to bring about the dissolution of a group which is against the best interests of the client. The example which first comes to mind is the delinquent gang and the alternatives are to try to modify the ambitions of the gang so that they are socially acceptable, or else to cause the group to break up.

The considerations which should govern this decision are again the interests of the clients rather than the personal predilections of the social worker. If genuine emotional needs of the members are met through their membership of the gang then the social worker would have a responsibility at least to try to resolve the differences between the mores of the gang and those of society in general. The way this might be achieved will be considered later in this chapter but, if the group is only held together, at least for some of the members, by satisfying some need in a pathological way, then the social worker's duty in respect of those members is to detach them from the group if not to break it up altogether. It is not always easy to distinguish one type of gang from another and indeed one may find a gang which is simultaneously meeting real emotional needs for some members and for others is acting as a basically disturbing influence.

A better example of a pathological group may be the association of drug-addicts as linked with the supplier. In such a group there is practically no emotional satisfaction to be gained from the group, in which the members may display the most profound antipathy for each other and certainly for the supplier. In these circumstances, the action of the social worker would probably be to inform the police, which would probably have the effect of disrupting the group through the arrest of the ringleader. However, in other circumstances the social worker may use his knowledge of group dynamics to cause the break-up of the group.

The obvious way would be to infiltrate the group, so that when the social worker is accepted as a member he is in a position to dispute the aims of the group with the leader. In the event, the social worker may succeed in altering the leadership or else by impeding the attainment of the group task could bring into play the basic assumption group which we considered earlier, which may well cause the group to disintegrate. In the delinquent or unlawful situation such a course of action should never be entered into lightly or without careful preparation because if the leader of the delinquent group wishes to counter the social worker's interference, he may well redouble his activities in order to accomplish the work task of the group and so the social worker's intervention may have the effect of increasing the mischief, at least in the beginning.

This basic decision of whether to support or help to break up a group is something which every social worker has to face, because quite apart from any other group with which he may be in contact, every social worker works with families. It is not uncommon for a social worker to conclude in effect that the dynamics of a family are so pathological that it is in the interests of the members that they should be separated on a long-term or permanent basis although the reasoning would not usually be presented in such stark terms. Such a decision is often taken in recommending that the local authority should assume parental rights over a child, but a more common situation occurs every time a social worker concludes that it would be advisable for a client to spend some time away from home. It is essentially the same decision as helping an adolescent to establish his independence of his family by leaving home, and the ways in which the social worker can operate in these specialised family situations will be considered more fully in Chapter 8.

AGENCY CONSIDERATIONS
The decision as to whether group counselling is appropriate in a

particular case is not left to the social worker to determine solely in terms of the client's interests, since agency expectations may well have a decisive influence.

One guide to the expectations which an agency or a branch of the social work profession have is the arrangements which it insists on for the education of new members of the profession and for the continuing education of the staff members it employs. It is disturbing that hardly any important social work agency in Britain insists on an adequate basic grounding in group counselling for its workers. Even though many of their clients face problems which would best be treated by group methods, the acquisition of such skills are left to the enthusiasm of individual social workers and clients are often inappropriately treated simply because of the limited skills of their social worker.

No doubt financial limitations are mainly to blame. In the short period usually available for the acquisition of social work skills it is probably not possible to teach more than one-to-one work, with some study of the family. However, to the extent that social work education reflects the demands of the agencies, the lack of group work training is almost certainly evidence of an under-valuation of group work methods. One would not wish to underrate the importance of tradition in social work but it is unfortunate if it is used to justify the limitations of the past being perpetuated to the detriment of clients.

Composition of the Counselling Group

THE DISCUSSION GROUP

Social group work is almost entirely concerned with counselling rather than interviewing as the compilation of a report or any other extraneous purpose is almost invariably carried out with clients individually. This is to minimise the degree of interaction which the social worker has to analyse and also to allow him to focus more completely on individuals in respect of whom he may have to make a recommendation as to future treatment. An exception to this might occur when the social worker has the opportunity to have a number of sessions with a client on whom he has to prepare a report, and then he might use one or two in a group situation to observe the interaction of the client with other members of the group. Otherwise, the social worker is almost entirely concerned in group work with using the group as a medium of treatment and this falls within our definition of counselling.

The first consideration is the composition of the group, in which the social worker has to take into account such factors as the number of members and their personality characteristics. For a sedentary group whose business is entirely or mainly discussion one would suggest approximate limits of six to ten members, particularly if there is only one social worker present. The minimum number of about six is proposed because below that figure it may not be possible to avoid a suggestion that the group session is no more than a number of individual interviews held together. Each client may feel constrained to talk only to the social worker and to be silent when another client is speaking, whereas one of the intentions of group counselling sessions is to allow interaction between the group members which the social worker can observe and promote.

The upper limit of about ten members is proposed because otherwise it is not possible for the social worker to pay even a modicum of attention to all the members. Even with ten members this can be a full-time task for the social worker with a lively group and prevent him taking his part in the group interaction. Another consequence of having too many members present at a group counselling session is that the group tends to lose its coherence and to splinter into sub-groups.

Apart from number, Kelman also lays stress on the balance of homogeneity and heterogeneity in the group. This may be expressed in many ways but in general involves choosing members because they have common interests and yet there needs to be variety in the group. The reasoning behind this is readily apparent, that with a common, homogeneous element, discussion would become too diffuse and it would be very difficult to establish an acceptable group task. On the other hand, without some variety, there would be a danger of the group becoming monolithic and limited by the uniformity of experience.

To translate this into practical terms, a social worker may wish to set up a group of foster parents to resolve some of the problems which they find in fostering. The common element of fostering is, of course, an element of homogeneity but this may be reinforced by choosing several members of the group from the same neighbourhood or from the same age-range. Elements of heterogeneity, of variety, might be provided by members with experience of fostering immigrant children or short-term foster parents, if the majority of the group were mainly interested in long-term fostering, all of which would be expected to throw some light on the central problem and also add to the interest of the discussion which none the less would have a common theme.

THE ACTIVITY GROUP

The social work group which is primarily concerned with an activity, particularly if it has a long-term programme which allows for freedom of movement, has much more flexibility with regard to structure and composition. It may indeed be of the same size and make-up as the sedentary discussion group but there are also many possibilities of delegated leadership with the social worker assisted by voluntary or professional help and the activity group as a whole consisting of a federation of small groups with a more or less unified purpose.

A social work camp illustrates this idea very well, with the social worker acting as camp leader supported by auxiliaries with responsibility for specialist functions or allocated to particular small groups. The division of the membership into tents or separated huts for sleeping would provide a natural small group structure and the setting up of groups for specialist activities would provide an alternative basis for division. Assuming that the camp lasted for a minimum period of several days, this would allow the camp leader to have direct contact with each sub-group and he would be kept informed of their progress by his assistant leaders.

One advantage of this form of organisation, provided that it is reasonably flexible, is that it allows more scope to the individual to take part in a group which meets his need and, if it is not possible to allow the members complete freedom of choice about group membership, it is easy enough to arrange that every member has experience of two or three different groupings for sleeping, eating and specialist activities.

From the social worker's point of view this type of organisation has the advantage that as well as providing comparative information as to how the individual responds in different group situations, he is also able to observe the interaction between groups which can be a very illuminating source of information about individual members. The relationship between groups is the essence of community work and is normally considered on a much bigger scale, but it can be very instructive even with a total membership of perhaps twenty people.

The example of the social work camp is only one illustration of how a large activity group may be organised. A social club would also normally be formed on the basis of a number of sub-groups, the membership of which might be extremely fluid and the movement between groups might be the most profitable subject to study, although it is doubtful if any one observer would be able to collate all the information even on this limited subject.

One of the most difficult problems of work with groups is the sheer abundance of material and the necessity to select particular aspects to study and follow through. This is difficult enough in the small group, but when there are a number of interacting sub-groups, the membership of which may be fluid, the selection of material to follow through requires great skill if valuable insight is not to be lost.

The Analysis of the Group Interview

It is not possible in the scope of this book to offer any model for an exhaustive analysis of group dynamics, which extends across the boundaries of at least three academic disciplines – psychology, social psychology and sociology. Instead it is necessary to refer the reader to specialist works in these subjects, a knowledge of which is essential preparation for any work with groups, and concentrate here on selected aspects of group dynamics which have a special bearing on group counselling. However, even a topic such as leadership has been the subject of many major studies and so it will be difficult in a few pages to avoid the charge of being at best arbitrary and at worst capricious.

LEADERSHIP IN GROUP COUNSELLING

The very fact of the group postulates leadership. The one cannot exist without the other, and for the same reason, that it is impossible to list every variety of group, so leadership has an almost infinite number of variations. In essence leadership is the expression of the will of the group and because the social worker is always concerned with the decisions which the group takes, so he must be involved in leadership.

In a different context, Max Weber defined the two types, charismatic and bureaucratic leadership. Charismatic leadership may be roughly described as inspirational, the sort of leadership which in a crisis inspires confidence that all difficulties will be conquered. Charismatic leadership is usually centred on a person whereas bureaucratic leadership may be collective and arouses confidence because of patient attention to detail and provision for all eventualities.

Social workers do not often choose to be charismatic leaders, although there are occasions in social work in which the difficulties have seemed so insurmountable, or the clients have seemed so depressed, that the only way to achieve results in the short term has been for the social worker to seize the initiative and lead the group into action.

One of the reasons why social workers are generally chary of seeking this form of leadership is that it isolates them from the rest of the membership of the group and so it is not possible to express their concern for individuals which is denoted by the social work principle of acceptance. Another disadvantage of charismatic leadership is that it highlights the phenomenon of scapegoating which, although it is invariably associated with group leadership, may be particularly difficult to handle in the group with charismatic leadership.

Scapegoating is a subject which has not been fully explored in the literature on groups, but because it may seriously affect the welfare of members of the group it is naturally of importance to the social worker. The roles of leader and scapegoat are inseparable, the one being the mirror-image of the other, although it is possible for one person to combine both roles so that, for instance, in politics, it is common for the failed leader to be reviled to the same degree to which he was once praised. However, it is more common for the displeasure of the group to be centred on someone other than the leader and one of the functions of the social worker in the group situation is to ensure that the success of the group in attaining its goals is not achieved at the expense of a scapegoat, unless the social worker himself chooses to occupy that role.

Just because bureaucratic leadership is by its nature less

dramatic, so the phenomenon of scapegoating is also less in evidence and, in a group situation in which the leadership potential of the members is not adequate for the needs of the group, the social worker may, particularly in the early stages, join with some of the members to form a collective bureaucratic leadership.

Even in these circumstances, the aim of the social worker would be to foster active leadership by the group members and as soon as it was practicable to adopt one or more of the other leadership roles which are possible in a group. The preferred role is often as an enabler or resource-figure, which could be described as the traditional role of the social group worker. For instance, in recreational work with adolescents, the social worker might accept responsibility for the provision of suitable premises and equipment even though the detailed programme would be a subject for the group to determine for itself. The social worker might be expected to be a source of ideas for possible activities and, when the group got into difficulties which it could not resolve, then the social worker would be called upon as a consultant or even as umpire to help settle disputes.

The role of consultant or counsellor is particularly appropriate in the discussion group where the social worker is often wise to avoid the role of executive chairman, which has charismatic overtones, assuming that the group is able to generate sufficient impetus to ensure its continued existence. However, consultants are also often the focus of hostility by the group.

The overall aim of the social worker who is working with a group is to help the group to function without his assistance and progress towards this aim may be measured by the worker's changing role. To begin with he may need to inspire it with enthusiasm for whatever task lies ahead, after which he may be concerned to hand over leadership to the members, retaining a consultative role for himself which may itself change to the role of observer as the group learns to become self-regulating until finally he can fade out of the group which no longer has a need of his services.

The Balance of Power in the Group

Just because group work consists in part of relationships between the social worker and individual members of the group, so much which was said about the one-to-one relationship holds true for groups, but in Chapter 3 a brief reference was also made to the significance of the work of Simmel in the analysis of group dynamics in terms of dyads and triads.

This is another subject which can only be touched on because of its extensive ramifications and refinements but without an appreciation of this method of analysis many of the alliances which manifest themselves in group counselling would be quite incomprehensible.

While admitting the danger of over-simplification, the basic thesis of Simmel, which has been more fully analysed by Caplow in an important study, *Two Against One: Coalitions in Triads,*[5] is that in any relationship between three parties there will be a tendency for each of the two stronger parties to seek an exclusive alliance with the weakest member. A lot depends on the relative strength of the three members, and other factors need to be considered, but if no single party is greater than the other two combined, then there will be a tendency for the weakest member to choose an alliance with the next weakest rather than with the strongest. One of the consequences of this in group counselling can be that avoiding the power position of leadership may make the social worker attractive as an ally and he may find himself being wooed by the factions in the group.

This situation gives the social worker the opportunity to influence group decisions without the disadvantages of an active leadership role but, for the social worker who does not appreciate what is happening, the danger is that he will be misled into thinking his ability to influence the group is due to the attractiveness of his personality.

The number of possible triadic relationships increases sharply with the number of members of the group and by his understanding of the dynamics of the group, the social worker is able to use his position as a member of the group to alter the balance of power as he thinks best in the interests of the group. It is from this method of approach that one may see how the social worker can use the basic role of group member in the interests of the group and this completes the spectrum of the social worker as leader, consultant and member.

Interaction Between Groups

Compared with the study which has been made of what goes on inside a group, comparatively little is known of interaction between groups and no doubt this accounts for the relatively underdeveloped state of community work, of which interaction between groups provides the basis. However, hypotheses derived from group psychotherapy and supported to some extent by experimental models suggest that the internal dynamics of a group are strongly affected by its relations with other groups and it is plainly the responsibility of the social worker to gain an understanding of how this operates. It is, for instance, well known that the homogeneity of a group is emphasised when its existence is threatened by another hostile group and it is not difficult to think of situations in which this phenomenon could be used by the social worker in the furtherance of his work.

The task of the social worker dealing with the relationships between groups is essentially the resolution of a paradox. Groups which are not in close contact tend to have exaggerated and unreal ideas of each other's activities. News of any internal difficulties in one group will tend to be construed by the other that it is falling apart and signs of success will similarly be taken as evidence that the other group has discovered a magic formula.

These phenomena are apparent in the relationship between political groups, and other situations in which there is a strong element of rivalry, but they are inherent in every inter-group situation and may be observed, for instance, in children's groups. However, the problem of distance leading to fantasy is nothing like so great as the difficulty of establishing relations between groups. The basic problem here is that anything approaching full communication would involve the groups losing their separate identities and to entrust communications to emissaries means that they are effectively detached from the group which they have to represent.

In social work terms it may be the task of a social worker to work with two groups which are both concerned with one problem. This may involve the coordination of the work of two committees in a traditional community organisation situation or the task may be to counsel two family groupings concerned with the problem.

The resolution of the paradox that both distance and proximity between groups would seem to present insurmountable problems to their cooperation seems to be to focus their energies on the problem rather than on their relationship. This is a pragmatic solution, but its efficacy can be attested by any social worker with experience of inter-group relationships and any social worker who doubts its truth should try for himself to establish a working relationship between two groups without focusing on a common problem to which they are able to make a distinctive contribution.

1 Home Office Prison Department, *Group Work in Prisons and Borstals*, 1962–6
2 Home Office Research Unit Report, *Survey of Group Work in the Probation Service*, 1966
3 Kelman, Herbert C., ' The Role of the Group in the Induction of Therapeautic Change.' *International Journal of Group Psycho-therapy*, XIII, No. 4, October 1963
4 Bion, W. R., *Experiences in Groups*, 1961
5 Caplow, Theodore, *Two Against One: Coalitions in Triads*, 1968

7 Matrimonial Interviewing and Counselling

Everything which has been said so far about the general principles of social work and specific techniques in particular situations is applicable to matrimonial work. Some of the specialist literature on this subject occasionally seems to suggest that matrimonial work is a world apart, calling for an approach which differs from other fields of social work. It is true that matrimonial counselling is of great importance both for the happiness of individuals and the well-being of society, but on both counts it is neither more important nor technically more difficult than many other problems faced by social workers. It is also true that there is a place for specialist skills for dealing with unusually complex and difficult matrimonial cases, but every social worker needs a basic competence in matrimonial work. Matrimonial difficulties may be the presenting or underlying problem in all fields of social work just because the institution of marriage is so common. Apart from the fact that it is not desirable, it is certainly not practicable to refer all matrimonial problems to a specialist in that field.

The attention of the reader is called to the juxtaposition of Chapters 7 and 8. Chapter 7 deals solely with the matrimonial relationship and should be read together with Chapter 8 on family counselling and interviewing. The dynamics of the whole family must be seen as a whole in any marital problem. It is all too common for the differences of the parents to be solved at the expense of the children and if this is to be avoided, the social worker must have intimate knowledge of the operation of the family group as a whole, and even in childless marriages, relationships with in-laws must be taken into consideration.

Even so, provided the rest of the family is not lost sight of, there is ample justification for examining the matrimonial relationship separately. It is the foundation of all family life and any social worker who does not appreciate the significance of the marriage partnership cannot hope to give assistance with family problems. Although all the general principles of social work are applicable, the matrimonial relationship is distinctive in that, alone of the family relationships, it is the only one which is the subject of choice. It is true that parents can, to some extent, choose whether or not to have a child but they cannot predetermine the sex of a child, let alone its personality, and with other blood relationships there is even less control.

It is on this basic fact of choosing to be married that all social work with matrimonial problems is constructed and it is first of all necessary to understand how the choice is made.

The Concept of Fit

The process which leads to the matrimonial partners choosing each other or agreeing to a proposal of marriage is usually known as the fit, that is the way in which the personalities of the partners interlock and complement each other and what they find attractive or acceptable about each other.

Anyone who is intending to do any social work which involves a matrimonial relationship needs to know how husband and wife came to be married, if they are to have any understanding of subsequent difficulties. Obviously the nature of the matrimonial relationship will alter as the personalities of the partners change and by tracing this process it may be possible to understand how incompatibility has come about.

HOMOGAMY AND HETEROGAMY

The concept of fit is generally agreed to have two constituent factors, which are sometimes known as homogamy and heterogamy. In fact, these rather abstruse technical terms just mean that when the individual is making his choice of marriage partner he is looking for someone who will match his own personality (homogamy) and also complement his personality by making up what he lacks (heterogamy). Both homogamy and heterogamy are well illustrated in the matrimonal interviews given in Appendices 3 and 4. The couple are of roughly the same age and share the same ideas about work and leisure. To use a very imprecise phrase, they are in agreement about general life-style, the main evidence for which is the very specific complaints which are made about the husband's occasional outbursts of violence, and husband and wife both say on separate occasions that, generally, they get along well with each other.

The heterogamous or complementary aspects of their personalities are just as evident. The husband is agreed by his wife to be usually placid and easy-going, anxious to avoid trouble, whereas she nags constantly and frequently makes an issue of trivial decisions, such as where to cross the road.

SOCIOLOGICAL AND SOCIAL ANTHROPOLOGICAL ASPECTS OF FIT

Homogamy and heterogamy are usually considered in terms of attitudes and personal relationships, but they may also be examined in terms of social class. The vast majority of marriages in Britain are between partners from the same social class and the same neighbourhood. The fact that the husband is usually a year or two older than the wife is probably no more than a reflection of the greater social maturity of post-adolescent girls, so that all of these factors are sociological expressions of homogamy. Heterogamy is similarly demonstrated sociologically through the complementary roles of husband and wife, with the British husband accepting primary responsibility for earning money and the British wife for looking after the home.

Social anthropologists have demonstrated very convincingly that there is nothing universal about this pattern and that in some cultures quite opposite roles are assigned to husband and wife. Even in British society there are important regional differences concerning important features of the roles of husband and wife, such as the expectation that the wife will go out to work, and it is very important for any social worker involved in matrimonial counselling to appreciate the sociological norms in the area in which he is working. This is true of all forms of social work but it is of special importance in matrimonial work as the continuance of the relationship is so often at stake.

The reference norms of matrimonial behaviour will certainly vary in important respects between different neighbourhoods in the same town, and even street by street. They are compounded of the most subtle nuances of mutual expectations, many of which will be unconscious on the part of the marriage partners, but these will still have to be understood by the social worker if he is to help them resolve their difficulties.

An important section of these expectations will be the taboos, which may range from the practically universal prohibition of incest to quite local disapproval of women going alone into pubs or men wheeling a pram. Only by understanding what is tacitly or explicitly forbidden in the marriage can the social worker appreciate the gravity of the transgressions of one of the marriage partners. In the case recorded in Appendices 3 and 4, it was obviously within the norms of the marriage to go to parties where a lot of drink was consumed, but any violence by the husband towards his wife was regarded as unacceptable by both of them. These norms are probably shared by most members of British society, but it is still of importance for the social worker to identify taboos and expectations in the marriage in order to relate them to general norms of society.

The Conduct of the Marriage

Any definition of fit and role relationship is in danger of making these concepts seem static and fixed when it is obvious that it is the developing incongruity of personalities which is the cause of trouble in many marriages. It is true that any individual has a basic personality set but this is only one of the many constituents of the personality of the adult. The fact that a high percentage of divorces takes place between middle-aged partners is no doubt due in part to the fact that they have developed away from each other and, even in marriages of only a few years standing, there may also be an element of incongruity, of no longer matching each other's needs, which has largely come about since the marriage.

For instance, any social worker who is frequently involved in matrimonial counselling will come across cases in which, by advancement in his work, a husband is tending to move into a higher social class to which his wife does not aspire, or else through premature illness, one of the partners is unable physically to fulfil role expectations. The possible variations are endless and because of the natural hazards of life, the changing nature of the matrimonial fit is a source of difficulty in every marriage, to which the partners have to accommodate themselves. The idea of living happily ever after is true only of fairy tales and it is evidence of the adaptability of the matrimonial relationship that relatively so few marriages founder on this problem.

THE SEXUAL RELATIONSHIP

Apart from the question of choice of partner, the other main distinctive feature of the matrimonial relationship is that it is normatively overtly sexual. A great deal has been written in recent years about sexual compatability in marriage and teaching about this should commonly form part of the training of all social workers. They are, however, two major pitfalls for the social worker in the area of the sexual relationship in marriage. The first is that, as well as the general norms of society, it is quite essential to have an understanding of the reference norms of the client who is in trouble. The reference norms for sexual conduct in a stockbroker belt are hardly likely to be the same as those of the mining village. Unfortunately for the social worker, there is usually no published information on this subject which is sufficiently localised and detailed, and until social workers themselves acquire the skills to gather and analyse this information, they will be dependent in the first instance on the acquired experience of their colleagues and, eventually, their own findings.

Just because sexual relationships are so private, and so closely allied to the inner workings of the individual personality, it is practically impossible for the social worker to view matrimonial relationships except in terms of his own experience and fantasy. Objectivity on the part of the worker in this area is very difficult to attain, even assuming it is desirable. In an attempt to remain impartial, the social worker sometimes puts on a front of emotional detachment which may have the effect of persuading the client of the worker's unwillingness to help.

The use of a consultant will often identify for the social worker those attitudes which represent his personal prejudices but, in the absence of objective data gained by research, there is still the danger that the client will be subject to the collective prejudices of the social workers which may well be reinforced by consultancy. There have been many examples of clients being treated, almost indiscriminately, with the latest nostrums fashionable in social work. On the subject of the sexual relationships in marriage as in all other areas of human experience, the social worker should at least be aware of the pressure groups advocating this or that, so that his help can be in line with the general principle of helping the client to decide on his own course of action.

In the matrimonial interviews set out in Appendices 3 and 4 there is not much explicit reference to the sexual relationship of the couple. As these are among the first interviews of the case, one would expect that the social worker would not broach such personal matters so soon, particularly as they both say that there is no difficulty in their sexual relationship. It is, however, interesting to look at the related topic of deciding to have children. In the interview with the wife set out in Appendix 3, it is generally agreed that the present childlessness is a subject of concern and although the topic is introduced rather arbitrarily on page 236 line 204 it obviously strikes a chord in the wife. However, in the double interview in Appendix 4, although the subject arouses some interesting responses in the husband, it usually seems to be introduced into the interview because of the determination of the social worker and against the wishes of the couple, so that one would ask if he were not imposing his will on them. (See page 246 line 194 *et seq.* and page 248 line 290.) It is not possible to answer this important question with the limited evidence which is available, but there is no doubt that the topic should be pursued further in future interviews, and possibly broadened to explore the couple's sexual relationship if they were willing. It would also have been of great assistance to the social worker to know the incidence of childbirth among this couple's reference group and answers to a whole host of related questions would have been helpful in identifying likely pathological areas.

Decision in Marriage Counselling

One of the questions, which the social worker dealing with a matrimonial problem has to decide, is whether to work directly with one or both partners. He may not, of course, have any choice because a husband or wife may refuse to see him, or else one of the partners is not available. Occasionally there are situations in which agency policy indicates that the work should be undertaken with only the husband or wife. We shall look at the relative advantages of working with one or both partners, and some other less common ways of working, but it is important to remember that in every case matrimonial counselling is essentially triadic, between husband, wife and social worker. It is not uncommon in some agencies for the social worker not to see the husband almost as a matter of policy, but even so there is no doubt that the triadic relationship still exists even though the relationship between the social worker and husband entirely depends on communication through the wife.

The significance of the triad in matrimonial relationships is well known to folklore. The role of mother-in-law is celebrated and the eternal triangle is a major theme in fiction.

Whether he deals with one or both parties to the marriage, the social worker is the third member of the triangle and he ignores the power aspects of this situation at the expense of his work. Most of the literature on matrimonial counselling concentrates on the dyadic relationship between the counsellor and client and if both partners are present they are treated as one person by emphasising their similarities and ignoring their differences. One-to-one relationships in matrimonial counselling are indeed important but, simultaneously, the effects on the third member of the triangle, even if he is not present, need to be remembered.

These points are well illustrated in the interviews given in Appendices 3 and 4. In the first, when the social worker sees the wife alone, one tends naturally to analyse the interview solely in terms of how the social worker deals with his client. It is quite instructive to consider the different picture which the social worker must have of the husband at the end of the first interview and at the end of the second. The husband is quite explicit on the subject: ' I do not know what my wife has been telling you, but . . .', showing his concern at how the wife was intending to use the social worker as her ally in her struggle with her husband.

Even a short acquaintance with the matrimonial work of the probation service suffices to show that the apparent aim of many of the women clients who seek help with matrimonial problems is to seek an ally against their husbands and probation officers are often requested to visit the erring husband to put him in his place. This is not necessarily wrong in appropriate situations, although it would invariably require careful thought, but it is only one of many ways in which the social worker can make most effective use of his situation in the triad.

Some of the complexities of the situation are illustrated by the two-person interview in Appendix 4 during which there is a constant struggle between husband and wife to enlist the support of the social worker, and it is a fascinating exercise to chart the shifts of power during the interview.

For the first three pages of the interview the conversation takes place almost exclusively between the husband and the social worker, with the wife making occasional interventions. An attempt by the husband on page 243 line 58, to establish a dialogue with his wife by asking her a question soon fails because both husband and wife are more concerned in enlisting the support of the social worker. On page 245 line 148, the social worker shifts his attention to the wife and when, on page 246 the husband tries to butt in, the social worker heads him off by continuing to direct his words to the wife. This continues until page 248 line 260 when the social worker–husband axis is restored with the wife very much the third person and even referred to as ' your wife '. The social worker shifts back to the wife on page 251 line 406, and the husband does not become the focus of interest again until page 253 line 503, when he dominates the scene until the social worker winds up the interview.

Either consciously or not, the social worker first takes up with one and then the other and in this way maintains a fluidity which gives him great scope. It is also interesting that the helpful, unassuming manner of the social worker has the effect of preventing a coalition of husband and wife against him as they do not see him as a threat. At a time during the casework when the emphasis is on establishing a therapeutic atmosphere this is obviously the correct role for the social worker but, at a later date, it might be advisable for the social worker to adopt a less amenable role in order to bring the marriage partners together, allied against him.

This is not an easy task for a social worker, as superficially it seems a denial of the principle of acceptance and it often takes a skilled consultant to help a usually mild-mannered social worker, such as we have in this case, to see that to be available and sympathetic to both partners might be a form of self-gratification which is inimical to the interests of his clients. One does not, of course, suggest that he should adopt a hectoring, bullying manner, but he may well have to decline further interviews firmly, on the grounds that they were having a divisive effect on the matrimonial relationship.

The main factors to be taken into consideration in deciding

whether to see one or both parties to the marriage at the same time are roughly the same as those listed in Chapters 5 and 6. By dealing with one person, it is much easier for the social worker to establish a professional relationship which enables the client to mature, and the opportunities presented by emotional crises can be more satisfactorily handled.

On the other hand, sole reliance on the one-to-one interview over a long period can be productive of crises because of the physical confrontation and these may be anything but helpful to the process of reconciliation. Similarly the one-to-one interview inevitably produces a distorted picture of the other partner which can only partially be corrected by seeing him. Joint interviews enable the social worker to observe the matrimonial interaction between the partners at first hand, although in a rather artificial situation, and also enable the social worker to observe his own impact on the marriage and to influence the matrimonial relationship directly.

Experiments have been carried out in which both parties to a matrimonial dispute have their own social worker and then there are occasional meetings at which both social workers and clients are all present together, although consultation is usually limited to the social workers. This method of working is extensively written up in the publications of the Tavistock Institute of Marital Studies and by Henry Dicks in his book, *Marital Tensions*[1] but, in general, financial considerations and limitations of staff time would generally preclude the use of two social workers on one case.

It is unlikely that the use of group counselling for matrimonial problems would economise on staff resources but the other potential advantages are so great that it is strange that group counselling is not commonly practised in this field. It may be thought that the close relationship between the marriage partners would militate against general group interaction but this would not apply in situations after separation had taken place. The problem of deserted wives in serious financial trouble is now common enough to justify group counselling and discussion as the usual means of creating mutual support.

Even before separation had been agreed upon, a group of individuals or couples who suffered from the same general problem, such as sexual incompatibility, might well find that a discussion with others in the same plight was helpful. Certainly at a time of constantly increasing numbers of marriage breakdowns it is an idea worth exploring.

The Crucial Decision

Just because marriage comes about through a choice of the partners so it can be ended in the same way, and the first question which has to be answered in every matrimonial counselling situation is whether the partners are seeking help in dissolving or strengthening their relationship.

This issue is quite universal and every form of society has had to devise machinery that recognises the breakdown of marriage. It may be that certain obstacles are erected to the legal recognition of the end of the marriage, and even that subsequent re-marriage to another person is forbidden, but no society refuses to recognise marriage breakdown.

Anyone involved in marriage counselling needs to be informed of the main connotations of marriage breakdown, legal, social, sociological and psychological, to name but a few, because anyone considering the possible ending of his marriage needs to consider the relative advantages and disadvantages. This will not take the form of a written balance sheet, because the various items are impossible to quantify and decisive irrational factors may even be unformulated, but the social worker is under an obligation to be at least as well informed as his client if he is to have any pretensions to expertise.

The marriage laws are extraordinarily complicated and there is no doubt that the ability to purchase the best legal advice can have a decisive effect on the outcome of a court-hearing. Even so, a thorough appreciation of the main principles of the laws concerning separation and divorce, and related subjects such as financial provisions in these cases, is needed by every social worker.

It is also important that the counsellor should be aware of the sanctions which society maintains against ending a marriage. Although it is universally admitted that marriages do break down, yet it is also generally believed that marriage and the family are the foundation of order in society as a means of socialising children. As a result, the apparatus for registering the end of a marriage often contains obstacles to prevent that step being undertaken lightly.

Much of this is common knowledge and indeed the social stigma of divorce or separation is probably the greatest deterrent, although this varies between social classes and from district to district, and the social worker needs to appreciate both the local and the overall situation. However, in addition, there are often financial penalties, particularly when there is only one relatively small income for the support of two separate households.

As well as helping the individual to adjust to the situation of ending a marriage, there are many other social work tasks associated with separation and divorce. For instance, it is now a responsibility of the probation service, in appropriate cases, to prepare reports for the divorce courts on the financial position of the parties and the interviews which are necessary for the purpose of preparing these reports are as difficult as any which a probation officer conducts. In addition to the emotive subject of money, there is the further complication of the other feelings associated with the ending of a marriage and, to make the task still more difficult, a report has to be prepared which can be challenged by both parties to a dispute, which often engenders great bitterness. Even so, most probation officers would agree that their task is not only to assist the court in making an equitable judgement but the interviews would also have an aim of helping the parties to work out their own adjustment to the ending of the marriage. In view of the number of separation orders and divorces granted each year, it may be that this service is capable of much greater extension in the future.

The Task of the Social Worker

The decision about ending or mending the marriage may present no problem at all. Both partners may have firmly made up their minds that they wish to be separated or divorced and, acting on the principle of self-determination, it is certainly not the task of the social worker to try to impose either his own or the conventional attitudes of society in enforcing a reconciliation. It is true that the social worker needs to satisfy himself that it is a firm decision which both partners appreciate but this should not be used as an excuse for pressing them to try again despite their better judgement.

Even though in a minority of cases a separation or divorce has been fixed upon before the social worker is consulted, there may still be plenty for him to do. As well as oiling the legal machinery and helping with practical arrangements, there are bound to be strong feelings at the severing of a relationship which was presumably once intended to be permanent and probably feelings of guilt and resentment have to be dealt with.

At the other extreme, the decision whether to part or try to work out a reconciliation may occupy the whole of the period during which the social worker is involved and still not be settled when he ends his contact with the case. There are some marriages in which this indetermination seems to be more or less permanent, but the majority of cases lie somewhere between these two extremes, when there is no fixed determination to part or stay together until the social worker has been consulted and the social worker's task is then to help the clients to make a decision and to carry through what they have decided.

It may happen that the marriage partners do not agree. One may seek a reconciliation while the other wants separation or divorce. Assuming that neither one has a change of heart it is usually possible for the partner who desires a separation to impose his will, but this can lead to very unhappy situations in which people live in hope of a reconciliation for years on end. The social worker then has the difficult task of deciding whether to try to help such a person to come to terms with the inevitable or to cherish a forlorn hope or a grievance, which might be a source of strength but which is more likely to depress or embitter his whole personality.

In any event, until the decision about separation or reconciliation has been made, it is not possible for the social worker to make further progress because his subsequent actions are governed in part by that decision, and the alternative courses of action are generally divergent. For instance, when there has been a final parting, it is possible for the social worker to deal with the client in a one-to-one relationship without worrying too much about triadic relationships, whereas when the task is reconciliation, then the dynamics of the triad are all-important.

The importance of helping the marriage partners to come to the correct decision about whether to make or break their marriage can hardly be over-estimated, as it is likely to be of continuing significance for them in their own view of themselves, the concept of self-worth which is a major factor in mental health. If the social worker does no more than help both the parties to the marriage to reach a decision with which they are satisfied then he has rendered them great service.

While there is no serious dispute that when the partners to a marriage have reached a firm decision to separate, this should be allowed, in effect this begs the question of how one recognises that such a decision has been reached. In almost every case, the decision to separate comes only at the end of a long process. Every marriage has its tensions and it is probably true that every marriage at some point comes close to breakdown. There is no recognisable dividing line between those problems which are resolved or accepted and those which lead to the breakdown of the marriage. The difference is generally of degree and persistence, and a lot depends on the personality of the partners and the surrounding circumstances. What may be in some circumstances no more than a minor irritation may become quite intolerable because of difficult housing conditions or chronic ill-health and it is well known that what bothers one person is a matter of comparative indifference to another.

The difference is by no means solely dependent on maturity, although this can be an important factor. An immature person may well find positive gratification in a situation which someone more mature would seek to avoid at any cost. For instance, the concept of neurotic balance in marriage is one which the social worker ignores at his peril and it can easily happen that what was originally an appropriate match becomes unbalanced because of the uneven development of the partners.

Recognising the point at which a decision to separate represents the settled intention of the marriage partners is impossible in any absolute sense. Statements of intention to separate are often made in many marriages in an attempt to alter the balance of power and the stability of the marriage will largely depend on the extent to which both partners are willing to accept the outcome. The guiding principle for the social worker is to focus on the clients and to allow them to make the decision for themselves.

The Social Worker's Prejudices

While it is quite acceptable for the social worker not to seek to minimise the obstacles to separation erected by society he must be very careful not to obtrude his own prejudices and the safest way is to recognise them rather than try to repress them.

In practical terms this could mean that a probation officer would not seek to short-circuit the business of applying for a court summons or legal aid, as both of these procedures have a short delaying effect which is presumably intended by society as an opportunity for second thoughts. However, the probation officer would also need to be very careful what impression he gave of the difficulties of the legal procedures because this could be an attempt on his part to persuade or even coerce the client towards a line of conduct which he favours.

In other agencies, particularly those which are not normally concerned with legal processes, the social workers would usually have to be careful to deal with their own feelings about courts dealing with matrimonial cases so as not to predispose their clients against seeking legal remedies.

It is not possible to deal with every way in which a social worker may allow his own feelings to over-influence his clients as this depends on the individual personality of the social worker. This is very much the job for a consultant, and while one would advocate that consultancy should be available in all forms of social work, the far-reaching effect of decisions in matrimonial and family work means that consultant help is specially necessary in these areas.

Agency Function

In many agencies there is an in-built predisposition towards reconciliation and, while this is understandable as a reflection of the interest which society has in maintaining the stability of marriage as an institution, the social worker has to be careful that he does not allow this to upset his work by making him attempt to influence the partners against a decision to separate. On the other hand, the social worker acts as a representative of his agency and needs to be in general agreement with its policies and so he should not disguise the interest which the agency has in reconciliation.

The way in which agency function manifests itself is likely to differ in every agency. In some cases it may be overtly stated that funds are available only to help with reconciliation, and clients who may be seeking help with separation or in making a decision are refused or discouraged in the reception procedure. The sort of thing which can happen is that the case will be taken on only when both partners are willing to be interviewed, which is likely to presupppose reconciliation. This is not unreasonable on the grounds that every agency must necessarily be selective about its clients and provided it is explicit, and that there are alternative sources of help to which the client may be referred.

However, it is not difficult to find instances in which ostensibly all clients with matrimonial problems are accepted, and yet there are forces at work in the agency to persuade the social worker to work for reconciliation. In the probation service, for instance, the way in which the probation officer has to present his statistics leaves him in no doubt that reconciliation is to be judged as success and, by implication, separation and divorce are failure, or at best a lack of success.

As in other forms of social work, the limits imposed by agency function may be used as a source of strength in matrimonial work. Time is the obvious example and it is not difficult to understand how the need to limit the length of an interview in order to free the social worker to serve other clients can be used to give shape to an interview which might otherwise be formless. It has been noticed in an earlier chapter how the impending end of a session may act as a spur to the client to become involved in the problem-solving working. Similarly, the fact that ideally one would use a particular way of working, but for administrative reasons this is not possible, can be used as an opportunity to discuss with the client why such a method of working would have been preferable.

It is, of course, important that this sort of argument should not be used to justify not making adequate administrative arrangements. In all of these instances, it is only the worker who has a fair amount of insight into his own subconscious motivation who will be able to strike the right balance and he will be largely dependent on the availability of adequate objective consultation.

Reconciliation

One of the purposes of this chapter is to show that interviewing and counselling in matrimonial situations is concerned with much more than reconciliation but, in many cases, reconciliation is the wish of the client and becomes the main focus of the social work. It is therefore important that we should try to identify the various alternatives which are available to the social worker.

At a time of increasing interest in emotional problems we should not overlook the use of material resources and services. Just because the subject of money is so highly charged emotionally, social work skills are often needed to enable the client to make the best use of what is available and many a marriage has foundered because there was not sufficient money to pay the bills. It is easy enough to say that it is part of the social worker's job in matrimonial counselling to assess the financial situation and either help the couple to spend their money more wisely or else to try to make more resources available, but the execution of this task calls for the greatest possible social work skill. As with problems of debt, to which it is closely related, good advice is dangerously easy and one can usually expect that the clients have been deluged with it by their family and friends. The social worker who gives advice without at least taking the trouble to establish an understanding relationship with his clients is almost sure to find himself in a position of conflict with them. It is probably true to say that the clients could offer the social worker just as good advice about the conduct of his financial affairs which he would be equally reluctant to put into practice.

It is, however, important in this context to distinguish between advice and information. Very often the social worker will know of resources of which the client is unaware, either to supplement income or for the provision of services which may meet a need with which he was unable to cope unaided.

In this connection, factual knowledge, both of national and local facilities, is the first essential and the social worker needs both imagination, to see how the available services can be used to meet the client's needs, and energy, either to bring the client and the service together or else to generate whatever resources may be lacking.

It may be that the situation needs no more than the application of an available resource or, as in the case set out in Appendices 3 and 4, there are no serious financial or material difficulties and the problem seems to be almost entirely emotional. In both of these situations, the relationship between social worker and client is vital, either as a means of enabling the client to make the most

effective use of the service or by using the relationship as the therapeutic tool.

We have already seen in Chapter 1 that the role of listener enables the worker to convey to the client that he is anxious to
understand the problem and that, by accepting the client as a person of intrinsic worth, irrespective of his conduct, the social
worker seeks to establish a relationship which will lead to an increase in the maturity of the client. Matrimonial counselling does
not differ from the general run of social work problems and the
social worker will seek to help the client to find his own solution
to the problem. However, given the persistent dilemma in matrimonial counselling of the triadic relationship, the self-denying
role which the social worker may adopt in order to establish social
work relationships with the clients as individuals may have the
effect of making the social worker an object of rivalry between
husband and wife and a further cause of difficulty.

This is a matter of the greatest importance in matrimonial reconciliation and the task of the social worker is constantly to
resolve the paradox that if he concentrates on the problems of the
individual he will endanger the relationship of the couple, and if
he is solely concerned with the partnership he loses his chance to
influence the actions of the individuals, which is the chief means
of bringing about change.

The answer would seem to be a delicate balancing act in which
the social worker endeavours to keep both perspectives within his
sights and as one shows signs of being overweighted so it is his
task to correct the balance.

It follows from this reasoning that, above all, the social worker
needs to be able to retain flexibility and he must resist attempts
to force social work in matrimonial problems into any set procedure. Individual and joint interviews and cooperation between
two workers, if resources allow, can all be used by the social
worker to prevent work with the individual marriage partners
from upsetting the marriage relationship.

There is, however, another side to this coin and the skilful
social worker can use the tension between the needs of the individual and the needs of the couple as a source of energy. The
point is well illustrated in the matrimonial case in Appendices 3
and 4. In the first interview, the social worker uses the one-to-one
interview to establish a relationship with the wife and to elucidate

the background material of the problem. By the end of this first interview there is little doubt that the wife sees the social worker as a helpful, sympathetic listener and he is aware of how she views the problem. A one-to-one interview with the husband could be expected to produce a very similar outcome. On the other hand the price which the social worker pays for this interview with the wife is to raise the husband's suspicions that his wife has gained an ally who will be used against him and it is no accident that the social worker deliberately uses the first part of the joint interview to conduct a dialogue between himself and the husband from which the wife is excluded.

The social worker is skilful enough not to endanger his relationship with the wife by excluding her totally and, as a result, the joint interview is, among other things, a rich source of material about the matrimonial disharmony. Taken together the two interviews are extremely helpful to the social worker, the one in giving a historical perspective and an opportunity to establish a personal relationship, and the other in showing the nature of the dispute as it happens. The one complements the other and, if the social worker had been committed to one method of working to the exclusion of all others, he would have been deprived of information which he needed in order to help.

One of the roles which the social worker has to be prepared to accept in matrimonial counselling is that of scapegoat. In a sense this is true of all social work. The positive listening which is described in Chapter 1 is a means of sharing the troubles of the client and anyone who has undertaken this work even for a period of several hours will know just how exhausting it can be.

This process also occurs in matrimonial counselling but can also take on a new form in connection with the triadic situation, when the social worker is working with both partners to the marriage and he may become scapegoat for both of them. In an extreme case, this may go so far as the married couple ascribing their difficulties to the social worker and allying against him, or more often using either one-to-one or joint interviews with the social worker as a safety valve, to express the difficulties and frustrations of the marriage, thereby taking some of the pressure off their home life.

Many social workers dislike matrimonial rows taking place during joint interviews and will actively try to stop them on the grounds that they are destructive. This may be so, but the social worker faced with this situation needs to be sure that he is not merely seeking to defend himself from an unpleasant situation. It may be in the interests of the couple to have their disagreement in his presence so that he can share the problem with them. In the joint interview set out in Appendix 4, one of the strengths of the social worker is that he does not remonstrate against the quite sharp disagreements which occur from time to time.

The difficulty of working both with the individual and the couple in matrimonial work no doubt accounts for the significance of the personal situation of the social worker to a degree which is uncommon in any other area of social work because he is involved in making a decision about marriage. To give just two examples, it is sometimes demanded that a social worker who is dealing with matrimonial problems should himself be married. This applies particularly to men social workers and is sometimes explained on the grounds that because of the conventions of society, a married woman client might be embarrassed to discuss her marriage with an unmarried man. However, the more common explanation is that only if the social worker is married will he have an adequate understanding of the problems of marriage. The answer to this is that social workers deal with all manner of social pathology and it could hardly be advocated that they should experience every form of deviance before they can help their clients. The very fact of being married will incline the social worker to view all matrimonial problems in terms of his own experience.

The second example is that it has, for many years, been a little known and much neglected provision of the law that matrimonial clients of the probation service should be dealt with by an officer of their own religious persuasion. Again, it is not difficult to understand both the superficial reasoning which gave rise to this regulation and the illogical and impracticable basis of the argument. However, with this regulation and the emphasis on the marital status of the social worker, the true motivation is almost certainly a realisation of the importance of the personality of the social worker in resolving the conflict between individual interests of the married partners and the interests of the marriage. While the specific applications of this concept may be misguided one cannot dispute the underlying principle.

1 Dicks, Henry, *Marital Tensions*, 1967

8 Interviewing and Counselling with Families

Some of the recent literature on social work with families might lead one to the conclusion that the family is a new discovery in social work. It is true that some of the techniques of family therapy are novel but the family has been a central concern of social workers from the earliest days. Mary Richmond defines social casework as ' work . . . which has for its immediate aim the betterment of individuals or families . . .'[1] and this certainly accorded with the practice of the Charity Organisation Society both in Britain and the USA. Octavia Hill did almost all of her social work in the homes of her clients and with relation to the whole family. The police court missionaries, the forebears of the probation service, tended to come into contact with delinquent individuals, but their concern was always to restore them either to their own families or to graft them into some other form of family life. This was the general pattern of social work in the nineteenth and early twentieth centuries, either to be concerned with the family as a whole from the beginning, or with the individual whose family life is disrupted. The first hospital almoners had the dual responsibility of checking if the family's means were sufficient to pay for private medical treatment for the patient and also to see how the sickness of the individual affected the functioning of the family as a whole.

A diminution of concern by social workers for individuals as family members seems to have come about with the increasing influence of ideas of dynamic psychology. In a way this is surprising because Freud and his followers stressed particularly the family relationship between parent and child. However, the explanation for this is in the method of psychoanalysis rather than in its theory. In classical psychoanalysis, the therapist concentrates solely on the individual patient in the dimly lit anonymity of the consulting-room, a setting as far removed as one can imagine from family life.

In imitation, social caseworkers concentrated more and more on one-to-one office interviews and attempted to deal with any maladjustment in the family through contact with the individual client. This tendency reached its peak in the USA in the 1940s and it is significant that in the famous series of articles written in 1949 for the *Journal of Social Casework,* referred to in Chapter 3, Swithun Bowers surveys and discusses the various definitions of social casework from 1919–49 with only passing references to the family and certainly with no suggestion of its basic importance for the social worker.

Since 1949, the family has again come into its own in social work, for a whole variety of reasons and the dynamic psychologists are now fully alive to the importance of the interaction of all the members of the family and not just the parent–child relationship.

This accords with the experience of social workers that some of the most intractable cases are those in which the client has lost all contact with his own family and has not succeeded in being accepted as a member of any other. Not everyone needs to live as a member of the family of which he is a member by birth or by marriage. One knows of many examples of successful adoption and, less frequently, of cases in which even such a casual relationship as being a lodger provides the necessary connection with a family group. However, without some such connection, it is as though the individual is denied a quite essential source of satisfaction and the only chance for the social worker in such a case is to help his client to become a member of a family group. There are many possibilities, but without some access to family life the prospect of long-term stability for an isolated client is practically non-existent.

It is, however, important, in the excitement of the rediscovery of the family in social work not to lose sight of other insights which have been gained by social workers over the years and some of the currently popular methods of working with the whole family need to be used in conjunction with well-established methods of one-to-one and group interviews. For one thing, one of the purposes of family life is to enable the children to mature to a point at which they are no longer dependent upon their parents and are able to found families of their own in which they are parents. This process of helping the nuclear family group to split up is not impossible in family group couselling but it is unreal to expect that the process will always be painless, and the social worker may be able to give more effective help by concentrating at times on working with individuals. The suspicious, fearful adolescent may well see the social worker as the natural ally of his parents and only by keeping away from them altogether will it be possible to allay these suspicions in some cases. Similarly, in cases of childhood maladjustment, the social worker may seek to give the parents a degree of insight into the situation which would be inappropriate for the child.

Although the social worker should invariably study his client in terms of his family background, work with the family group as a whole is only one of a number of techniques which every social worker should possess, at least at a basic level, so that the client may be given whatever help is most appropriate. This means that social work with families includes everything which has gone before in this book, skill in one-to-one relationships, dealing with matrimonial problems, and with groups other than the family group. With this foundation, family group counselling and interviewing falls into place as an additional skill, to be used differentially when needed.

In the nuclear family in which there is more than one child, there are three basic relationships. The matrimonial relationship and the relationship between parents and child has been dealt with from almost every conceivable aspect in the vast literature of human growth and behaviour. However, the relationships between the children of the same family have received comparatively little attention even though it is obviously a rich source of information about many human problems. The difficulties of the only child, of the step-child, of the child who is separated in age by a large gap from his brothers and sisters, of the child who is physically or mentally abnormal in any way, are all reflected in relationships with the other children of the family and yet we know very little about this area, which probably contains the origins of many of the problems of concern to the social worker.

It is one of the most important discoveries of psychoanalysis for social work that all human relationships are seen to some degree in terms of an individual's relationship with parent, spouse or child. This is the origin of the concepts of transference and counter-transference and, while it is an essential part of social work education and consultation that the social worker should be aware of the distortions brought about by his own emotional history, so that the basis of counter-transference is constant for him, his client's view of the world is something which differs in every case. Thus the social worker needs to know about his client's family relationships, not only for their own sake but also because, unless he knows, for instance, how the client responds to his father, the social worker may not understand the client's conduct towards the social worker whom he may perceive as a father figure. This is a crude example to serve the purpose of illustration whereas the reality is much more subtle and all sorts of considerations of maleness and femaleness of both father and mother, brothers and sisters and the client's own children may all enter into the client's relationship with the social worker or with any other person with whom he is in contact.

As well as the one-to-one relationships in the family, it is also important to remember that the family is a group, albeit a rather specialised group, but still with all the charcteristics which the social psychologists and sociologists have shown to be common to all small groups. This means that the whole of the chapter on groups is relevant to the study of the family and it may be helpful to show the particular application of group phenomena to the work of counselling and interviewing with families.

In many cultures, and particularly those of Europe and America, family leadership tends to be associated with the role of the father, and the social worker dealing with the family needs to analyse leadership in the family group and whether it is contributing to the family pathology. This may occur in a whole host of ways. It may be that the father is too dominant and will not allow the adolescent children freedom to develop their independence or else, because of illness or choice, the father may have abdicated from his leadership position creating a power vacuum which causes difficulty for the whole family.

It is, however, misleading to think of leadership simply in terms of the position of the father as an individual. Leadership is a function of the group as a whole and changes according to the task in hand so that all the members may assume leadership attributes in particular situations and, while the father is usually charged with the responsibility to support the family financially, social anthropological studies have shown that in a sub-culture such as east London, social organisation is on a matriarchal basis and that on marriage a man becomes a member of his wife's family rather than the other way round.

Similarly, studies of immigrant families in England have shown that the ability of children to absorb language so much more readily than adults can mean that the children of immigrants are often used as a principal means of communication with the rest of society and in this way have a leadership role which it is very important should be recognised by any social worker seeking to help these families. Thus, quite young children will take their parents shopping and accompany them to the doctor or any social work agency with which the family has dealings, and the social worker or whoever is concerned would be well advised not to treat such a child merely as an interpreter but as a key figure in the leadership structure of that family group.

There are many other examples of the children adopting leadership functions in families. Usually in default of one or both parents, older children may well accept responsibilities far in advance of their age, such as quite young girls acting as mother to the family. It is much rarer to find boys taking the place of their fathers. This may be explained in part by the greater emotional maturity of adolescent girls compared with their brothers, but is also due to the economic structure of western society, that it is practically impossible for a boy to earn sufficient to take the place of his father in supporting the family financially.

All of this has significance for the social worker and to take the last point first, social agencies concerned to keep a fatherless family together should consider supplementing the family income if there is an older boy who can otherwise take the place of the father. However, the connection between the father's earnings and his role as head of the family in some respects is so close that the money would have to be channelled through the father-substitute if he is to be expected to have any authority.

Analysis of the various factors involved in leadership can have many lessons for the social worker, and particularly for the younger social worker. For many years the expectation was that social workers would adopt the role of a parent figure and limitations on the age of recruitment meant that social workers were more of an age with the parents than with the children of any family in which they were working. This is now changing. There is an increasing number of qualified social workers in their early twenties and it is often quite false for them to assume quasi-parental roles. This is not invariably true, as a dependent client may be quite willing to see a younger person as a parent figure, but it is often much more appropriate for the younger social worker to adopt the role of a helpful older son or daughter and as such make an invaluable contribution to the welfare of the family.

All forms of leadership can be appropriate to the social worker who is trying to help families. For instance, with a family which was completely depressed as the result of years of adversity, charismatic leadership at least in the early stages of the case might serve to strike a spark and, through the enthusiasm of the social worker, make the family willing to look again at their position in society. This approach could be justified only if the social worker was prepared to give the members of such a family the long-term support which would enable them to bring about a change in their position in society. Without this backing-up work, when the initial enthusiasm wore off, they could be in a more depressed state than ever as the result of yet another disappointment. However, assuming the long-term support, charismatic 'leadership on the part of the social worker may be just what is needed to get the case moving.

The connection between enthusiasm and youth may explain the curious fact that young and quite inexperienced students are often able to achieve results in cases which more experienced social workers have, in effect, written off as hopeless. It seems as if their freshness, their obvious desire to help, and their refusal to be daunted by the negative experience of others, all of which are aspects of charisma, can have the effect of galvanising people who have been impervious to the patient efforts of others, often over long periods of time.

On the other side of this coin, it is equally true that the enthusiasm of the student or the young social worker can wane as quickly as it grew and it then becomes the responsibility of the supervisor to see that the case is not just discarded in favour of some new interest and the complementary task of keeping alive the family's new-found spark of life is continued until they have been able to consolidate their gains. This process, which is neither more or less important than charisma, is an aspect of bureaucratic leadership. Its hallmark is patience and while its gains are less dramatic, they are likely to be longer lasting. In the welfare state, the role of bureaucratic leader for social worker will also consist in part of helping the family to unravel the complicated regulations which seem to be an integral part of the provision of help by statutory authorities.

Unravelling seems a very apt description of bureaucratic leadership and may be applied to emotional and relationship problems just as much as to material and financial difficulties. The relationship between stepmother and child which has gone wrong for ten years will never be sorted out in a single session, however emotionally charged it may be. But such an occasion may well provide the incentive for the many future occasions when the social worker listens to the often repeated complaints of misunderstanding and ill-will from both parties, either separately or together or in the family group, in an endeavour to help them work out a relationship which they can, at least, find tolerable, even if it is not a source of strength.

A case of this sort also illustrates the idea that the concept of leadership is inextricably bound up with the concept of the scapegoat. One major contribution of the social worker in work with families is often that he is willing to allow the members to express negative feelings such as anger, resentment and envy without any fear of retaliation. By offering this alternative focus, it is hoped to drain some of the rancour from family relationships and give a chance for some positive feelings to be expressed. In practice, things hardly ever work out so smoothly and, although there is often no great difficulty in helping the family members to express their negative feelings to the social worker, there is no guarantee of an automatic or quick lessening of tension in family affairs. A social worker who takes on such a task can find himself operating under a considerable burden for long-term goals which are often difficult to recognise, particularly for someone closely involved in the situation.

It is not only the social worker who adopts the role of scapegoat in the family and in any case it is not necessarily an unhealthy phenomenon that another member should have this role. A natural part of the process of family life is that parents should accept responsibility for the transgressions of their children and part of their leadership function as parents is that they should take the main brunt of the hazards which affect the family as a whole.

It is when the leaders of the group refuse to accept the scapegoating aspects of their leadership, and in the family this does not apply only to the parents, that difficulties commonly arise. Perhaps the best-known example is when one of the children is singled out as the scapegoat for the family and then such a child can be made to suffer both materially and emotionally to an astonishing degree in extreme cases. Cinderella is the archetype of such cases and in many of the battered baby cases, it seems that the scapegoating mechanism is at work.

In this situation there are many possibilities for action. The most extreme is to remove one of the members of the family group. In battered baby cases, it is not uncommon for one of the parents to be sent to jail and, if a parent is not imprisoned, then the child is often removed. This gross disturbance of the family group, which may even be carried to the length of separating all the members, can be defended on the grounds that their attitudes towards each other were so ingrained that there was no hope of altering them without drastic measures, and certainly the absence of one of the members of a group may give a social worker the opportunity to bring about a realignment in the family group so that it does not have to operate in this way in the future.

Another possibility, which we have already considered, is that the social worker should take over some of the functions of the family group scapegoat by willingly becoming the repository of the fears and difficulties of its members, and the counselling session in which the social worker adopts a positive listening role is the obvious way to achieve this goal. However, there is also a third alternative, that the social worker can use his position as a temporary member of the family group to bring about a realignment of its power structure.

Some indications of how this can be done have already been given in the previous chapters on groups and matrimonial work, in which the concept of triadic relationships was briefly discussed. In the simple matrimonial situation there is only one main triad, the husband, wife and social worker, and it is possible to enumerate the possible power combinations quite easily, although even concentrating on matrimonial problems one quickly comes up against additional complications if parents-in-law are taken into account and in the family, the role of the children must also be considered.

Some indication of the complexity of the power-structure in families can be given in numerical terms. In a nuclear family consisting of man, wife and one child, there is only one possible triadic relationship, in which all the members are involved, but even here there are three possible alliances of two members against one. In the family group of four members, there are four triadic relationships to be considered with twelve alliances and the possibilities increase greatly as additional members are brought in.

It is not traditional to discuss social work with families in terms of power struggles and alliances, but any case study will almost certainly show that the social worker does this, although usually instinctively rather than by conscious design. Indeed it follows from the fact that the family has all of the characteristics of a group that the social worker needs to be able to utilise the analytic concepts of the social psychologist in order to understand what is going on in the family group.

It may be possible for the experienced social worker who has undertaken a lot of work with family problems to rely on his instinct. Even then one wonders if his instinctive knowledge could not have been gained at less cost to his clients, but for the newly trained social worker there is a positive obligiation for him to understand the dynamics of the family group which he is seeking to help and to be aware of how this intervention may alter the balance of power.

It is not as if the social worker can opt out of this aspect of the situation. Whether he likes it or not, and whether he recognises it or not, his work will inevitably create a disturbance in all the family relationships. Rather than denying or ignoring this disturbance, he will do better to recognise it and seek to utilise it as a means of helping the family as a whole.

Although we have so far adopted a rather untraditional approach to the analysis of family dynamics, in practice it accords well enough with what social workers are accustomed to doing. For instance, when the family is having a problem in adjusting to the adolescence and emerging maturity of one of the children, it may be that the social worker would offer the adolescent a relationship in which he would be treated as an adult whose opinions were worthy of serious consideration, in the hope that this would to some extent remove the need for the adolescent to impose his adultness on the rest of the family. Alternatively, in the same situation, the social worker may give most of his attention to the father, recognising the threat to him of another male adult in the family and by offering the satisfaction of his support show the father that his position is not necessarily undermined.

In order to illustrate the various points, it has been necessary to describe common and clearly recognisable situations. These certainly exist but family dynamics are also manifested in subtle nuances which quickly change. In the last chapter we showed how in the interview set out in Appendix 4 the alliances within a triad changed at least three times during the space of a single interview.

On a longer scale, the changes due to time may cause major shifts in the power structure of a family. The infant becomes a child with constantly growing influence until he becomes adolescent and then usually leaves the family group to found a family of his own, while the parent may expect in later life to have a steadily declining position of influence.

All of these general trends are subject to the particular developments of the individual family and may contribute to a pathological situation. They all need to be understood by the social worker who is trying to help the family reach a solution to its problems. It is, however, a mistake for the social worker to suppose that a family has a single personality. One sometimes sees a diagnosis that a family is neurotic or psychotic. These words may be convenient labels but they ignore constantly changing interaction between the family members, which both gives a family its distinctive attributes and offers the social worker his main opportunity to help the members to alter their relationships so that they may individually derive greater satisfaction from their membership of the family group.

Like all groups, the family has no existence apart from the interaction of its members. It is true that in its dealings with the outside world, which could be described as its foreign relations, it sometimes pretends a unity, which in fact does not exist except for this purpose. The social worker seeking a convenient diagnostic label, such as neurotic, may be misled into thinking that the image which the family seeks to project to the rest of society is in fact a true description of family life. This process of labelling the family as though it were an individual is sometimes known as ' anthropomorphising '. Such a description can be made only from outside the family and it would be very rare that the social worker would be able to help from that position.

The social worker who is kept outside the family group will have no opportunity to study the system of communication in the family in which it is almost certain that the difficulties of the family will be reflected. We have already looked at some of the problems of communication in Chapter 3, but there are some aspects of this subject which are particular to the family group situation. For instance the family is, in general, the only group which shares its living accommodation. Social workers have long realised how much information can be gleaned from a home visit in which the evidence of family group life is all around for the perceptive observer to see. One can also learn a great deal about the set-up in the family from such simple things as the seating arrangements which the family make for the social worker's visit. For instance the probation officer calling to see why a twelve-year-old boy has not been to the probation office recently, finds the situation set out in the following diagram

boy

mother

father   probation officer

Father is sitting in the armchair. The boy is sitting at one end of the settee, with his mother sitting between him and the remaining seat on the settee, which the probation officer is invited to occupy. The course of the interview confirmed the family set-up which can be deduced from the diagram – that the father is expected to conduct the conversation with the probation officer while the mother acts as a shield for the boy. Any attempt by the probation officer to speak to the boy involves a physical contortion and is easily blocked by the mother, who can answer for him. So long as the three members of the family maintain this unity against what they perceive as the common danger, the probation officer is powerless but, instead of simply feeling frustrated and possibly labelling the family as neurotic, the social worker could learn some valuable lessons from this situation. It may be that the probation officer in such a case would decide that in the beginning stages more progress could be made by seeing the family members individually, or even in twos, rather than all together, at least as long as they were united in trying to stop him from establishing a relationship with the boy. Divide and rule is a phrase which comes to mind in this case and one trusts that if a social worker adopted this tactic, he would be aware of the danger of trying to force his way into the family group as a means of satisfying his own needs.

In this case a lot would depend on the nature of the problems which the family was experiencing. If they were able to manage reasonably well to live in harmony with their neighbours and were not seriously impeding the development of any of their members and particularly the boy, then the probation officer would have no right to use his knowledge of the dynamics of the family group to establish a place for himself. Instead he should accept the implied rejection expressed by the seating arrangement and confirmed by their management of the interview and keep out of the family interaction. However, in this case the boy was seriously delinquent to the extent that the court was likely to remove him from his home, and on this basis, the probation officer felt justified at least in trying to overcome the initial resistances of the family.

It would be wrong to construct too elaborate a hypothesis on one piece of evidence like the seating arrangement of the family group interview, which could be interpreted in several different ways. However, when the structure suggested by the seating is borne out by the conduct of the interview then the social worker would attach more weight to it and it would be very interesting at future interviews to note any changes which the family proposed in the seating plan.

In another case a child care officer was asked to call to see a married couple to discuss the possibility that they should adopt a child. When he called he found three people present, a man, his wife and a lodger. The seating arrangement was as follows:

man

wife   lodger

social worker

with the three members of the household seated on individual chairs and a fourth placed for the social worker to complete an approximate diamond shape. During the course of the interview it soon became apparent that the husband objected to his wife's relationship with the lodger and was seeking the adoption as an excuse that would force the lodger to leave the house. As an illustration of this, during the interview the husband tried hard to establish a relationship with the social worker. In particular, he was anxious to cut across any conversation between the wife and the lodger and while he had no objection to the social worker speaking to his wife, he endeavoured to stop him speaking to the lodger. In this way the dynamics of the interview are all illustrated by the diagram of the seating arrangements and the husband's task in controlling the interview would have been much harder if the seating arrangement had been different.

The Sociology of the Family

As well as dynamic and social psychological considerations, the social worker who wishes to help with family problems needs to know a lot about the sociology of the family. This is also a subject which it is outside the scope of this book to treat comprehensively but there is now an extensive literature with which social workers should be familiar. At the most, one can refer only to some topics of special importance and some of the special hazards which lie in wait for the social worker.

The definition of the family needs careful consideration if there is not to be a confusion of thought. In fact, the sociologists have shown that the term can have many connotations all of which have their own implications. The most common forms of the family which are of value to the social worker are the nuclear family, the family of procreation, the primary family, the extended family and the family of orientation.

The term nuclear family has already been used in this book to refer to the two-generation family of husband, wife and infant children. Sometimes the phrase ' fatherless family ' may be used to refer to a two-person family group, mother and child, but generally the nuclear family consists of at least three members. The significance of such very small family groups has increased in recent years for a number of reasons. Increased social mobility puts a premium on cohesiveness and smallness and housing limitations make more extended family groups impracticable Similarly, economic considerations and the birth-control movement all stress the advantages of the small, nuclear family.

The family of procreation is essentially a biological term, referring to the family of which one is a blood member. In most cases it is identical with the nuclear family, but in cases of adop-

tion, for instance, there is a distinction which is of great importance to the social worker.

Although in modern Britain the primary and extended family
have generally declined in relative importance to the nuclear
family, for most individuals they are still of considerable significance. The primary family may be defined as blood-relations who
live in the same household and usually extends to three generations, including grandparents in contrast to the two generations of
the nuclear family. However, it may also include cousins and
uncles and aunts who live in the same household. The extended
family, as its name implies, is an even wider concept which includes all close relatives, particularly those who live in the same
neighbourhood and may even be understood to include close
friends and neighbours who may not be related at all, but who
might, for instance, enjoy the title of honorary aunt and uncle.

The importance of these other forms varies family by family
and the social worker has to analyse each case individually to
appreciate how the various forms of the family are of significance.
There are also regional and class norms which the social worker
can find it very profitable to know. Willmott and Young[2] have
analysed kinship in east London and Elizabeth Bott[3] has made a
number of studies of communication networks involving families.
Many social workers involved in overspill housing estates are
aware of how many problems arise, particularly in the early stages,
from the feeling by the nuclear family of isolation from the extended family with whom all their lives have previously been
spent. On the other hand, in a higher-class area such a problem
could hardly occur and the influence of the extended family on
daily life would be negligible.

Again it is possible to make only broad generalisations to which
there are many exceptions and the social worker needs to know his
area in great detail so that he knows what is usual and what is the
exception in family life. The advantage of this knowledge is that
the social worker does not have to work solely on the basis of his
own experience and prejudices. This applies particularly to the
family of orientation, a concept which is likely to become of increasing importance as the incidence of separation and divorce
increases. The family of orientation is already familiar to the
social worker in several forms and its best-known use is in adoption, in which an attempt is made to substitute the family of

orientation completely for the family of procreation, to the extent of removing the child's birth certificate and substituting the certificate of adoption.

Fostering is a much less extreme form of the same procedure, although the term includes every gradation from child-minding for a few days while a mother is in hospital, to *de facto* adoption in which the only difference is the legal one that no court order has been made. However, the term ' family of orientation ' may have quite different connotations. For instance a lodger may come to be regarded as a member of the family group and while this relationship is not usually sufficiently permanent to act as a satisfactory substitute for the natural family, there are many exceptions. This is potentially of great importance to social workers who often have difficult cases in which the main problem is that the client has either not belonged to a primary family or has broken off relations with them. The experienced social worker who has to deal with such cases often tries to establish a relationship with one or two families in his area who are willing to take lodgers into their family, usually temporary, but occasionally with a view to longer stay. In the case of fostering, a whole administration system has been evolved, but in other fields the arrangement is likely to be much more *ad hoc*.

Divorce and separation are other subjects in which the objective approach of the sociologist can be of great assistance to the social worker. They are topics which inevitably arouse strong emotions if only because the serious tensions which occur in every marriage mean that the social worker has himself probably had to contend with such problems in the family in which he was a child and in the family in which he is a parent. In consequence, it is very difficult to find an impartial treatment of the subject and even sociological studies are liable to be partisan but with the guise of objectivity. This situation demands a competence by social workers to evaluate sociological studies rather than simply accept their findings. It also has important consequences for social work education.

If the whole family is the client, the social worker needs to decide if their individual interests are so indistinguishable that he will never be in the position of helping one to the apparent detriment of the others. Certainly appearances would argue otherwise and it is not difficult to postulate situations in which the interests of the different members of the family seem to be opposed. Where the mother of a young child is mentally ill but still capable of carrying out her mothering functions, the social worker will have to decide if he should encourage her to enter hospital for her own sake even though this will mean an emotional upheaval for the child. Such problems are incapable of resolution without a firm grasp of the basic principles of moral philosophy, and family life can provide some of the severest tests of the principles of self-determination and confidentiality. At what age should the child be helped to establish his independence of his parents? While one might object that this is a matter for the family to decide for itself, there are many cases in which the social worker has been vested with authority and cannot avoid being involved in the decision. Similarly, the social worker who is working with the family will soon find that any attempt to maintain absolute confidentiality between the various members is insupportable and, unless he has thought out for himself those areas in which it is vital, he will find himself in a sea of confusion in which the principle is abandoned altogether.

The reason the family is of such importance is that it has been confirmed by the social anthropologists that almost without exception, in every form of society, the family is the only effective means of socialisation. The only partial exception is the Israeli kibbutz system about which there has been considerable discussion and even the kibbutz does not attempt to displace the natural family altogether. Apart from this, no successful alternative has been found and the most satisfactory substitutes seem to be those which most nearly imitate the natural family.

There is, however, no agreement on which factors in family life are of most importance in this vital process of socialisation. Despite intense study, all the social sciences have their supporters and detractors. Psychology in several forms, sociology, social anthropology, law and economics have all claimed at various times to provide the most satisfactory basis for analysing family life and it makes an interesting occupation for the social worker to observe the relative ascendancy of one of the social sciences, to be followed inevitably by comparative neglect. In fact, each gives a vital but only partial explanation of how the family operates and in our present state of knowledge it is necessary for the social worker to know the main findings of each of the social sciences, keeping them all in perspective.

Family Group Counselling and Interviewing

It is natural that in view of the revived interest of social workers in working with the family as a whole and the recent experimental work in group dynamics that these two interests should be combined in family group counselling.

As with most new ideas or old ideas in a new form, the advocates of working with the family group as a whole have sometimes let their enthusiasm swamp their better judgement and exaggerated claims have been made that no other method of working is valid and, unless the whole family will participate, then no help can be given. Such statements are contrary to the spirit of the principles of social work and can only be of disservice to a social work method which is an important addition to the therapeutic range of social workers, but no more than that, and certainly not a replacement for other methods.

A more balanced approach is to examine the relative advantages and disadvantages of family group counselling and interviewing so that the social worker will be able to identify situations in which this will be the most helpful method of working. In essence, this consists of nothing more than the social worker meeting with the whole family group in order to resolve a problem with which the family is unable to deal. The meeting place may be in the social work agency or in the family home and making this initial decision needs considerable skill. A general consideration is that in the early stages the family group may feel more comfortable in the agency with its greater anonymity but may be willing to let the worker see more of themselves in their home as confidence is established.

Interviewing in the agency will generally have to be static, with all the group remaining seated out of consideration for other workers in the agency and this can prove both inhibiting and artificial, particularly for younger children who are not used to sitting still for long periods. Such restrictions are not necessary in the family home and the social worker can learn a lot from the kaleidoscopic change of groupings which can take place in a household even in the course of an hour. As the social worker comes to be more accepted by the family so he may be allowed to move about the house and Laing[4] has described how he conducted a diagnostic interview with different members of a family around the house.

The family group which the social worker chooses to work with may be the nuclear family, the family of procreation, or orientation, the primary family or even, exceptionally, the extended family. Again this is a decision which will have to be made according to the circumstances of the case and it is obviously one to which the social worker must give a great deal of thought.

Generally speaking, most of the literature on the subject of family group therapy takes for granted the fact that the family will be a small group with a range of four to ten members, according to the size of the household. This accords well with the size of most family groups except the extended family and several cases have been reported, in the American journal *Family Process,* of what is described as tribal network therapy. These involved a number of sessions, each of which lasted for several hours or more, in which not only cousins and other relations who lived nearby were invited to join the primary family but also friends and neighbours. A team of therapists then took part in what can best be described as a psychological free-for-all at the end of which the therapists held an evaluation session of which the dominant factor was the complete lack of confidentiality.

The difficulties of organising such sessions as a general rule are obvious. The cost both financially and in terms of manpower resources would usually make such a project impracticable and the psychological hazards are frightening. However, rather than writing off such experiments as displays of irresponsible enthusiasm, they can be of great interest to the social worker. For instance, they are an attempt to develop group therapy with the extended family group and one can imagine family situations such as those which are described in *Family Process* in which the total energy of the primary family is directed towards reinforcing the mental illness of one of its members, and the social worker may logically seek to use the extended family as a counterforce.

Although tribal network therapy is perhaps the most unconventional form of family therapy in present social work practice, the work of other therapists can also seem rather strange. We have already mentioned Laing's method of wandering around the house, and Virginia Satir in her book *Conjoint Family Therapy*[5] advocates what she calls family games. For instance, she noted the fact that in quarrels the participants would refuse to look at each other, or to use the technical phrase, would reduce their eye-contact. In treating such cases, Mrs Satir would ask the family to re-enact a situation in which a disagreement took place but on this occasion to make sure that they look at the person towards whom their remark is addressed. As an extension of this idea, it was postulated that eye-contact was generally representative of all physical contact and so on other occasions she would ask the family members to hold hands or otherwise be in physical contact while they simulated a quarrel. The hypothesis is that the contact, whether by eye or by touch, made it very difficult to maintain the quarrel and this would both give the family insight into their difficulties and also provide them with a remedy which they could use for themselves.

The main disadvantage of family group interviewing or counselling as a method of working is that it is difficult for the social worker to concentrate on a specific problem within the family. As a diagnostic tool, and as a means of getting to know the family as a group and how they interact, it is very helpful but the actual treatment plan may need to be much more detailed.

For instance, the problem in the family may be centred in the matrimonial relationship or one may have an adolescent who needs to establish his independence of the family group. In both of these cases, although the social worker will keep the general family picture in mind, in the one case he will probably concentrate mainly on the married couple and in the other on the individual adolescent. Other sub-groupings are possible and, in the family in which the main difficulty is the illegitimate child of one of the parents who is not accepted by the other, the social worker may concentrate on the parents and this one child, even though the opposing attitudes of the parents are reflected by the other children. The reasoning might be that if the parents' attitudes can be resolved then the other children can subsequently be helped to adjust their relationship.

Although family group therapy is usually written about in terms of family reconciliation, there is no reason why the social worker should not help the family group come to a decision to split up. The natural process is when the children leave home to found their own families, but other divisions, such as separation between the parents or removal of the children from their parents, also occur from time to time. It is possible for the family group counselling session to be used to help the members reconcile themselves to the wisdom of this decision. However, it is unreal to expect that all such decisions can be postponed until they have the full consent of all the group members and in these circumstances it may be that a family group session would have the effect of intensifying feelings of deprivation without allowing them to be resolved.

The great advantage of the family group session is that it allows the social worker to see family interaction for himself and not through the necessarily biased account of any one of the members. It is necessary to remember that family interaction represents all sorts of emotional levels. The social worker who has spent a few hours with a family group would be wrong to persuade himself that he knew everything about their relationships, but it would be surprising if a perceptive worker did not have clues about the most important ways in which the family operates.

It is practically impossible to understand the nature of communication between the family members without the social worker seeing them together as a group and, as the basic problem in family life so often consists of a defect in communications, this must always be allowed for in the diagnostic study. One of the problems of family life which has received a lot of attention in recent years is the ' double-bind '. In essence the double-bind occurs when a person receives two or more simultaneous but contradictory instructions. This is like a game which the player cannot win, although the consequences are likely to be much more serious than any game. The double-bind is now generally accepted as an important cause of mental illness in which the patient takes refuge from an intolerable situation. Similarly, in a delinquent subculture, a parent may express conventional disapproval of such delinquent acts as stealing but by his actions shows that he is willing to profit from such actions. One may also observe situations in which a mother calls the child to her, possibly with endearments, while her facial expression and body posture show that there is no such welcome.

Situations of this kind may threaten the whole stability of a family and yet the family members may be quite unconscious of their actions. The contradictory messages may also be expressed in such subtle and transient forms that only a skilled observer intimately acquainted with the family would be able to discern them. However, the potential threat of the double-bind to family life is such that if the social worker identifies its presence, this would

constitute a powerful argument in favour of family group counselling as a means of dealing with the problem.

Finally, the advantages of working with all the members of the
family together means that the problems of one or two members
will not be relieved at the expense of the others. Mention has
already been made of the scapegoat and very often social workers
have gone to great trouble to remove a child from a family in an
attempt to ease the pressure, only to find that the family immediately pick on another member to occupy this role.

In an apparently opposite direction, but one which is potentially
no less dangerous, one sometimes find parents who are ambitious
for their children and who push them to an extent which threatens
both their natural development and family relationships. Again, it
is no help simply to relieve the pressure on the child who is the
object of the parents' ambitions at a given moment. Instead the
parents' drives need to be redirected and this is probably best done
in the context of the family counselling session when all the members of the family can consider how they can best meet each others'
needs.

Family group interviewing, as distinct from counselling, will
best be used when the whole family needs to take action with
regard to some event external to the family. For instance, if the
family is making an application for adoption, the social worker
would be foolish not to see the family as a group in order to discuss the application on at least one occasion. There would certainly
be no objection to seeing the parents alone, or even the children
alone, to ascertain their views and one would not say that one part
of the work was more important than another but even so, there
would be no substitute for seeing the family as a group and
ascertaining the group reaction to the inclusion of an extra
member.

As the social work techniques of intervention in family life become more effective, so the social worker will need to employ
all the available knowledge of social science and the principles
of social work to ensure that his work is really for the benefit of
his clients. Now that social work techniques can induce change in
individuals and groups, it is too dangerous to employ half-
educated, dogmatic social workers.

1 Richmond, Mary, *Social Diagnosis*, 1917

2 Willmott, P. and Young, M., *Family and Kinship in East London,* 1957
3 Bott, Elizabeth, *Family and Social Network,* 1957
4 Laing, R., *Intervention in Social Situations,* 1969
5 Satir, Virginia, *Conjoint Family Therapy,* 1967

9 Case Records

Case recording is an essential corollary to counselling and interviewing and yet, apparently, such a constant source of difficulty and frustration to social workers that it is worth examining the reasons why it needs to occupy such an important place in social work.

Like many other worthwhile enterprises, appropriate recording is not easy to attain and if the social worker is merely trying to comply with administrative rules for their own sake then it is not surprising that the exercise will seem like wasting time and energy which could be spent more profitably on other occupations. However, effective counselling and interviewing cannot be achieved without adequate records. Obviously each agency, and indeed each individual social worker, will evolve an individual method of compiling records which will reflect differences in agency function and individual methods of working, but the main considerations which govern case recording are remarkably uniform in all areas of social work. Discussion of the reasons for recording and of the different components of a record may help to show that recording is not simply the administrative chore which some social workers seem to infer.

The Reasons for Recording

The most important reason for making a record of an interview or counselling session is that it helps the social worker with his diagnostic thinking. One hopes that the worker will have prepared for the interview and that he will have considered the significance of what is happening during the course of the interview but none of this is a substitute for careful diagnostic thought after the interview is over. The reasoning is entirely practical. Any experience of interviewing and counselling shows that an essential factor in preparation is to allow for what the client will bring new to the interview and, while interviewing and counselling is in progress, the social worker has so much to do that diagnostic thinking can be given only relatively little attention.

A certain pressure of work is not necessarily to be regretted. Although serious over-work can result only in either total neglect of some areas or an all-round series of rush jobs, yet a certain pressure has the advantage of keeping the social worker in touch with reality and it should be one of the concerns of the agency administration to maintain this balance. It is also desirable that the process of diagnostic thinking should have to take place mainly through the medium of record keeping. The reason for this derives from the nature of diagnostic thinking, which is not primarily a solitary rumination by the social worker on the problems of the client for which a plan of action will be evolved. The functionalists have shown the folly of that sort of approach which demands, among other things, that the social worker should split himself into two people, one of whom is involved with the client while the other is detached and sits pulling strings which will make the situation come right.

Apart from the impossibility of effecting this split in the personality of the social worker, it is now generally recognised that there is no solution to social problems in the sense of living happily ever after or even that the problem which brought the client and social worker together is solved in the sense of restoring some previous happier state. Change, adjustment and time are all integral factors in diagnosis, the full significance of which social workers are only just beginning to recognise theoretically even though they have been dealing with them practically for as long as social work has been practised. Just because these considerations play such an important part in counselling and interviewing, so the process of recording, which should recapture them for the social worker, is an excellent time for him to incorporate them in his thinking.

It is sometimes stated that the primary purpose of recording is to enable a colleague to take over the case if the original worker is suddenly incapacitated. The counter-argument is that this is primarily a hypothetical conjecture which does not correspond to the reality of the situation. For one thing it has been pointed out that the number of social workers who are run down by a bus or who otherwise die suddenly and unexpectedly is infinitesimal and certainly would not justify the massive insurance premium of record writing. The suspicion is that the social work administrators have their own reasons for wishing records to be kept as a measurable standard of work and then seek spurious professional arguments in order to persuade the social workers.

Both of these arguments miss the true point of keeping records as a source of information for professional colleagues. It is quite true that only comparatively rarely would a social worker have to take over a case without prior warning and without the possibility of consulting the previous worker. Even then it is probable that the record of the last and therefore the most significant interview would be missing, as even the most efficient administration cannot totally eliminate the gap between concluding an interview and making a record of it. However, what is more to the point is that social workers frequently have to cooperate with their colleagues in their work and the written record, as a thought-out, edited summary of the latest work is the best means of communication.

The cooperation may take many forms. It may involve coordinated working, as in a matrimonial case in which two workers are working simultaneously with the marriage partners, or in some group counselling situations there would be two or more workers with the group. At the present time, if only for economic reasons, such situations are rare, but cooperation means much more than that. Holidays, training courses and sickness all mean that social workers have to be away from the agency, but the work still goes on and another worker will have to step in for a time. In these circumstances the written record is indispensable. For one thing, the departing worker cannot foresee all the difficulties which are likely to arise and so he cannot forewarn his colleague. Even if he could it would not be desirable, as the two social workers will inevitably have different ways of dealing with problems. This is natural enough if one considers that the major tool of the social worker is his own personality and so the best method of transferring the case is to provide the measure of objectivity which is given by the written record as the means of referral. Otherwise, in a verbal briefing, the social worker who is to take on the case has difficulty sorting out what is the personal bias of his colleague. It will also be possible, when the unforeseen crisis arises, to read the record in the light of what is happening at a time when the original social worker is not available.

The question of supervision is discussed more fully in Chapter 10, but it can be noted here that the written record of the individual interview is the supervisor's principal source of knowledge about the problems of the clients of the agency and how the social worker is tackling them. It is true that the social worker may add verbal comments to the written record and may draw his own conclusions about how they should affect the policy of the agency and be affected by it. However, assuming that the written record is a reasonably accurate reflection of the way in which the social worker sees the case, then it constitutes a part of the foundations on which agency practice is constructed and the raw material out of which agency policy is formulated.

Consultation is also considered at greater length in the next chapter but the importance of the written record to the consultant lies in its objectivity. This is not to suppose that anyone should regard the record as a reliable factual account of what occurred. A very few simple experiments would be sufficient to dispel that illusion, but the written record, by being fixed and in the past, provides a basis for the discussion between the social worker and the consultant.

Research in counselling and interviewing has so far proved very unrewarding. The difficulties of fixing boundaries, of isolating measurable significant factors and having to accommodate to the extraordinary complex interaction between worker and client, to name but a few of the difficulties of research in this area, have generally proved insurmountable. Many attempts have been made and some of them are very ingenious in concept and construction but in most areas of interviewing and counselling it would be very difficult to demonstrate any discernible benefit from the research, either to social workers or their clients.

This is no argument against research and one could easily list a whole series of problems with which social workers would be more than happy to have the help of reliable research findings. To name a few, the selection of clients and some way of matching them appropriately with social workers and, most important of all, some means of quantifying numerically the results of counselling and interviewing, would all be of immense value but it seems unlikely that much experimental progress will be made in the near future. However, the area of social science in which research has proved of great value to social workers is in small-group therapy. Sociology and social psychology have made findings of great significance and a lot of the current practice of social group work is based on their results. Similarly social surveys and censuses have given the social workers a better understanding of the society in which they and their clients live, but in counselling and interviewing there has been no such help, at least of the same magnitude.

No doubt this picture will change as the research workers are able to analyse more effectively the extremely complex nature of a counselling session and it is almost certain that an integral part of this process will be an analysis of social work records, if only to check the conclusions. It is a matter of frequent comment among social workers how much valuable material is locked away in their records and one hopes that the social scientists and social workers between them will be able to find a way to utilise the information more widely. It may be that one of the results will be to change the form of the records if they are to be used as an effective research tool.

The other main reason for keeping records is for the purpose of communication with people who are not social workers but who are concerned in the case. In fact, this very general statement includes an almost infinite variety of possibilities, ranging from the members of other professions to individuals who have an interest in one particular case because of their particular relationship with the person in trouble.

Many social workers are employed in what are sometimes known as secondary settings. For instance the medical and psychiatric social workers in hospitals are often seen as providing an ancillary service to the doctors, although increasing knowledge of the causes of both physical and mental illness is likely to lead to a redefinition of this model. However, hospitals are still primarily institutions for the practice of the skills of doctors and nurses, in which social workers play a secondary role and, as such, it is important that the work of the social workers should be tied in with that of the doctors.

Verbal communication is generally found to be inadequate in these relationships but on the other hand most social workers in hospitals would not make their own professional records available to the doctors. The reason for this is that the social work records are likely to be inappropriate for this purpose. They will almost certainly contain many matters which are not of direct interest to the doctor, in exactly the same way as many of the pharmacological and physiological details of the medical records are irrelevant to the social worker and both need to rely on the other to help them to see the wider significance of their own speciality. For this reason the medical social worker, in addition to her own records, would also make additions to the medical notes based on her own professional expertise but for the general benefit of the medical team treating the patient.

On the other hand, a social worker, in a local authority social services department, works in a primary social work setting in which social work is the central professional interest and in which other professions play an ancillary role. In this case also it would probably be thought inappropriate to make the professional records of the social workers freely available even to all the other social workers from other agencies who may be involved in the case. However, it is also unlikely that there would be any formalised means of communication such as the medical social worker's contribution to the medical notes, as contact with other agencies is likely to be much less consistent and less well defined.

Any examination of the actual records which social workers keep for the purpose of communication with other agencies and other professions is likely to reveal an extremely haphazard state of affairs which is nothing more than a reflection of the uneven nature of professional development in different agencies and different areas. The connection between social work practice and administration is now generally accepted and record keeping is an excellent example of the way in which better administrative arrangements will result in more effective social work and the all-round improvement will be reflected in a more rational system of record-keeping.

The Nature of Case Recording

One of the most enduring compliments which social workers have paid to their nineteenth-century predecessors is to leave substantially unchanged their system of case-recording. In essence, the basic system which is used in almost every agency was formulated by Octavia Hill for the Charity Organisation Society a century ago and shows every sign of lasting as long again.

The reasons for this remarkable constancy in a profession which is sometimes accused of embracing every fashionable new idea, however transient, are the essential simplicity of the system and the fact that it accords so well with the nature of the work. The outline form also allows considerable variation in order to accommodate the particular interests of an agency so that the record can combine both the general facts, which all social workers would recognise as necessary, and specialist information.

The system is basically tri-partite, a front sheet, a diagnostic section and a running record and it may be helpful to describe how these are made up and the purposes which they are intended to serve.

THE FRONT SHEET

The front sheet is meant to consist of basic data which are likely to remain constant for the duration of the case. In every agency it would contain the names of the client, his address, his age and date of birth, his employment or school, his home and family situation, probably his religious affiliation and a note of his hobbies and interests.

All of this is meant to give a quick, but all-round, picture of the client in his present social setting and in addition there would almost certainly be an attempt to give an idea of how this state of affairs had come about. There would, for instance, be information about his health record, his schooling and employment record and, most important of all, a summary of the family history giving an account of the relationship of the client between the various members of his family and how this had come about. There would probably also be a brief account of the personal histories of other family members.

Finally, there would be information related to the specialist interests of the agency. In an agency which frequently dealt with problems of poverty then obviously there would be requirements for detailed information about family income and financial liabilities while a probation record would be expected to place more emphasis on details of contact with the law, and a child care agency would probably need a minute account of family relationships and a personal history which gave details of the pregnancy and birth of the children involved.

It may be seen that the difference between one agency and another is generally one of emphasis. In total they would all cover the same ground, of the client in his social environment seen in terms of his personality development, but with each agency concentrating more on the aspects in which it is specially interested.

One would not expect a trained social worker to use the front-sheet of the case record like an application form which has to be fully completed before any help can be offered. To adopt that procedure would be to go contrary to the idea of allowing the client to state his problem in his own way after only the briefest enquiry to ascertain that he has been appropriately referred to the correct agency. For this purpose, the social worker would need to know nothing more than name and address, which in any case would probably have been ascertained by the receptionist, and thereafter the client would be encouraged to state his problem in his own way. This would almost certainly involve touching on many of the points raised on the front sheet which the social worker would note. In most instances this can be done mentally, although the complexities of family relationships in a large family are likely to tax even the best memory and the client is unlikely to be surprised if the social worker asks permission to note down the names and ages of all the children, for instance, when the subject arises.

The key phrase is ' when the subject arises '. The client who, early on in the social work process, is faced with an interrogation of his family circumstances and history is almost certain to see himself as being caught up in a bureaucracy, whereas the rationale of the front sheet is that it summarises information of importance in all cases. If this is so, the subjects which it covers will arise naturally and the social worker can accept the responsibility of sorting out the information into the form of the front-sheet, rather than force the interview with the client into a strait-jacket of administrative convenience.

The exception to the subjects which arise naturally are those which are of great importance to the client and one thinks immediately of the primary family relationships. Obviously one would not expect someone to talk about such intimate matters with a comparative stranger, and as a rule a client will need to feel confidence in the social worker before he can discuss his true feelings about his parents or his children or his wife. However, the reason for including these topics on the front sheet are to remind the social worker that even if they are not raised initially they are still of great importance and the social worker will certainly not know his client until he knows something of these matters.

There is little doubt that the form of the case-record has a considerable impact on the interaction between the social worker and his client. Perhaps surprisingly, there has apparently been no experimental work done on a subject which is of great significance to social work practice, but it seems certain that social workers shape their work in accordance with the form of their records. This is both understandable and desirable, but it places an onus on agencies to revise the form of their records from time to time. With some agencies one has the impression that not only has the outline of the record not changed since Octavia Hill but the details have not changed either. For instance, in probation, the front sheet includes some questions on housing accommodation which were formulated in the 1930s to provide data for an examination of the relationship between delinquency and housing conditions. In fact the survey was never completed but probation officers have been left with a series of questions, the instructions for completing which are both very complicated and quite inappropriate to modern housing conditions. The choice for the probation officer is either to complete the questions according to his own system or else become involved in an enquiry which is of no possible benefit to his client or anyone else.

In view of changing social conditions, five years would seem to be a reasonable minimum for a detailed review of the appropriateness of the form of the front-sheet. It is desirable to have quite a long period of stability in order to allow policies to be worked through, but equally the case-record forms of an agency need to be closely related to social conditions as they actually exist. The task of revising the front sheet is one on which both field workers and administrators should be involved and it would provide an invaluable opportunity for each to come to grips with the demands of others' situation. It may also be possible in the future that the clients might be represented in this process, although at the moment this can be little more than a pious hope.

It is unfortunate that the housing survey contained in the English probation records has proved so abortive as there is no doubt that the case-records and particularly the front-sheets ought to be used for the purpose of collecting data. Apart from the fact that case-records are potentially a rich source of data which are so far practically untapped, to be involved in research work of this sort is an important way in which the social worker can meet his obligations to help to adjust society to meet the needs of individuals. At the present time, the social responsibilities of social workers tend to be seen mainly in terms of social protest and community work. In many instances this is, of course, quite valid, although as with the remainder of a social worker's activities it is important that his actions should not be primarily for the purpose of self-gratification. It would certainly be no less a contribution to the course of social justice to distil the lessons to be learned from one or a series of interviewing and counselling sessions and make them generally available for the common good.

DIAGNOSIS

The second part of the case-record should be an account of the social worker's diagnostic thinking. We have already remarked on a number of occasions just how difficult it is for social workers to find adequate time to think about the extremely complex problems with which they are involved. Obviously when they have to write reports they should try to think through the case as a whole and if they are wise they will take a minute or so to prepare themselves for each individual interview. The other time when a social worker is almost forced to give thought to a case is when an unexpected crisis blows up and the social worker has to take action.

One of the advantages of setting aside a regular time for thinking about each case is that it may be possible to anticipate future trouble and possibly forestall it, but primarily so that such a valuable and scarce commodity as the time which a social worker has to spend with his clients will be properly planned in the interests of the clients, the worker and the agency as a whole.

It would seem that an assessment of each case once every three months would be about the most that could be expected if one is expecting to measure substantial movement in attitudes and relationships, and yet three months is not long enough to have any serious danger of losing the case from the social worker's attention. In cases in which there is a great deal of activity, then the regular process of diagnostic assessment may occur more frequently although there is something to be said for reviews which are removed from each other a little way in time as this allows the worker greater objectivity.

Before describing in detail the way in which a diagnostic assessment may be made, it should be said that this is not the only form of diagnosis which occurs. The moment a social worker comes into contact professionally with a client with a problem, his mind will be working to distinguish the causes and nature of the problem and ways in which the problem may be solved, and this process continues throughout the case. The diagnostic section of the case-record is much more a record of the results of the diagnostic thinking which has been continuing throughout all the interviewing and counselling sessions, although it is also an opportunity for the social worker to step back and take an overall view of the case at that moment in time.

Like Janus, the periodic diagnostic assessment needs to face both ways. It needs to look back particularly at the period since the last review to see just what has happened, what changes have occurred, which lines that the social worker has pursued have proved helpful and what the errors and omissions have been. In most cases this will not involve more than one or two hundred words but it will have the advantage of refining the social worker's approach. Unprofitable lines of enquiry can be dropped and greater attention can be given to methods of working which look more profitable. In fact, the review of the past leads automatically to the other function of the diagnostic assessment which is planning for the future, both short term and long term. The efficient social worker will use the relative leisure of the periodic review to formulate an overall plan as a base on which the usually hurried preparation for the individual interview can be quickly but soundly erected.

This description of the use of the second part of the case-record for the purpose of diagnosis and evaluation has so far been written without reference to supervision and consultation. In the next chapter we shall see how it fits in to these concepts, but one should also face the reality that for many social workers supervision and consultation hardly exist. While one deplores this situation and would certainly not propose that they can be dispensed with, it is worth noting that the system of periodic diagnostic review which we have just described is one means whereby a social worker can gain a measure of objectivity about his own work.

THE RUNNING RECORD

The third part of the record is intended to be an account of events in the case as they happen and, in addition to accounts of interviews in the agency and in the home, there would also be a reference to telephone calls, letters, hospital visits, court appearances, contacts with other agencies and anything else which occurred in the context of the client and his relationship with the agency.

Because the aim is to give a picture of the case as it unfolds itself, so this third part of the record does not claim to demonstrate the relative significance of various issues like a quarterly diagnostic assessment. Another person reading the running record should be able to reach his own conclusions, independent of those of the social worker who wrote the record, because he should have an account of all the events in the case. However, there is one important respect in which the running record is not simply an objective account of everything which happened. Any case-record which attempted to record everything which happened would quickly become unmanageably bulky and there would simply not be the time for anyone else to read it, let alone master the contents.

The running record can therefore only be a summary and while the aim is to make it as objective as possible, any summary invariably reflects the outlook of the summariser. It is important to note that the aim of the running record is to make it objective rather than impersonal. Confusion over this point sometimes inclines inexperienced social workers to excise their own share in the proceedings and their account of a one-to-one interview can seem like a monologue by the client at which the social worker was not even present. However, the necessity to include an account of his own participation in an interview or counselling session, coupled with his own editing of the total result, makes objectivity a very difficult goal for the social worker to achieve.

The golden rule in keeping a running record is to keep it up to date. The record which is more than a week in arrears is already lacking one of its most important constituents for the colleague who has to take over the case. If a sudden crisis has occurred and the social worker dealing with the case is not available, then his substitute is likely to read the diagnostic assessments to see what the social worker was doing, read the front-sheet to make himself familiar with the family and social context of the case and then finally read the account of the last interview to see what indications there were that a crisis was impending. There will often be no more time to study the record further and if there is no account of the last interview, then the substitute may well waste valuable time in going over the same ground twice with the client and possibly repeating mistakes.

Just as serious, failure to keep the running record up to date vitiates the purpose of giving a picture of the case as it happened. There may be some satisfaction in writing up an account of an interview which accords better with the way events turned out rather than as they were envisaged by the social worker at the time of the interview. However, for anyone trying to follow the thought processes of the social worker, this subsequent adjustment will serve only to confuse the issue. It is quite impossible to write up a record which is several weeks in arrears. The incidents of an interview will have been overtaken by later events and both client and social worker will have developed to an extent that makes it impossible to recapture the past.

On the other hand, it is generally considered to be unwise to dictate the summary of an interview immediately after its conclusion. The object is to obtain a proper balance between the various parts of the interview and without some lapse of time it is almost certain that the social worker would over-emphasise the closing stages, instead of achieving a true perspective. An ideal arrangement might be to have an interval overnight when the material would still be fresh but the social worker would be able to give a rounded account of the interview as a whole. There would also be the advantage of doing a difficult job at a time when the social worker was fresh and probably least liable to interruption.

Too much should not be made of the pressures of social work in objecting that such an arrangement is impracticable. The busier the social worker the more care he has to take that his administrative arrangements are efficient and anyone who has had to write accounts of interviews which took place several weeks previously will know how much extra work is involved. Even so one must recognise that in the best organisation it may still not be practicable to bring the running record up to date every day, but one would be apprehensive about an administrative system which allowed them to be more than a week out of date.

Most social workers develop a system of record-completion which suits them personally, and every agency tends to develop a general pattern. New social workers often feel the need to write their records by hand, usually because this is the only way they can manage the unfamiliar and important material with which they are dealing, but the pressure of work and greater confidence in their verbal ability makes them more willing to dictate. Even so, it requires considerable skill to be able to dictate an accurate summary of an interview without any memory aid and many social workers use a system of key words to remind themselves of the topics which need to be included in the record of the interview. A cryptic sentence such as ' illness – details – feelings – history – family – husband – children ' would be the work of a moment to write but would be quite sufficient to remind a medical social worker that in her interview with a patient they talked about the patient's illness with specific reference to the physical details and the patient's feelings about them. This may have been followed by an account of the history of the illness and then the interview had changed to a discussion of the patient's family at home, how her husband was managing and what the effect was on the children.

An interview or counselling session which covers all these topics is hardly likely to have lasted less than half an hour and the record summary will probably need to be two or three hundred words long, but the worker may find that by using the key-word system he is able to make his dictation on the basis of less than a dozen words for even quite complicated interviews.

It is a vexed question whether social workers use dictating machines or dictate their work to clerical assistants. At first sight it may seem that the dictating machine is preferable on the grounds that it does not require the presence of the clerical assistant, so that the social worker can dictate just when it suits himself. It is also cheaper in that the time of the clerical assistant is not taken up with receiving dictation. However, a lot depends on the arrangements which the agency makes for the reception of clients and, if this is a duty of the clerical assistants, then there is a case for retaining dictation so that the clerical assistant may be kept up to date with regard to professional policy. Formal briefings could not possibly enable the clerical staff to keep up with the subleties of changes in agency policy and simply to type up what is recorded on the dictating machine will convey almost nothing, whereas the social worker who is aware of the importance of reception can use dictation to the clerical assistant as a means of conveying attitudes about clients and how they should be treated.

There is, of course, no reason why some combination of both methods should not be used and the social worker should be free to choose to use a dictating machine or dictate to a clerical assistant as the occasion demands. Certainly one would hope that, when social work skills are in such short supply, every facility both in the form of office equipment and clerical help was available to support the social worker in his work.

The purpose of the running record is to describe the client as he was in that particular interview or counselling situation, together with an account of the connective links of letters, telephone calls and contacts with other agencies and institutions. All of this will show the client as he is in relationship to society and it is important to remember this when writing the running record. No client exists without social contacts and it is with the satisfaction which the client gains from these contacts that the social worker is concerned. Accordingly, even in the one-to-one interview in the agency, attention should be paid to the relationship with the social worker and this interaction should be included in the running record. Similarly in group situations, the record should be written up from the point of view of the client's interaction with the other members of the group, including the social worker. One would thus find that when all the members of a group were clients of the agency then all their case-records would be written up differently as they would all cover the same events, but from the points of view of the different individuals concerned. Any attempt to write a standard account of what happened which would be equally applicable to all the participants would either be so generalised as to be worthless or else no more than an account of the author's prejudices and would be comparatively useless in the case record.

Social workers are often less able to write summaries of group interviews or counselling than individual sessions. Perhaps it is that until recently they have often had less experience or simply that they are more conscious in the group how difficult it is to be aware of everything that is happening and as a result their records of group events tend to be much more rambling. This is a pity because the observation of the client in the group is of major importance to the social worker.

Process Recording

So much has been written about process recording in social work that the temptation is to believe that there is general agreement about what the phrase means. In a sense this is true. Many social workers would define process recording as an attempt to record the process of the interview with the assumption that this contrasts with the summary of an interview which would be included in the running record. It is also generally true that process recording is much more detailed than the accounts of interviews which appear in working case-records, but the often unspoken assumption that process recording is somehow objectively more true than a summary will not stand up to investigation.

Process recording is primarily of use in learning social work skills such as interviewing and counselling, and its application will be considered in the next chapter, but there is so much misapprehension, even about what it consists of, that it seems necessary to get that preliminary hurdle out of the way. The student or social worker who is writing a process record of an interview is generally asked to do three things. The first is to write a straight account of what happened during the interview. This would include the conversation, as nearly verbatim as possible, with indications of pauses and emphasis, but also things like facial expressions and body movements. The student is then asked to account for the client's behaviour, why he said what he said and in what particular order and to discuss its significance. Finally, the student is asked to explain why he said what he said, why he responded in a particular way, why he asked the questions he did and why he directed the interview in that way.

It should already be apparent that it is not possible to comply with these instructions in any absolute sense. With regard to the client's motivation, to answer the question fully would require a degree of knowledge greater than that of the trained psychoanalyst and that could not suffice to give a total explanation of the client's behaviour. Even with the most straightforward task of describing what took place we have already seen that the amount of interaction is simply too great to allow full recall even if one could do away with the distorting effect of the social worker's own perception.

If the supervisor or consultant, for whom a process recording is prepared, really needed to have a full and accurate account of the interaction then he would do better to have a tape-recorder and a television camera secreted in the interviewing room, but this would be to miss the point of the exercise. Process recording is not for the purpose of forcing the student towards some ideal model of practice, which in fact does not exist, but of helping the student to make the best use of his own personality to help his clients.

It is true that there are professional social work standards which need to be maintained, and intending aspirants to the profession must be instructed in the professional code even though in the case of social work it is not yet complete, but this is not the primary task of process recording. If it were, it would be altogether easier to train the student by making him observe his supervisor at work and after some time to allow him to interview in the presence of the supervisor. However, it is generally recognised that the presence of an observer so alters the structure of the interaction that it is comparatively valueless as a teaching method.

Process recording can be guaranteed to demonstrate the prejudices and bias of the person who writes it and the skilful teacher will have no shortage of material to demonstrate to the student just how his work is influenced by his own predilections. The amount of objective straight recording which anyone can achieve is very small and the rest of the process recording must consist of material taken from the worker's own personality, as there is no other source.

To begin with, the student is often conscious only of the size of the task with which he is confronted and his total preoccupation consists in getting it down on paper. This is usually the most revealing phase of all, because he is so involved in the recording task that he is unaware how many of his attitudes show through. However, the first session with his supervisor is usually sufficient to show him just how much of the interaction is a reflection of his own personality and that interviewing and counselling is so much more difficult than it seems. There is also likely to be a period of denial when the supervisor's interpretations will be rejected with more or less justification and with varying degrees of warmth. In turn, this is often followed by a period when the student has an intellectual appreciation of how he can use his personality more effectively to help his client, but he is not yet able to carry this out in practice. Indeed, one can say that it is an unattainable ideal for the social worker that his own personality should never intrude to the detriment of his clients, but the student often becomes aware of major lapses when he has been carried away, usually on subjects about which he feels strongly or with clients who arouse strong emotions in him.

This disparity between what the student knows and what he can achieve often reveals itself when he is writing up the process recording. Knowing what his supervisor is likely to say there is a practically irresistible temptation to alter the account to conform with what should have happened rather than what did happen. The experienced supervisor will expect this phase and instead of becoming upset at any duplicity on the part of the student, will see it as a powerful learning experience which will do more to modify the student's attitudes and methods of interviewing and counselling than any amount of exposition.

The preoccupation of social workers with process recording has been so great that it is necessary to state the undoubted limitations of this method of recording. Process recording is primarily of use in social work teaching and has a place in supervision and consultation but it is not appropriate to routine case-recording. There are a number of reasons for this. For example, the sheer number of words involved in process recording would mean that the case would be unmanageable as no one could be expected to plough through the tens of thousands of words which would represent just a few interviews. Even assuming anyone had the time and the inclination, it is also certain that he would become so bogged down in the minutiae of the interaction of the personalities of the worker and client that he would almost certainly lose sight of the major issues of the case.

Confidentiality

Some of the general considerations relating to the social work principle of confidentiality have been considered in Chapter 2 but the subject of the confidential nature of social work records raises such important and immediate problems for social workers that it is worth treating it separately.

The general conclusion about confidentiality which we reached in Chapter 2 was that the profession of social work is still at a stage at which it is not possible to formulate definitive answers to the many difficult questions which arise. The same is true of the specific question of social work records, that at present we can do no more than state the questions and some of the factors which a social worker will have to take into consideration in coming to a decision.

The unsatisfactory nature of this state of affairs, in which a profession is unable to give detailed guidance to its members on a matter of considerable importance, is self-evident and yet it is surely better to recognise the reality of the situation rather than assume an agreed professional approach which will be found to be illusory at the time when it is most needed.

With regard to the members of the same agency, there seems to be no acceptable alternative to declaring that they all have an absolute right of access to the case records of all their colleagues without distinction of seniority. To legislate otherwise would involve defining objective criteria of the situations by which social workers have access to the case-records of the agency and this would either involve making the records the personal property of the worker who compiled them or of the senior members of the hierarchy. Neither of these propositions is acceptable on professional grounds but one is still faced with the difficulties which arise from free access to records.

Gossiping about clients is universally condemned, and universally practised in social work agencies but there is no evidence that making case-records available to the staff exacerbates this problem. In fact, the contrary is more likely to be true, that gossip will flourish more on half-truths than on full information and that it is scarcity value which gives gossip its main appeal.

A much more hopeful approach to this very difficult problem lies in the content of social work education in providing opportunities for each social worker to work out for himself what confidentiality means in terms of gossiping about clients' affairs. In any case, even if he is denied total knowledge about the rest of the agency's records, no security procedure can stop a social worker from gossiping about his own clients' affairs.

Attitudes about the confidential nature of their clients' affairs practised by the social worker are much more likely to communicate themselves to the clerical staff than the double standard of ' do what I say, not what I do ', which operates at present in many agencies. The literature of social work has little to say about clerical assistants and yet they are an integral part of the social work system. It is obvious that they are fully conversant with the most intimate details of the clients' personal lives because of the records which they handle, and yet very little formal attention has been given to their selection, training and method of working. In other professions a great deal of reliance is placed on the fact that they assimilate the code of conduct of the profession with which they are working so that one is hardly surprised when a doctor's secretary bases her conduct on medical ethics. In time this will doubtless solve the problem for the social workers but until a satisfactory professional social work code is formulated it becomes the responsibility of every social worker to give his clerical assistant the maximum help in this area and to remember that his own example will carry much greater weight than anything he says.

The principle that all the professional workers in an agency have an absolute right of access to all the social work records, which they can extend to their ancillaries such as clerical assistants and students, removes any problem of confidentiality in respect of supervisors and consultants appointed by the agency. Just because they are either professional social workers or members of related professions which have an identical approach to the question of confidentiality, they have a right of unrestricted access to all the social work records. It is true that there are managerial and other professional problems involved in supervision and consultation, which we shall consider in the next chapter but, with regard to confidentiality, the safeguard lies entirely and solely in the professional standing of the person concerned as to the use which he makes of the material to which he has access.

Much more difficult problems arise in the case of non-professionals who believe that they have a right of access to the case-records of a social worker and it is very important for the social workers to think out the basic issues involved if they are not to betray the confidences of their clients. For instance it would sometimes happen that the lay members of the board of management of a voluntary agency would believe that the case-records were actually their property, and in a statutory agency the members of the managing committee might be able to point to regulations specifically stating their right of access to a worker's records.

Faced with such a situation, particularly if it has even the tacit support of professional supervisors, it is not surprising that many social workers would not dispute the issue, but one of the hall-marks of a profession is its claim to distinguish between just and unjust laws. It is important to remember that no doctor would feel free to disclose medical information despite the most extreme pressure and there have been instances in the last few years of journalists being willing to suffer imprisonment rather than act contrary to their professional code by disclosing sources of infor-mation, despite specific laws to the contrary.

It is likely to be some time before social workers will achieve this degree of professionalism but as their methods are generally appreciated to be becoming more effective, so it is likely that pressure will increase to make them disclose the information in their records, although an awareness of this pressure may have the effect of making the social workers close their professional ranks and really think through many issues which they have so far largely evaded.

Some of the most difficult situations are likely to occur in the courts, where all the rigours of the law are immediately available to coerce the reluctant social worker. In a way this is surprising because the lawyers as a profession are well aware of the import-ance of professional confidence and have used their privileged posi-tion to have their own profession specially protected by the law. In fact, it often happens that a judge will intervene to protect a social worker from having to produce his records in court but it is unsatisfactory that this protection needs to depend on the goodwill of the presiding judge in a particular case.

In Chapter 3, we noticed the interesting development which has occurred in matrimonial cases in the High Court in which there are frequently problems of confidentiality about attempts at recon-ciliation in which a probation officer has been involved. Because it was held that the preservation of family life was a matter of public policy, the matter was held to be privileged, but it was also held that the privilege was that of the clients, not the social worker, and if they both chose that the information should be dis-closed, then the social worker had no choice in the matter. This

solution seems entirely appropriate and it is significant that a difficult professional problem was resolved by focusing on the rights
of the client.

Even on this comparatively straightforward issue it is not difficult to see some residual problems, mainly revolving around the
question of the circumstances in which consent was given and the
ability of one of the parties to make an appropriate decision for
himself. One can also imagine in exceptional circumstances that a
probation officer would decline to disclose his records on the
grounds that it would be prejudicial to the rights of children or
some other third party who was not present.

It is practically impossible to separate the acquisition of interviewing and counselling skills from the rest of social work and we have seen in the earlier chapters of this book how aspects of interviewing and counselling spill over into other areas of social work. However, if social workers believe that interviewing and counselling requires more than good intentions and a kind heart, or even proximity to an experienced worker, though all of these are essential constituents, then there is an obligation on the social work profession to spell out how these skills may be acquired.

From an examination of the way that social work practice has evolved, it is possible to distinguish four distinct components in the process of learning interviewing and counselling. As one would expect, they are interlocked and mutually dependent and although they fall into a natural progression, each component may be studied at any time during a social worker's career at a level consonant with his professional development.

In the order in which they are usually encountered by the social work student and the beginning social worker, the stages are the theoretical basis of interviewing and counselling, the supervision of the student undertaking practical work, the supervision of the social worker in the agency and consultation by the social worker about his work.

Class-room Teaching

It is now generally accepted that every social worker needs adequate education in all the social sciences in order to be able to function competently and one of the major problems of social work education is to balance the time necessary for this theoretical teaching with the urgent need for social workers in the agencies. In a sense any solution is bound to be inadequate because the growth of knowledge is such that it is possible to spend one's whole time in the study of one aspect of one of the social sciences and so any all-round expertise is increasingly difficult. On the other hand, the medical profession have shown that it is possible to be generally competent in a number of related specialisms and, despite the cult of the expert, the general practitioner continues to survive and flourish.

One of the ways in which this result can be achieved is to make sure that the related subjects are taught with the needs of the practitioner in mind. The average medical student is not intending to become a specialist pharmacologist or a histologist and yet he wants much more than a watered-down beginner's approach to these subjects. Medical education has shown that by constant exertion on the part of both the profession and the scientific specialists it is possible to gain a professional working knowledge of a number of related subjects.

As yet, social work education has not achieved this happy position and in many educational institutions it is still under the tutelage of one of the social sciences. It is hardly likely that social workers will be able to enter into any sort of equal discussion with sociologists or psychologists so long as either claim the right to teach the social workers their business. However, the fault has not been entirely one way. Many social workers have made quite violent swings from sociology to psychology, and now apparently back to sociology, as the sole foundation of their work, and, too frequently, the intensity of their enthusiasm for the new discipline has only been matched by their rejection of what they previously accepted. Similarly their desire to accept leadership from some other profession, whether medical, psychiatric or legal, has hampered the development of social work as a profession in its own right.

Much of this is now changing. Social workers are increasingly claiming the right to have the main say in education for their own profession and while the claim is not being conceded without fierce struggles in many educational establishments, there can be no doubt that important concessions have been won and more are on the way. This is welcome news but it places great responsibility on social workers to think out just what it is that they need from the social sciences.

We have already seen in this book how a knowledge of philosophy, sociology, social psychology and psychology is necessary as a basis for interviewing and counselling but it would be idle to pretend that much more than a beginning has been made on how social work students should be taught these subjects and even less work has been done at more advanced levels. Even for the beginning student there is little agreement among social workers on how such important subjects as law, economics, anthropology and political theory should be taught and the latest preoccupation with management means that for practical purposes, senior social workers are not concerned with social science theory.

All the social sciences need to be taught as basic knowledge for the social worker, who will use them amongst other things to enlarge his personal philosophy to encompass his professional work. This point cannot be exaggerated because without a sound personal philosophy, the social worker has no means of resolving the moral, social and even political conflicts with which he is constantly faced. Even if he decides to determine all issues by reference to some form of authority, he must know on what basis he accepts this authority. The search for a personal philosophy is a lifelong quest which reflects the personality of the individual, his social setting, and his education, and as these alter so his philosophy will change.

One of the most cogent reasons for a social worker to know his own philosophic position is to help him decide a dilemma which occurs in almost every case, whether the client should be helped to adjust better to his social situation, or whether the social situation is unjust and should be altered to make life easier for the client. The danger of stating the problem in these terms is that the alternatives may seem mutually exclusive.

In practice it would be impossible to find a social work case in which it was not necessary to bring about both individual and social adjustment and it is the balance between these which provides the major test of the social worker's own philosophic judgement. The concept of a perfectly just society has never seemed even remotely within reach under any known political or social system and, therefore, even leaving out of account the individual imperfections of his clients, the social worker will aways have to strive for a more just society and always contend with the knowledge that it will not be immediately attained and so he must help his client live with the unjust situation. Put in such stark terms, this may seem a statement of the essential futility of social work, but from another point of view it can be argued that it is the striving for individual happiness and social justice which provides the justification of the social work profession.

Because of changes both in the social sciences and the problems with which social workers are called upon to help, it is important that students are not only given factual information but also equipped to re-educate themselves as knowledge and social conditions change, and this applies just as much to the methods of social work as it does to social science theory.

At the height of the domination of social work by dynamic psychology between 1940 and 1950, there was, in effect, a schism between the followers of Otto Rank, known as the functionalists, and the orthodox Freudians, usually known as the diagnostic school. It is appropriate to describe the controversy in religious terms as it had all the features of a theological dispute, particularly the heated intolerance by both sides for the other's point of view. The battle raged most fiercely in the USA, where the functionalists had their headquarters at the University of Pennsylvania at Philadelphia and the Freudians were mainly centred on Columbia University in New York and the University of Chicago School of Social Service Administration. In its heyday the struggle was both ideological and strategic. Extravagant claims were made and one of the aims of both sides was to gain control of as many social work agencies as possible.

As with many fierce controversies, the struggle ended when enlightened figures on both sides saw the merits of their opponents' case, that the fundamental issues were not irreconcilable. Mrs Perlman's *Social Casework: a Problem-solving Process*,[1] published in 1957, was probably the first major publication from the diagnostic stronghold of the University of Chicago to accept many of the premises of the functionalists and Ruth Smalley's *Theory for Social Work Practice*[2] is quite acceptable to the diagnostic school, even though it is written by the successor of Jessie Taft, the high priestess of functionalism.

Only occasional echoes of this war found their way to England, where the diagnostic school held undisputed sway and English social workers may have congratulated themselves on remaining free from a dispute in which so much energy was consumed, apparently to such little purpose. While there is indeed no reason why

English social workers should ape their American counterparts, it would be a pity to regard the diagnostic/functionalist controversy as barren. Rank's idea of the mobilisation of the client's will is complementary to Freud's stress on the personality of the analyst as the major tool in therapy. Similarly, the diagnostic formula of study, diagnosis and treatment needs the functionalist stress on the dimension of time if one is to grasp how each of these concepts is implicit in the others.

It is only by involvement in the social work process that social work theory will come to life for the student, but without adequate theoretical exposition, practical experience will be meaningless. There is, therefore, a heavy responsibility on the social work teacher to help his students to see the relevance of social science to social work and to be able to analyse the social work process from many points of view.

TEACHING RESEARCH METHODS
Another serious omission in the education of most social workers is in research methods, and this will have to be remedied if social work is ever to rebuff the entirely justified criticism of the social scientists that social work theory and practice as at present constituted is largely a combination of hunch and prejudice. However, it is also worth remarking that forays by social researchers have been generally unhelpful mainly because those who undertook the research were apparently insufficiently conversant with social work practice. Too often their work has been irrelevant and one can only conclude that the research has been shaped more by the available research techniques than any attempts to solve the problems of social workers.

For example, at face value the study by Kogan and Hunt on *Measuring Results in Social Work*[3] would seem to tackle one of the central problems of social work, but a closer examination of the text of this study reveals a basic confusion between the concepts of success and movement, two very different ideas. It is significant that this study has not been followed up by other agencies.

Social work involves so many complex processes that the still primitive, although rapidly developing, techniques of social research are inadequate for the purpose of analysis. Interviewing and counselling are as complicated as any aspect of social work and more progress is likely to be made in research technology if the difficulties are recognised. Carl Rogers has purported to show a scientific basis to counselling in his book *Client-centered Therapy,*[4] but he really avoids the issue of communication in the counselling situation, the sheer volume of which defeats the researcher, quite apart from the subtleties which are so difficult to quantify.

At one time it seemed that the only hope for constructive research in social work, and particularly in interviewing and counselling, lay in teaching social workers the techniques of research, as social scientists who were not trained in social work seemed unable or unwilling to recognise the complexities of counselling. There is a sense in which this is true, although in its most obvious meaning the statement is unduly defeatist. On the other hand, social workers seem to be insufficiently instructed to know what they want. The success of any product ultimately depends upon the existence of demand for consumption and while there may be a dispute about how such a demand comes about, there is no doubt that, in general terms, social work education has not included a sufficient appreciation of the language, methods and limitations of social research.

Again one returns to the subject of how much can be included in a social worker's education and while there is great scope for a more effective use of available time, it is rapidly becoming obvious that even the two-year period, which is only now gaining acceptance as the minimum acceptable period, is too short if such important subjects as research methods are to be adequately taught.

HISTORY OF SOCIAL WORK

Finally, at a purely academic level, it is necessary for the social work teacher to instruct his students in the history of their profession. Present professional practice is very much the result of pragmatic development and can be fully understood only in those terms although an understanding of social history and political and economic history is obviously a useful corollary. Unfortunately, because of the scarcity of resources, social history has sometimes been taught as a substitute for the history of the development of social work and this has sometimes had the effect of leaving the social work student in the dark about many of the reasons for contemporary professional practice. In view of the scarcity of constructive research it is doubly important that the student should know of the successes and failures of his predecessors.

ROLE-PLAYING

From all of this it can be seen that there is no shortage of theoretical material for the social work teacher in the academic setting but, however well instructed the student may be in the theory of social work, there is no guarantee that he will be able to put his knowledge into practice. Ultimately there is no alternative to practising on the clients of an agency, with appropriate safeguards and supervision, and this has been one of the distinctive features of social work practice in all periods of history. In England, social casework training in its modern form began when Octavia Hill found that she was personally unable to deal with the tenants in her improved housing scheme and took on a number of voluntary assistants whom she soon discovered she had to train in the methods she had herself pioneered. Her training methods have been generally adopted both in England and abroad.

Even though the training of a social worker must include contact with clients before the student is fully trained, it is possible to impart a number of the practical skills of interviewing and counselling without coming into contact with the public. Such exercises are usually known as role-playing and the greater availability of audio-visual equipment means that role-playing is likely to play a much greater part in the training of social workers in the future.

In its simplest form, role-playing involves using the members of the student group to enact a counselling situation which then becomes the subject matter for discussion and teaching. Quite a lot can be achieved with this basic method, particularly if the social work teacher takes on the role either of client or social worker, as two students, particularly if they have no experience of interviewing and counselling, sometimes have difficulty in creating the atmosphere of a social work interview.

A more serious difficulty is to recall the contents of the interview with any accuracy and much better results can be obtained if the role-playing is tape-recorded and a typescript is prepared of the dialogue. This has the additional advantage of allowing the students the opportunity to work in private. From experience, it seems that after a little practice they have no difficulty in working in the presence of a tape-recorder. The preparation of an accurate typescript is certainly an onerous task but the resulting gain in the value of the teaching material justifies the effort involved.

Points which such a recording and typescript may be expected to illustrate graphically are particularly those involved in communication and the problem of working through the medium of the social worker's personality. It is, for instance, easy to show from the typescript the number and complexity of messages which are transmitted, even in the shortest dialogue. The recording itself can be used to exemplify the effect of different tones of voice and of emphasis, which may be underlined by the choice of material and the way it is presented both on a large and a small scale.

It is possible to use a recording and typescript many times over with succeeding classes and, as the collection of recordings is built up, some will be seen to be of particular value in illustrating particular aspects of interviewing and counselling. For instance, aggression in an interview often proves very disturbing to the social work student and a tape-recording which illustrates some of the forms of aggression and the various ways in which the social worker can respond, may well be given an important place in any social work teaching programme. However, if the secretarial resources are available, there is a great deal to be said for allowing each group of students to prepare their own material. The advantage of involving the students in the teaching process, which invariably results from involving them in role-playing, more than outweighs the cost involved.

It is true that the social work teacher has only limited control over the material which is produced and he has to rely on the co-operation of the students and trust that their work will illustrate the teaching points he wishes to make. In fact, the richness of any interview material will almost certainly guarantee the latter point and it is much more likely that his problem will be to discuss the material fully in the time which he has available. The fact that he is always using fresh material will help to keep his teaching from becoming stale.

As well as using role-playing for the purpose of general teaching about interviewing and counselling and other aspects of social work, a tape-recording of a role-play interview and a typescript can also be used to help the individual student with the use of his own personality as a means of helping his clients. If the social work teacher makes the minimum specification about the contents of the interview, then the interaction is almost certain to reflect how the student would react in a real interview and some of his abilities and weaknesses will be evident and can be picked up in individual tutorials.

It may be objected that knowing his teacher will be listening to the interview, the role-play may represent what the student thinks he ought to produce, or even that he is doing what he believes his teacher thinks is right. Such arguments presuppose a degree of sophistication and skill in managing an interview which most trained social workers would envy. However, even allowing that there are elements of truth in this objection, the experienced social work teacher recognises that for many students there is a time-lag between intellectual understanding and emotional acceptance, particularly in such a personalised skill as interviewing and, therefore, discussion centred on role-playing will generally make the learning process smoother. Assuming that there is an irreconcilable gap between the student's convictions about interviewing and counselling and what he believes is required of him, role-playing will almost certainly reveal this discrepancy, which is far better dealt with before the student has a chance to work out his difficulties on his clients.

The other main advantage of role-playing, however it is carried out, is implied in its name. The concept of role is one which the sociologists are constantly bringing to the attention of social workers and adequate instruction in role theory is now an essential feature of social work education. This also is a subject which needs to be grasped by the social worker, both intellectually and emotionally, and it is very interesting in a role-playing session to see the extent to which the students become involved and identified with roles which are far removed from their own circumstances. It is particularly valuable for them to experience the roles of various types of clients, which can give them an empathy and an understanding which they will not easily obtain otherwise and which will be a humanising influence in their later professional practice.

It is still the function of the social work teacher to help the student to understand what is of general significance in the case record but it is just as important to see how this interacts with the narrower issues of the community in which the client lives and with what might be unique to the particular case. For this reason each social work teacher needs to prepare his own selection of cases and, increasingly, he will rely on material produced by the students with whom he is dealing. In interviewing and coun-selling, the process record is probably the most useful agent, be-cause, as the name implies, it deals with the social work process, how the worker interacts with the client and how this interaction is used to help the client with his problem, either directly through counselling or indirectly by using the interview for the mobilisa-tion of external resources.

In the last chapter we saw that the process record is of com-paratively little value as an objective record of what occurred dur-ing the interview and for this reason, and because of its bulk, it does not form an appropriate part of the agency records, but as a teaching aid it is invaluable. Its particular merit is that it enables the social work teacher to see how the student tries to use his own personality to help his clients and the difficulties which he en-counters both within himself and externally.

As well as individual tuition, process recording can also be used for group teaching, provided there are adequate safeguards to pre-vent the individual student from being unduly exposed in the group. Many of the teaching points in the record are likely to be of significance to all the members of the teaching group, who are presumably at a roughly comparable stage of development. The immediacy of the teaching material is its great merit and, while there is generally no difficulty in finding suitable illustrations for the points which the teacher wishes to make, there is no reason why the process recording cannot be supplemented with other material. However if the teacher feels the need for supplementary material all the time, one would wonder if his teaching plan were appropriately correlated to the needs of the students as shown by their work.

As audio-visual aids become more generally available, they are likely to play a greater part in all social work teaching and par-ticularly interviewing and counselling. We have already discussed the use which may be made of tape-recorders and the fact that they record only auditory communications has the advantage from the teaching point of view of making the material more manageable by cutting out visual messages mainly conveyed by facial expres-sions and bodily movements. However, because in the past there were no suitable teaching aids generally available for recording visual communication, this area has tended to be neglected. Some efforts were made to use appropriate films and, while they were helpful and certainly better than nothing, they lacked the immediacy and relevance which are the chief merits of a tape-recording made by a student group for their own use. The advent of closed circuit television has done something to remedy this situation and some fascinating studies can be done not only of visual communications but also of the visual effects of physical contact, an area which is practically untouched in the literature of social work even though many social workers are aware of its potential in practice.

Cost and technical limitations, such as bulky equipment and relatively immobile cameras, still make practical teaching in visual matters more difficult than auditory communication, but technical advance in this field is so fast that it promises to affect social work teaching radically in the next few years. Lightweight portable equipment will mean that it will be possible to record visually interviewing and counselling situations other than the static office interview, and will enable the class-room teacher to keep pace with such developments as family group counselling sessions.

Mention should be made of the one-way screen which has now been in use for many years as a means of observing interaction visually and, while its value is undisputed, the one-way screen also suffers from the limitations that by itself there is no means of recording what happens for future analysis, so that it is mainly of value when used in conjunction with closed circuit television.

Student Supervision in the Agency

The words supervision and consultation have so many connotations in social work that it is necessary to define their use in this book. One may assume that all social work education includes an appreciable time in an academic institution and for our purposes what happens there is referred to as teaching. This is an entirely arbitrary use of language, as every aspect of social work has a teaching content, but if one disclaims any intention of implying greater value to one part of social work rather than another, then for the sake of clarity such distinctions may be allowed.

Supervision is most conveniently discussed under two headings, the supervision of the student by the field-work instructor and the supervision of the trained social worker by the agency supervisor. While there are common elements in these processes, there are more dissimilarities and it may prevent confusion to consider them separately.

Finally, consultation is different again from the supervision of the trained worker and ideally should be the function of a specialist who is not a member of the agency to which he is acting as consultant.

The field work supervision of the social work student in the social work agency is essentially an intermediate process between the academic orientation of the teaching institution and full professional practice in the agency. The degree of tutelage in student supervision generally reflects this transition and should vary from quite careful hand-holding in the initial stages to relative freedom and a greater stress on initiative towards the end.

However practically orientated the social work teaching may be, it is no substitute for actual contact with real clients and the purpose of role-playing and similar exercises is not to act as a subsitute for genuine practical work experience but to smooth some of the edges and try to reduce the extent to which the students learn at the clients' expense.

The other main purpose of student supervision is to introduce the social work student to agency function in practice. The most that the social work teacher can do is to discuss agency function in general terms. This is very important and it is essential that the student should appreciate the general theoretical considerations involved, but it is unlikely that they will mean very much to him until he sees how they are carried out in practice. For instance, the teacher will tell him that any agency has to define its clientele and that amongst other things this involves problems of client selection and rejection and will call for particular skills in the professional staff. However, it is only when the student has to decide whether a particular referral is appropriate to the agency in which he is working that he will fully appreciate all the factors involved.

On the specific issues of interviewing and counselling, agency function is, if anything, even more important as it is one of the most important sources of objective definition in an area which can seem entirely formless, particularly to the new student. Left to himself the student will have no idea how long an interview should be, with the result that he will spend hours talking to a client who engages his interest, or as little time as possible with clients whom he finds unsympathetic or whose problems seem to threaten his competence. Alternatively, if he has learned the lesson that interviewing and counselling should be client focused, he will be inclined to allow the client to dictate the length of the interview.

All of these factors are likely to play a part in determining the length of an interview, but to depend on them alone is altogether too abitrary and idiosyncratic and the field-work supervisor will also help the student to see how the availability of total resources and the agency decisions about priorities also play a part in determining the length of an interview. For example, the number of staff whom the agency employ and the total number of clients are the real determining factors, at least in establishing the norms for interviewing. While it is highly unlikely that any attempt will be made to coerce any worker or student to adhere rigidly to the average in a particular case, the existence of such standards can be of great assistance to the student in planning his work most effectively in the agency setting.

Agency function in interviewing and counselling involves many more subjects than the length of an interview, although that has been discussed at some length to illustrate in detail how field work supervision works. Other topics which would come under this heading are the nature and extent of financial and material help which the agency can provide from its own resources, criteria of success, and the nature of the problems with which the agency exists to help.

It is a common misapprehension that agency function is solely restrictive. Some restrictions are, of course, essential, as resources both of man-power and money are never unlimited but, as we have already stated, even the limitations can have the positive basis of helping the social worker to give shape to his work. However, supervision both of the social worker and the student has another side, in that it provides the most effective medium for the transmission of information from the field worker through the administrative hierarchy. This subject is more appropriately dealt with in the next section of this chapter, but it should be noted that the student undertaking field work in an agency has a distinctive part to play in the formulation of agency policy, and one of the duties of the field work supervisor is to help the student to understand this function and to facilitate the communication between the student and the rest of the agency.

The contribution is not so much in professional practice, in which the student can be expected to give little that is new, although the freshness and enthusiasm which students often bring to an agency should not be underestimated, and their work is often more painstaking and thorough than that of the professional staff. The fact that they have more time often more than compensates for their inexperience. However, their major contribution, which many agencies see as the chief bonus from taking students, is as a link with the colleges and universities and they are often able to keep the agencies in touch with the latest ideas. This is not to suggest that contacts with students should be used by social workers as a substitute for keeping up with their own professional reading, but in the nature of things the students will have more time for discussion and it can be very stimulating for the social workers in an agency to have contact with the wider influences to which the social work student is subject.

The usual medium for student supervision is the process record, particularly in the beginning stages, because it allows the supervisor to relate the innumerable parts which together make up social work practice. The way in which the student supervisor uses process records of interviews and other situations is admirably shown in great detail by Bessie Kent in her book *Social Work Supervision in Practice*[5] in which one is taken step by step through the supervision sessions of one student.

The relationship between the student and the supervisor is the main feature which distinguishes student supervision from social work practice. Whereas the worker–client relationship is one-way, in that the worker has no right to expect direct emotional satisfaction from the client, this is not true of student supervision. The supervisor positively needs to have expectations of the student in order to help him achieve his maximum performance and there is no reason why there should not be a warm personal relationship which will often last long after the period of supervision has come to an end.

The alternatives to process recording as a means of enabling the supervisor to monitor the student's progress are either to have the supervisor present when the student is conducting an interview, or else to have the session recorded. At first glance, the presence of the supervisor would not only allow him to judge the student's work but would also give him an opportunity to compare the student's record of the interview with what actually took place.

However, there are numerous objections to this apparently attractive scheme. The most serious is that the presence of the supervisor will radically affect the dynamics of the interview. Even if the supervisor is quite silent, the one-to-one interview becomes triadic and the supervisor's silence may very well have a more pervasive effect than if he took a part.

A more subtle objection to the presence of the supervisor when the student is interviewing is that it perpetuates the idea that experience in social work somehow brings about greater objectivity of perception. In one sense this is true, in that the experienced social worker is usually more able than a student to identify his own emotions, but any suggestion that he would have fewer personal emotions would be professionally slanderous and, if it were true, the worker should resign at once. The presence of the supervisor would mean that he would have to allow for the effect of his own emotions on his perception of the interview as well as those of the student, whereas with process recording it is so much easier to focus on the student–client interaction.

The presence of a tape-recorder, provided it is unobtrusive, raises none of these problems and the ethical proprieties, even with the consent of the client, which are the cause of a serious division of opinion in social work, are really outside the scope of this book, except to say that the issues raised by this hotly disputed subject, are much more far-reaching than is generally appreciated. However, a tape-recorder by itself would be no substitute for process recording as it only records speech and sounds and, even assuming much more versatile visual recording apparatus, one is still left without the subjective impressions that are the chief value of the process recording.

This is not to denigrate the value of objective recording and it seems likely that when some of the ethical problems involved have been thought through, their use will become much more extensive, both as aids to student supervision and other aspects of social work education, but they can never be more than aids, however useful, as the essence of student supervision lies in the relationship between supervisor and student. Because the social worker can use his own personality only as the medium for all his dealings with his clients, so the most effective way to learn to use his personality is through his relationship with his supervisor.

Although so much emphasis has been given to the use of process recording in student supervision, its use is much greater in the early stages and, as the student approaches professional qualification, it will generally be discontinued. This is not because process recording has no place in mature professional practice as it can form part both of agency supervision and consultation, but rather because social work education forms a continuum in which there should not be any sudden transformation from student to fully-qualified social worker.

For the social work student, process recording represents dependency on the supervisor in which the student presents a total picture as he sees it and allows the supervisor to select what he thinks is of importance. This is exactly what is required in the initial stages, particularly as the student will inevitably indicate in the process recording those features which he felt were the most important. However, as the student progresses in professional competenc⸱ he needs to learn to place greater reliance on his own judgement ⸱nd this includes the selection of those items which he judges to be of greatest significance. In fact the summary to be included in the running record involves just such judgements and so it is natural that student supervision should move on from process recording to brief summary. This transition also does not need to be abrupt and such phrases as abbreviated process recordings are sometimes used to denote the intermediate stages.

Agency Supervision

Although the difference between the field work supervision of the student and the supervision of the professionally qualified social worker in the agency is a matter of emphasis rather than of principle, it is sufficiently important for the two subjects to be dealt with separately. The fact that nothing miraculous happens to a social worker on the day he qualifies is amply demonstrated by a study undertaken for the Institute of Medical Social Workers, *The First Two Years*,[6] in which the need for support for the newly qualified worker is one of the main findings.

Reduced to essentials, student supervision is a process of helping the student to develop his practice within the limits of professional social work which the supervisor will help him to discover, and involves the imparting of information about agency function in the agency in which they are working. While it is now generally acknowledged that the student has a contribution to make, this cannot compare with the contribution to be expected of the qualified worker. The main object of this period is the professional education of the student, although this is by no means inconsistent with the welfare of the clients with whom he is in contact.

On the other hand, the supervision of the qualified social worker is primarily a managerial rather than an educational process, although too much should not be made of this distinction. Management and professional education both include elements of the other and the likelihood is that their similarities will receive more stress in the future. However, at the present time, education is still seen more as a one-way process, whereas in management, the central importance of two-way communication is accepted, at least in theory.

In some agencies even professional supervision is seen primarily as a one-way process to ensure that the decisions of the administrators are carried out by the field-workers and it would follow from this that the greatest sign of confidence which an agency could show in one of its workers would be to emancipate him from supervision. While there is an obvious internal logic in this procedure, it involves a misconception of the true purpose of supervision, which is to act as the link between agency policy and the realities of the situation in which it has to function. Social change is a constant and permanent factor which every agency must recognise and, without the information which only the field worker can give, administrative decisions are in serious danger of being irrelevant to the needs of the time.

This process of two-way communication is anything but straightforward, and certainly should not consist solely of the field workers attempting to have their fashions and prejudices reflected in agency policy. It is true that they have access to the essential basic information, but only with much greater skill in research methods will they be able to refine their information so that it can be used as the foundation of policy decisions. Similarly, those who have the responsibility of making policy decisions need to be able to use the information supplied by the field workers as the basis, for instance, of decisions about the allocation of resources so that their logic will be generally recognised. The role of the agency supervisor is thus quite vital to the well-being of the agency and one of the changes which one can expect in the future is that much more attention will be paid to the skills involved in bringing about this amalgam of administrative and professional practice.

The major complication of agency supervision is that all staff members, even with the same professional training, cannot be expected to make an equal contribution to the formulation of agency policy. The worker with ten years' service will generally be of much greater value than one with six months and this is one of the reasons for salary differentials, although there are many other factors to be considered, both in assessing professional worth and determining salary scales.

The process of supervision necessarily combines the tasks of assessment with acting as a communication medium, and both tasks are continuous. Because the worker's professional development goes on after qualification, and should continue throughout his career, there should be no question of a once-for-all assessment to be got out of the way, although some agencies have adopted a procedure of annual assessment, which may be an attempt to encapsulate this element of supervision and thereby separate it from its other functions. The English probation service with its system of confirmation after one or two years' service, after which a probation officer is practically irremovable from office, substantially introduced a once-for-all assessment at a basic level which has advantages in the professional freedom of officers, but which also goes a long way to explain the acknowledged difficulties of the senior probation officers in their role as agency supervisors.

Any attempt to separate the functions of two-way communication from the hierarchical structure of the agency is likely to cause more difficulties than it solves because it would involve separating the personal interests of the social workers from their professional duties, when the tendency is increasingly towards helping them to see how their professional work can be carried out only by the full use of their personalities.

The alternative to separation is to accept that the two elements of agency supervision may seem incompatible but as they are both essential, it is as well to bring the resulting contradictions and tensions out into the open instead of pretending they do not exist. Grasping this nettle can have many advantages both in terms of improved communication flow, staff satisfaction and improved decision making at all levels.

If agency supervision is to become an integral part of agency functioning, then the supervisors will need special training which the social work profession will have to provide. The tendency has been to promote experienced social workers to supervisory posts without any special training and it is only recently that it has been recognised that social work skills were not all that was needed for the duties of supervision.

As a result efforts have been made to import middle management skills, and ideas have been borrowed from industry, trade and the other professions. All of this is fine, and social work as a whole has benefited from the interest that has been taken in supervision. However, a third stage is necessary in which theoretical concepts of management have to be married to the practical realities of social work practice and agency structure. There are some signs that this process has begun but there is still a lot to be done before the position can be regarded as entirely satisfactory. The benefits of better supervision would be apparent in all aspects of social work. The administrative structure would almost certainly be less rigid and as the information supplied by the field-workers was seen to affect administrative decisions this would both encourage the field-workers and would incline them to be more open in their accounts of their work.

So far, this discussion of agency supervision has been almost entirely in administrative and managerial terms which may seem remote from the subject of interviewing and counselling, but administrative change can be assessed only in terms of an improved social work service and this will be reflected in improved interviewing and counselling. It could mean, for instance, that the social worker was expected to deal with a caseload according to his time and talents and with better facilities ranging from appropriate clerical help to a properly furnished office.

In return one would expect that he would give a better service to his clients which would be reflected in the records, themselves a tool of management and a source of data for research.

Consultation

By definition, consultation is not possible between two members of the same agency. This is not because of any clash of function, as in supervision, which might be resolved with positive advantages, but because the essence of consultation is that the consultant should be outside the structure in which the social worker is operating. It is precisely because consultation has important administrative connotations that it must be separated from supervision.

Many of the agencies which have made use of consultation have engaged members of other professions, particularly psychiatrists, but also lay analysts, psychologists and other medical practitioners. This was understandable when the social work profession was in its infancy. There is a lot to be said for the independent standpoint of another profession and one trusts that social work will foster its exchanges with doctors of all sorts and other professional bodies and that, in turn, they will come to welcome the opinions of social workers.

However, social work has now reached a stage of development when consideration can be given to setting up a system of consultation from within the profession. Several models are possible, of which the medical profession has some interesting examples. For instance, the role of the consultant in the hospital service shows clearly the dangers of incorporating the consultant in the structure of the organisation. The hospital consultant is in fact usually the chief practitioner but, because of his designation, it is practically impossible to achieve a genuinely consultative service in the hospital. Outside the hospital it is quite a different matter and there the consultant is free to give an expert second opinion because he is not involved in the day-to-day business of the general practitioner.

One difficulty in social work, at least in England, is that there is no reservoir of well-trained social workers outside the agency structure. It would presumably be possible for agencies to exchange the services of workers to act as consultants but, with the present shortage of experienced social workers in most agencies, it is unlikely that such a scheme will get started, unless possibly it is done on a reciprocal basis.

Another alternative is for some agencies to specialise in this role, which might prove attractive to some of the voluntary agencies. The cost would be fully covered by fees which would be justified by the improvement in the professional service as the result of consultation. Although this would create a financial relationship between the consultant and the social worker with whom he was working, it would be sufficiently indirect not to affect their relationship unduly, which would in any case be protected by accepted standards of confidentiality.

The sort of model which might be used is that of the independent management consultant firm, of which there are many examples in business and industry, in which the services of the consultant are purchased. There is certainly scope for management consultancy in social work but our concern here is with providing a professional consultation service for the field workers of an agency. Because the primary interest is in professional social work matters, so the consultant needs to be a trained and experienced social worker.

There are two main reasons why consultation needs to be independent. First, it is very helpful for a social worker to be able to discuss the problems of his clients in a wider context than that of the agency in which he is working. It is essential, from time to time, to refer back to the basic principles of social work and it is useful to consider a case from the standpoint of other agencies with which the consultant may be familiar. Secondly, consultation helps the social worker to have an objective point of view when considering a particular case.

Objectivity is really the distinctive contribution in social work consultation. However well trained the social worker may be, and however much he tries to view his work objectively, when he is involved in a particular case it is not possible both to engage his own personality in the helping process and to retain the detachment of the observer. To attempt to do so will either cause the worker to delude himself or else to withdraw from the relationship with the client.

The experienced social worker should know a lot about the quirks of his own personality, but every case is different and if the consultant did no more than act as a mirror to the worker so that he could see his own actions more clearly, he would more than justify his role. In fact most workers need to have the consultant take more positive action by interpreting the actions of the social worker in the case. One cannot be dogmatic about this. Just because the consultant is not directly in contact with the client, so he can do no more than suggest interpretations, explanations and possible courses of action. The social worker has to decide what is appropriate and the value of the process comes from the interaction between consultant and worker rather than from the single contribution of either side.

Consultation also helps the worker take an objective view of agency function, as it is all too easy for a client to be treated according to the interests of the agency. This is not to suggest that agency function is necessarily antipathetic to the interests of the client, and one trusts that the interests of the client are a major factor in the formulation of policy, but it is still possible, for instance, that administrative convenience will make the agency tend to push a client in a direction in which it does not suit him to go. There is not usually anything very sinister about this and compromise is almost always possible, but without a consultant there is no counter-pressure to agency policy to make the client conform, except the client himself who may, or may not, be able to resist.

It is this sort of situation which distinguishes consultation from supervision. Because the supervisor is himself a staff-member of the agency he will have nothing like the same freedom in helping the social worker view a case both from the point of view of the client and of the agency. This is not because he has lower professional standards than a consultant, but because he is himself a member of the agency whose policy to some extent represents his ideas that it is therefore unrealistic to expect him to view his own agency with the same detachment as an independent outsider.

Similarly, in a perfect world it would be possible for a worker to discuss his case with his supervisor quite freely and without regard to his own career prospects and his own standing in the agency, in which the supervisor is almost certainly a more senior member of the hierarchy. However, in the world as it is, any social worker will feel much happier at discussing his problems with a consultant who has no place in the agency hierarchy and whose communication with the social worker is confidential.

1 Perlman, Mrs H. H., *Social Casework: a Problem-solving Process,* 1957
2 Smalley, Ruth, *Theory for Social Work Practice,* 1967
3 Kogan, L. S. and Hunt, J. M., *Measuring Results in Social Work,* 1950
4 Rogers, Carl, *Client-centred Therapy,* 1952
5 Kent, Bessie, *Social Work Supervision in Practice,* 1969
6 Moon, M. and Slack, K., Institute of Medical Social Workers, *The First Two Years,* 1965

Appendix I

UNIVERSAL DECLARATION

OF HUMAN RIGHTS

On December 10, 1948, the General Assembly of the United Nations adopted and proclaimed the Universal Declaration of Human Rights, the full text of which appears in the following pages. Following this historic act the Assembly called upon all Member countries to publicise the text of the Declaration and ' to cause it to be disseminated, displayed, read and expounded principally in schools and other educational institutions, without distinction based on the political status of countries or territories '.

PREAMBLE

Whereas recognition of the inherent dignity and of the equal and inalienable rights of all members of the human family is the foundation of freedom, justice and peace in the world,

Whereas disregard and contempt for human rights have resulted in barbarous acts which have outraged the conscience of mankind, and the advent of a world in which human beings shall enjoy freedom of speech and belief and freedom from fear and want has been proclaimed as the highest aspiration of the common people,

Whereas it is essential, if man is not to be compelled to have recourse, as a last resort, to rebellion against tyranny and oppression, that human rights should be protected by the rule of law,

Whereas it is essential to promote the development of friendly relations between nations,

Whereas the peoples of the United Nations have in the Charter reaffirmed their faith in fundamental human rights, in the dignity and worth of the human person and in the equal rights of men and women and have determined to promote social progress and better standards of life in larger freedom,

Whereas Member States have pledged themselves to achieve, in co-operation with the United Nations, the promotion of universal respect for and observance of human rights and fundamental freedoms,

Whereas a common understanding of these rights and freedoms is of the greatest importance for the full realisation of this pledge.

Now Therefore,

THE GENERAL ASSEMBLY
PROCLAIMS

THIS UNIVERSAL DECLARATION OF HUMAN RIGHTS as a common standard of achievement for all peoples and all nations, to the end that every individual and every organ of society, keeping this Declaration constantly in mind, shall strive by teaching and education to promote respect for these rights and freedoms and by progressive measures, national and international, to secure their universal and effective recognition and observance, both among the peoples of Member States themselves and among the peoples of territories under their jurisdiction.

Article 1. All human beings are born free and equal in dignity and rights. They are endowed with reason and conscience and should act towards one another in a spirit of brotherhood.

Article 2. Everyone is entitled to all the rights and freedoms set forth in this Declaration, without distinction of any kind, such as race, colour, sex, language, religion, political or other opinion, national or social origin, property, birth or other status.

Furthermore, no distinction shall be made on the basis of the political, jurisdictional or international status of the country or territory to which a person belongs, whether it be independent, trust, non-self-governing or under any other limitation of sovereignty.

Article 3. Everyone has the right to life, liberty and security of person.

Article 4. No one shall be held in slavery or servitude; slavery and the slave trade shall be prohibited in all their forms.

Article 5. No one shall be subjected to torture or to cruel, inhuman or degrading treatment or punishment.

Article 6. Everyone has the right to recognition everywhere as a person before the law.

Article 7. All are equal before the law and are entitled without any discrimination to equal protection of the law. All are entitled to equal protection against any discrimination in violation of this Declaration and against any incitement to such discrimination.

Article 8. Everyone has the right to an effective remedy by the competent national tribunals for acts violating the fundamental rights granted him by the constitution or by law.

Article 9. No one shall be subjected to arbitrary arrest, detention or exile.

Article 10. Everyone is entitled in full equality to a fair and public hearing by an independent and impartial tribunal, in the determination of his rights or obligations and of any criminal charge against him.

Article 11. (1) Everyone charged with a penal offence has the right to be presumed innocent until proved guilty according to law in a public trial at which he has had all the guarantees necessary for his defence.

(2) No one shall be held guilty of any penal offence on account of any act or omission which did not constitute a penal offence, under national or international law, at the time when it was committed. Nor shall a heavier penalty be imposed than the one that was applicable at the time the penal offence was committed.

Article 12. No one shall be subjected to arbitrary interference with his privacy, family, home or correspondence, nor to attacks upon his honour and reputation. Everyone has the right to the protection of the law against such interference or attacks.

Article 13. (1) Everyone has the right to freedom of movement and residence within the borders of each state.

(2) Everyone has the right to leave any country, including his own, and to return to his country.

Article 14. (1) Everyone has the right to seek and to enjoy in other countries asylum from persecution.

(2) This right may not be invoked in the case of prosecutions genuinely arising from non-political crimes or from acts contrary to the purposes and principles of the United Nations.

Article 15. (1) Everyone has the right to a nationality.

(2) No one shall be arbitrarily deprived of his nationality nor denied the right to change his nationality.

Article 16. (1) Men and women of full age, without any limitation due to race, nationality or religion, have the right to marry and to found a family. They are entitled to equal rights as to marriage, during marriage and at its dissolution.

(2) Marriage shall be entered into only with the free and full consent of the intending spouses.

(3) The family is the natural and fundamental group unit of society and is entitled to protection by society and the State.

Article 17. (1) Everyone has the right to own property alone as well as in association with others.

(2) No one shall be arbitrarily deprived of his property.

Article 18. Everyone has the right to freedom of thought, conscience and religion; this right includes freedom to change his religion or belief, and freedom, either alone or in community with others and in public or private, to manifest his religion or belief in teaching, practice, worship and observance.

Article 19. Everyone has the right to freedom of opinion and expression; this right includes freedom to hold opinions without interference and to seek, receive and impart information and ideas through any media and regardless of frontier.

Article 20. (1) Everyone has the right to freedom of peaceful assembly and association.

(2) No one may be compelled to belong to an association.

Article 21. (1) Everyone has the right to take part in the government of his country, directly or through freely chosen representatives.

(2) Everyone has the right of equal access to public service in his country.

(3) The will of the people shall be the basis of the authority of government; this will shall be expressed in periodic and genuine elections which shall be by universal and equal suffrage and shall be held by secret vote or by equivalent free voting procedures.

Article 22. Everyone, as a member of society, has the right to social security and is entitled to realisation, through national effort and international cooperation and in accordance with the organisation and resources of each State, of the economic, social and cultural rights indispensable for his dignity and the free development of his personality.

Article 23. (1) Everyone has the right to work, to free choice of employment, to just and favourable conditions of work and to protection against unemployment.

(2) Everyone, without any discrimination, has the right to equal pay for equal work.

(3) Everyone who works has the right to just and favourable remuneration ensuring for himself and his family an existence worthy of

human dignity, and supplemented, if necessary, by other means of social protection.

(4) Everyone has the right to form and to join trade unions for the protection of his interests.

Article 24. Everyone has the right to rest and leisure, including reasonable limitation of working hours and periodic holidays with pay.

Article 25. (1) Everyone has the right to a standard of living adequate for the health and well-being of himself and of his family, including food, clothing, housing and medical care and necessary social services, and the right to security in the event of unemployment, sickness, disability, widowhood, old age or other lack of livelihood in circumstances beyond his control.

(2) Motherhood and childhood are entitled to special care and assistance. All children, whether born in or out of wedlock, shall enjoy the same social protection.

Article 26. (1) Everyone has the right to education. Education shall be free, at least in the elementary and fundamental stages. Elementary education shall be compulsory. Technical and professional education shall be made generally available and higher education shall be equally accessible to all on the basis of merit.

(2) Education shall be directed to the full development of the human personality and to the strengthening of respect for human rights and fundamental freedoms. It shall promote understanding, tolerance and friendship among all nations, racial or religious groups, and shall further the activities of the United Nations for the maintenance of peace.

(3) Parents have a prior right to choose the kind of education that shall be given to their children.

Article 27. (1) Everyone has the right freely to participate in the cultural life of the community, to enjoy the arts and to share in scientific advancement and its benefits.

(2) Everyone has the right to the protection of the moral and material interests resulting from any scientific, literary or artistic production of which he is the author.

Article 28. Everyone is entitled to a social and international order in which the rights and freedoms set forth in this Declaration can be fully realised.

Article 29. (1) Everyone has duties to the community in which alone the free and full development of his personality is possible.

(2) In the exercise of his rights and freedoms, everyone shall be sub-

ject only to such limitations as are determined by law solely for the purpose of securing due recognition and respect for the rights and freedoms of others and of meeting the just requirements of morality, public order and the general welfare in a democratic society.

(3) These rights and freedoms may in no case be exercised contrary to the purposes and principles of the United Nations.

Article 30. Nothing in this Declaration may be interpreted as implying for any State, group or person any right to engage in any activity or to perform any act aimed at the destruction of any of the rights and freedoms set forth herein.

Appendix II

S.W. Mr. Crawford?   1

Mr C. Yes.   2

S.W. Do come in.   3

Mr C. Thank you.   4

S.W. Won't you sit down?   5

Mr C. Thank you.   6

S.W. I understand that you made an appointment earlier this   7
morning.   8

Mr C. Yes, yes I did.   9

S.W. Er, how can I help you?   10

Mr C. Well, I don't know whether you can. I went to this day-   11
nursery school today to see about putting my kids there while   12
I'm out at work. I have a nine-to-five job . . . and er . . . and   13
they wouldn't take them, they wouldn't accept them, they said   14
there was no room so . . . er . . . I made a few calls and they   15
said come and see you . . . you seem to be the only person   16
around who could . . . be bothered to help so . . .   17

S.W. Well, what's happening during the day with them at the   18
moment?   19

Mr C. Well, at the moment they're with the neighbours next door   20
. . . and I don't think . . . er um . . . she can really cope, she's   21
got three of her own and er I don't want to impose on her any   22
longer, you know . . . I want something a bit better for them   23
. . . they're in this kitchen all day long, you know . . . and er   24
well . . . I'd rather get them in something better.   25

S.W. I see, this must be very awkward for you.   26

Mr C. Well, yes, it is yes, and it's . . . it's the kids I'm really   27
worried about . . . they're not getting much of a life at the   28
moment you know . . . so what can you do . . .?   29

S.W. How old are your children, Mr. Crawford?   30

Mr C. Well . . . Robert is four and Debbie's three and er . . .   31
well this is the problem you know that they're at that age   32
where they need somebody with them all the time and er . . .   33
I'm just not there.   34

S.W. Well, it is a problem isn't it because it's quite a time before   35
they go to school?   36
Mr C. Yea, yea.   37
S.W. How long has your neighbour been looking after them?   38
Mr C. Well, you see my wife left me about eighteen months   39
ago and she's been looking after them since then.   40
S.W. Does your wife have any contact with the children at all?   41
Mr C. No, no she doesn't er . . . I saw her about twelve months   42
ago but she hasn't seen them since she left. The point is . . . I   43
went round yesterday to this place and er . . . and I saw the   44
man in charge, whoever he was, and I said there must be . . .   45
surely you can fit in my two kids here, you know. He said . . .   46
no, no, no, we haven't got room, you know, crowded already,   47
can't get any money and all this and that er . . . I   48
thought well hell, you know . . . what am I going to do with   49
them . . . er . . . isn't there anywhere in town where I can   50
put them? . . . there must be some sort of agency where they   51
can spend the day . . . I just can't have them with this woman   52
all the time and they are going to go on the streets at the age   53
of three or four.   54
S.W. No, obviously not, have you thought of having a child-   55
minder rather than putting them in a nursery?   56
Mr C. Well . . . who are these child minders . . . I've read   57
something in the papers er . . . you know . . . are they pro-   58
fessionally trained . . . or are they just housewives doing it   59
on the side . . . making a bit of money, 'cos I don't want them   60
. . . if this is the case I could just leave them next door in the   61
kitchen, you know . . .   62
S.W. Well, all the child-minders must be registered now so that   63
we do have some means of checking that they are suitable.   64
Mr C. But can you guarantee that they will be looked after?   65
. . . I mean, you know . . . they are my kids after all.   66
S.W. Well, with registration everything has been done that's   67
possible to ensure that suitable people will be employed.   68
Mr C. Yea, well . . . do they come to the house or do you put   69
them with them? Do I have to sort of take them round every   70
morning?   71
S.W. Well, I think we could do either really. We could find   72
someone that you could take them to each morning before you   73
went to work and then collect them at night . . . or alternatively   74
you could have a sort of a housekeeper coming in.   75
Mr C. No . . . I'm not having that, no . . . no. I don't want any-   76
one coming in just coming in and looking after them like that   77

. . . they're either going somewhere for the day or . . . well I   78
don't know you know . . . I'm not having them coming in.   79
S.W. Well in that case perhaps we can arrange for you to take   80
them to someone each day.   81
Mr C. Um yes. I suppose that's the only way then . . . if that's the   82
only thing you've got to offer. What about these nursery   83
schools? . . . you know . . . I went to that one down Mount   84
Bank is that the only one you have?   85
S.W. Yes, unfortunately it is.   86
Mr C. But there's a hundred thousand people in this town, you   87
know . . . just to have one nursery school . . . I think it holds   88
about sixty kids this chap said. Well I am not going to try   89
and work out the percentage of anything . . . but I think it's   90
pretty disgusting that just sixty places or whatever it is for that   91
many children . . . I don't know what the situation is but it   92
seems to me that there are going to be a lot of people like me   93
around whose wives have run off or left them or died on the   94
spot or something but . . . if that's all you've got then you've   95
got . . . all you've suggested so far is . . . a nursery school   96
which isn't there which I've been to already . . . you've sug-   97
gested having a housekeeper to come in which I will *not*   98
have under any situation at any time . . . and you've suggested   99
putting them out with somebody I'm not . . . who I don't know   100
you know . . . I mean what else is there? Somebody said I   101
should have sent them away . . . adopted is the word you call   102
it I think . . . but that's out for a start anyway . . . if they try   103
to take my kids away I'll brain 'em.   104
S.W. Yes, it's true that part of our job is to . . .   105
Mr C. Oh well . . . if you're going to be like that . . . I thought   106
you know I'd get some help when I came here . . . if all I'd   107
known you were going to be some interfering busybody who'd   108
try to take my kids away then I'm sorry there's just no point   109
coming at all.   110
S.W. How would you feel about having a child-minder, Mr   111
Crawford? Because obviously you have your work to go to and   112
it is a big job looking after two children.   113
Mr C. Yes what I want to know is . . . is this child-minder just   114
going to come in and make some report on me and it's just   115
going to lead off to them being carted away to adoption.   116
S.W. Oh, like you we'd only be interested in the welfare of the   117
children, Mr Crawford.   118
Mr C. Well . . . if by welfare of the children you mean adoption   119
then I'm sorry, that's just not on. You seem to have rapidly   120

shifted from child-minding to adoption and er . . . I don't 121
know . . . I thought in coming here I'd find some help . . . I'd 122
find somebody who could help me place my kids for the day 123
not to have them carted away as you keep seeming to have sug- 124
gested. And I don't want people coming in and spying on me 125
which is all you have to offer . . . I'm sorry. 126
S.W. How are you managing at the moment? Have you had any 127
help from relatives at all? 128
Mr C. Of course I didn't get any help from relatives . . . they 129
send me letters saying I should look after the kids better but I 130
don't take any notice of them, they're my children and I'm not 131
having them interfering . . . and anyway I've told you this be- 132
fore . . . I don't want to keep recapping on this . . . I just want 133
a few suggestions . . . reasonable suggestions . . . 134
S.W. So you could manage better if you did have a child-minder 135
during the day? 136
Mr C. Well that's what I came here for . . . I didn't just come 137
here for . . . a lecture on morals . . . a lecture on adoption. 138
S.W. So if we arranged for someone to act as child-minder for 139
your children you could take them every morning, could you? 140
And then collect them at night? 141
Mr C. Of course I could, that's what I came here for. 142
S.W. What about at nights . . . because obviously you'll want to 143
have some life for yourself . . . perhaps we could arrange for 144
someone to babysit for you. 145
Mr C. No . . . no . . . I'll work that out myself . . . I have a 146
few friends who can do this . . . I just want to keep this 147
official child-minding down to a minimum. Look, I told you 148
time and time again all I want is I go to work every day I 149
cannot take my children to work . . . I want somebody to look 150
after them in the day . . . I don't want people coming in . . . I 151
don't want them snooping on my private affairs . . . and I'm 152
perfectly capable of looking after them at all other times. 153
S.W. Well, how would you feel about me coming with you to 154
introduce you to any child-minder? 155
Mr C. Well of course . . . well of course I'd want to see these 156
people first . . . I don't want to take my children round to 157
anywhere . . . I want to see what sort of place they're going to 158
spend the day in. 159
S.W. Is there any time that would be most convenient for you? 160
Mr C. What for? 161
S.W. To see the child-minder. 162
Mr C. Well . . . if you suggest a few times that you're free I 163

can soon . . . rearrange my affairs to suit this.   164

S.W. Well, it will be easier for you not to take time off from   165
work, won't it, Mr Crawford.   166

Mr C. Of course yes.   167

S.W. So perhaps if we arrange for some time at night?   168

Mr C. Yes.   169

S.W. Er . . . tomorrow evening?   170

Mr C. Er make it the next night.   171

S.W. All right . . . Thursday. Would eight o'clock be convenient   172
for you?   173

Mr C. Yes, yes that's fine.   174

S.W. Here?   175

Mr C. Yes, I'll come . . . I'll come around and pick you up and   176
we'll go and see whoever you choose.   177

S.W. Well . . . I'm glad you came into see us about this . . . so   178
unless there's anything else at the moment I'll see you on   179
Thursday.   180

Mr C. Er no . . . that's all. Thank you very much . . . 'Bye.   181

Appendix III

S.W. Good afternoon.   1

W. Good afternoon.   2

S.W. Now, you have come to see me for some reason – I don't   3
know quite what – there seems to be trouble at home. Would   4
you like to tell me about it?   5

W. Yes – it's, I am getting worried at the moment because my   6
husband on certain occasions is inclined to drink too much, and   7
when he does he sets about me in a way that just makes me   8
purely frightened, because I just feel I am not strong enough   9
to fight against it. Purely sort of physical violence that's   10
frightening me.   11

S.W. H'm.   12

W. I can't and if I were stronger I wouldn't be quite so worried.   13
I am not going to be able to do anything about it if it happens   14
again.   15

S.W. Has this only happened recently?   16

W. It's happened . . . after we had been married about eighteen   17
months it started.   18

S.W. How long have you been married now?   19

W. Three and a half years.   20

S.W. What were things like when you first married?   21

W. Well, nothing of this sort arose. This usually happens if we   22
go out to parties and go and have a few drinks in a pub.   23
It is fine till we get home and then it usually starts with small   24
sort of niggling things, and things didn't niggle us quite so   25
much until we had been married a bit . . . things to find that   26
were niggly.   27

S.W. I see. [Pause] When did things first seem to be going   28
wrong?   29

W. Well, there has never been any difference in our normal   30
day-to-day relationship – it just seems to be I suppose about   31
eighteen months after we were married my husband started   32
drinking. He doesn't drink a lot by any means normally, but   33
at parties when there is a load of drink going round – this   34

sort of thing happens – I can't think why . . . it's usually my 35
reprimanding him for looking at other women, not that he 36
has been doing anything particularly wrong except looking at 37
them. I suppose I have got a very jealous nature and resented 38
it, and this sort of thing blew up and then the only way he 39
seemed to resolve it would be by setting about me. 40

S.W. H'm . . . that seems to be the only way he copes with it? 41

W. I think so, because normally he takes any amount of 42
nagging from me, and I am inclined to nag a bit, and I sup- 43
pose if you are drinking you can get rid of sort of reasoning, 44
and you can tackle it that way. 45

S.W. Have you any children? 46

W. No. 47

S.W. H'm. 48

W. We both want them and it is a question of deliberately post- 49
poning them, which sometimes I find a bit of a strain, but it 50
is just that we don't live in conditions – it's a flat and it's not 51
ideal to bring up children in. 52

S.W. I see. Do you go out to work then? 53

W. Yes – I work all day. 54

S.W. You work full time? 55

W. Yes, I do. 56

S.W. Are you ever short of money, would you find? 57

W. No, not by any means – we are quite well off compared 58
with other people who put up with a lot less than we do. 59

S.W. Are you happy with your living conditions? 60

W. Yes, oh yes! We've got ideal conditions for a couple with no 61
children, but it just wouldn't be ideal, although people do do 62
it on things that are far worse than ours – we don't feel we 63
could manage it at the moment. 64

S.W. But there's no disagreement about this? 65

W. No, no, except as I say occasionally I do flare up about it 66
and think, blow the money and blow living three floors up. 67

S.W. H'm. Before you married did you ever feel that your 68
husband drank too much? 69

W. No, I don't even feel it now. I feel that on occasions he 70
drinks more than he ought to, but it's nothing . . . except 71
when it happens that is the only time it ever causes trouble, 72
I don't throw it at him at all any other time because it never 73
occurs to me that it is a problem. Just when it happens it up- 74
sets me rather and makes things difficult. 75

S.W. He doesn't drink a terrible lot? 76

W. No. 77

S.W. . . . but sometimes when he's had a drink things go wrong? 78
W. Yes, well, if . . . he just goes over the top. It usually happens at 79
a party which goes on late into the night and everybody prob- 80
ably drinks too much. The only thing, of course, that I don't be- 81
lieve I do drink too much. I have got a thing about alcohol 82
isn't really necessary to enjoy oneself, so I incline then to be- 83
come more and more sober instead of more and more drunk. 84
S.W. H'm. What sort of person is your husband? 85
W. Er . . . I don't know. He is sort of generally very tolerant, 86
sort of easygoing sort of person, without too many obvious 87
worries. Not nervous in any way I wouldn't think. Normally 88
quite easy to live with. 89
S.W. You'd be very sorry now if anything prevented your living 90
together? 91
W. Yes, I would. But at the same time, that is to say immediately 92
after something like this happens, then I get a bit worried 93
and I don't quite know what to do about it. 94
S.W. You found that you nagged him fairly often? 95
W. I do. I keep on a bit – not so much nagging as keeping on. 96
S.W. What of sort of thing is it about? 97
W. Ordinary sort of things, like keeping the flat tidy, and I am 98
forever going round with dusters and brooms and things like 99
this, and it must be very annoying to anybody else, but I can't 100
help it. I have always got the Hoover out and thinks like that. 101
S.W. Was it always like that at home before you were married – 102
very tidy? 103
W. Er . . . No, I have always been like that – I admit my cup- 104
boards and drawers are in a dreadful state but as long as the 105
doors' shut on them I am happy – as long as everything looks 106
neat and tidy. 107
S.W. H'm. 108
W. I do try to overcome this, but I can't help it, I am still in- 109
clined to do it rather a lot and sort of tell him to tidy his books 110
up and put his clothes away and put his jacket on a hanger and 111
this sort of thing. 112
S.W. You worry about what other people think about you? 113
W. I don't think it's that at all. I think it's just I've got the feel- 114
ing that if I'm going to get any order into my life I've got to 115
start with the basic things, like keeping my surroundings tidy, 116
and then perhaps I can keep myself well regimented and well 117
organised, and I do feel that this sort of attitude helps me in 118
things, if I am tidy in my surroundings then I can work tidily. 119
S.W. Do you try to organise your husband in the same way? 120

W. I don't . . . I try not to but I do tend to do so, I suppose. 121

S.W. H'm. 122

W. Certain hobbies and things that I participate in as well as I am 123
inclined to do rather more shouting than necessary and order- 124
ing about. 125

S.W. H'm. 126

W. . . . but I realise just normally these things don't cause 127
problems – only if trouble arises over something else and 128
this crops up. 129

S.W. H'm. What do you normally do of an evening – do you go 130
out together? 131

W. My husband plays in a band but I take great pleasure in 132
following and participating in it. We both enjoy music, and if 133
we're not going out with the band then occasionally we do go 134
out to listen to other bands, but normally our social life is 135
taken up with my husband actually playing and my going to 136
listen. 137

S.W. You don't take any part? 138

W. Well, I do sing with them occasionally, but that's really be- 139
cause I am there. You know, because I'm there I thought I 140
might as well do something about it. 141

S.W. Are you a good singer? 142

W. Sometimes I am – I have my off nights of which I am very 143
conscious. 144

S.W. I see. 145

W. Of course the thing is he drinks a great deal when he is with 146
the band, but because he is playing I suppose it's all . . . you 147
just don't get drunk because you are drinking because you are 148
thirsty, and I suppose when we go to parties and he is not play- 149
ing he feels he can drink the same amount without its having 150
any effect, and it usually does have some effect because he is 151
not working like he would be with the band. 152

S.W. H'm. Is he happier when he is working? 153

W. He'd be entirely lost without the band – it's completely time 154
consuming. I don't quite know what either of us would do 155
without it – I suppose find some other hobby – it would be 156
difficult to imagine what. 157

S.W. It's an outlet for both of you. 158

W. Yes it is, definitely. 159

S.W. Are your parents still alive? 160

W. Yes. 161

S.W. Do you see much of them? 162

W. Not very much, no. Both my parents and my husband's 163

parents live in the same town, and when we go down to visit 164
them, we visit both at the same time. 165

S.W. H'm. Are you very close with your own mother? 166

W. I'm closer with my own mother now since I've been married 167
than I was beforehand. I've never been particularly close with 168
my father. 169

S.W. I see. 170

W. But . . . on quite good terms with them. 171

S.W. Were there many troubles when you were becoming in- 172
dependent as a teenager at home? 173

W. Yes, there were . . . um . . . mainly with my father, who even 174
in fact after I was married and I went down home I was told 175
not to put my elbows on the table one lunchtime, even though 176
I was married, sort of. I don't think my father's ever accepted 177
the fact that I have become independent and I don't think he 178
can see there's anything other than a daughter and a sort of 179
young one that still needs to be brought up. 180

S.W. H'm. 181

W. . . . although in fact both my parents are in their mid-forties, 182
they're not old by any means. 183

S.W. H'm . . . more Victorian in manner than . . . 184

W. M'm . . . due to their own upbringing, I feel. 185

SW. H'm. Why do you say that? 186

W. Well, not so much in the case of my father who was sent to 187
boarding school when he was eight, but my mother was 188
brought up in a sort of almost typically Victorian atmosphere, 189
very large family, very large house and everybody . . . father sat 190
at the head of the table and it was sort of ruled rather like that. 191

S.W. H'm. 192

W. . . . and I think she's viewed my father in the same way and 193
allowed him to do the ruling in her own family. 194

S.W. H'm. You think that's wrong? 195

W. I think . . . I think there should be a working relationship as 196
far as children are concerned. You know, it's no good one 197
saying the whole time ' Ask your father ', and ' See what your 198
father says ', because I think a child's then inclined to go and 199
try and wheedle father round and know that mother will sort 200
of do whatever he says. I think parents ought to work things 201
out beforehand. It's easy to talk of course, because I'm not one 202
yet. 203

S.W. H'm. You're very conscious of that? 204

W. Yes! I am, yes! 205

S.W. H'm. 206

W. I get decidedly broody sometimes   207
S.W. H'm. Does the fact that your husband spends a lot of time   208
   with the band worry you at all, or do you feel that going with   209
   him is better for you?   210
W. Yes, I don't resent the amount of time he spends on this one   211
   bit, and I enjoy participating in it. I can feel that another   212
   reason why if we had children my participation would have to   213
   stop and I would begrudge this, I think.   214
S.W. H'm.   215
W. I do . . . as long as I can do this I am quite happy, I don't   216
   mind how much time – I don't go out with him every time   217
   he plays.   218
S.W. H'm.   219
W. . . . . simply because I have housework and things to do, but it   220
   never worries me how often he's out playing, how much time   221
   he spends on it.   222
S.W. H'm. You said you were a little jealous in some ways.   223
W. Not in some ways, I am just jealous of other women, that's   224
   the only thing I am ever jealous of. It's the only thing that   225
   ever causes real trouble between us.   226
S.W. H'm.   227
W. It's something . . . he's got a completely non-jealous nature,   228
   and I can't even reciprocate by sort of going my own way,   229
   because it wouldn't have any effect on him at all, I'm quite   230
   sure.   231
S.W. H'm.   232
W. . . . . so I do resent any attention he pays to other women   233
S.W. Have you ever had reason to feel that you couldn't trust   234
   him?   235
W. No, no, I haven't, except that I've got this dreadful thing   236
   and I believe that no men are to be trusted completely as such,   237
   because I think men are sort of incapable of turning things   238
   down if it's offered to them on a plate, as they say. I don't   239
   think a bloke could turn it down and I am *always* conscious of   240
   the fact that perhaps my husband might be offered this on a   241
   plate and wouldn't be able to turn it down, and I'd feel   242
   frantically jealous, that's not a very rational way of thinking,   243
   but I would sort of almost go berserk over it. Any trouble   244
   between us is caused by my sort of trying to prevent this   245
   occurrence which has never really shown itself to be there.   246
S.W. H'm.   247
W. But I just keep feeling it might be.   248
S.W. And you feel this contributes to the fact that your husband   249

does fly into tempers about this sort of thing?   250
W. Yes. It must be annoying for him for me to keep on, but   251
unless my attitude changes drastically it is going to keep on,   252
and we are going to keep having these terrific flare-ups and   253
be stuck with it.   254
S.W. You're taking the blame for most of this now. Do you feel   255
that your husband is at fault?   256
W. I don't think he is at fault any more than any other person is. 257
Really I don't know, I think my attitude is that if he feels   258
that, he knows that if he gets drunk he gets intolerant and he's   259
going to hit me or go for me in any way, I do feel that perhaps   260
he could try not to, if he is with me at a party or somewhere,   261
he could try perhaps not to drink so much, and then of course   262
the situation wouldn't arise. If he's not with me and he gets   263
very drunk, well then what he does is up to him really. I can't   264
feel that I would be to blame if he did do anything   265
wrong because I wouldn't be there to stop it. But if he's with   266
me I think he could sort of consider this sort of thing might   267
happen and try to avoid it.   268
S.W. Your husband's not a very forceful man then?   269
W. No, not really.   270
S.W. No   271
W. Normally both very placid.   272
S.W. H'm. Your father was a more forceful man, I understand,   273
than that, and you resented it.   274
W. I didn't resent the fact that he was forceful because I don't   275
think this is a fault, but I . . . what it boils down to is I   276
suppose my father was never really interested in what myself   277
and my sister have ever done. He wasn't a family man by any   278
means. He was sent away to boarding school when he was very   279
young and I don't think he ever really had a family life. He   280
also has a . . . He runs a couple of pubs so he doesn't lead a   281
normal working life, he's out very often and when he was in   282
he was tired and he wanted to relax and he wasn't very inter-   283
ested in anything that we were doing. If I tried to tell him he'd   284
sort of say ' yes, dear ' and get on with his reading or doing a   285
crossword or something.   286
  ⎰ *S.W*. And that was your only experience of any marriage   287
  ⎱   from inside before yours.   288
    W. Yes, it was.   289
S.W. Do you feel that was very different to your husband's?   290
W. Yes, although my mother . . . I consciously tried to model   291
myself on my mother's way because my mother is to me the   292

perfect housewife and mother without being sort of silly about 293
it, but looking back on it I realise she's a fantastic manager, 294
both in being a wife to my father and a mother to myself and 295
my sister; though I wouldn't call theirs the ideal family set- 296
up, my mother's half of it I think was done quite well. 297

S.W. H'm. You think that your mother would have run the 298
house far better if she had been given more freedom by your 299
father? 300

W. Yes, or more support really, not so much freedom – actual 301
sort of participation by my father. I think this is very im- 302
portant. I think if people are married they have got to sort 303
of fifty-fifty sort of thing in everything. 304

S.W. H'm. Do you feel this is happening in your marriage? 305

W. Yes it is when we are both reasonable and it's only as I say 306
when tempers get aroused and the whole things just seems to 307
fall down around us and there doesn't seem to be much point 308
to it at all. 309

S.W. H'm. 310

W. But when it's going along normally, like my cooking a meal 311
and my husband eating it and enjoying it, you know, which is 312
very basic, but this sort of thing I think is quite important and 313
it goes along fine, or we've got any other problems to talk 314
over – you know the demon drink that seems to cause the 315
trouble. 316

S.W. Do you find it easy to talk this sort of thing over with your 317
husband? 318

W. Yes, I do normally. 319

S.W. H'm. 320

W. I may have this thing about drink as well because as I say 321
my father's run pubs and my mother was born in a pub and its 322
been in the family the whole time, and I've always had this 323
thing drummed into me about how drink can get the better of 324
people . . . perhaps not too tolerant of it. 325

S.W. It's very easy, of course, to see the things you're afraid of. 326

W. Yes, it is, it's not so easy to do anything about them. 327

S.W. H'm. Of course you've married a man who is in the most 328
important characteristics, anyway, the opposite of your hus . . . 329
of your father. 330

W. Yes, absolutely. 331

S.W. You're running against difficulties now because your 332
marriage really seems to be the opposite in personalities . . . 333

W. Yes. 334

S.W. . . . . to your parents. 335

W. Yes.   336
S.W. You feel partly to blame for this obviously, m'm – none the   337
less, there is this situation which you feel you can't cope with.   338
Your husband is coping with the problems that seem to arise   339
in a way that obviously isn't acceptable to you.   340
W. Yes.   341
S.W. Is there any way that you can see that that can be improved?   342
W. Well, I don't . . . no, I can't, and I don't really know at all   343
what can be done. If I'd lived near my parents, say, I would   344
have gone to them for a couple of weeks I suppose, and sort of   345
seen if that had pulled him to his senses . . . um, because I   346
don't have sort of anybody I can run to I don't know quite   347
what to do. Quite frankly the thing is that it just scares me   348
stiff. It's pure physical fear of really being injured badly or   349
done in, because obviously my husband is stronger than I am   350
because he's a man.   351

    S.W. You are aware of this possibility . . . um . . . before   352
    you start complaining, we'll say, about the things you   353
    see?   354
    W. Yes, I am aware.   355

W. Well, the last time it happened I was very aware of this. I   356
was frightened. I did everything in my power to steer off it.   357
It was after a party and I said absolutely nothing to him, and   358
he was very drunk and he wanted to get home so I followed   359
him. He took about three wrong turnings on the way home. I   360
didn't say a thing, I just followed him and got home.   361
S.W. H'm.   362
W. Then suddenly he just sort of hit me for some reason.   363
S.W. H'm.   364
W. And then when we did get home the final thing was I let   365
him in with my own front door key because he didn't have   366
his and he went in and put the latch up on me and I was left   367
out on the landing for four hours in the middle of the night.   368
S.W. H'm.   369
W. So I don't think it seems to me at the moment this sort of   370
thing can't be avoided at all, except by not drinking which   371
he doesn't seem prepared to do.   372
S.W. Had nothing at all led up to this behaviour of his?   373
W. Yes. Well, it had . . . at a party as I say I feel myself able   374
to enjoy myself without necessarily going after some other   375
bloke or drinking too much. I can sort of chat to people quite   376
happily for quite a long time, but he seems to enjoy parties if   377
it means he can get hold of another woman, not do anything   378

wrong really by any means, but I just grow very jealous. 379
S.W. H'm. 380
W. And then of course I say something about this and it all starts 381
from there. 382
S.W. H'm. 383
W. But when I realised that I was getting a bit, you know, it 384
might be getting a bit dangerous I did stop completely and we 385
hardly spoke a word to each other, but it didn't stop him 386
obviously feeling some sort of resentment towards me. 387
S.W. H'm. No, there are obviously faults on both sides from the 388
way you have described it to me, and I think you feel that your 389
own behaviour has contributed to it. 390
W. Yes. 391
S.W. What I *can* do is to write to your husband and ask him if 392
he would like to come and see me with you. 393
W. Yes. 394
S.W. . . . and this would give me the opportunity to meet him 395
and discuss this with both of you. 396
W. Yes. 397
S.W. Do you feel that this would be the right thing to do? 398
W. Well, at first I think his initial reaction . . . he'll be rather 399
annoyed that I felt I couldn't talk this out with him myself, 400
but I think perhaps once he decided to do it then he wouldn't 401
mind at all. 402
S.W. H'm. Well, thank you, I'll do that then, I shall write to him 403
today asking to see you both next week. 404
W. Yes. 405
S.W. Perhaps next Friday would be convenient. 406
W. Yes. 407
S.W. And by that time we hope that at least you will be able to 408
have discussed this from both points of view by then. 409
W. Yes, I hope so. 410
S.W. Thank you. 411
W. Thank you. 412

Appendix IV

S.W. Good afternoon.   1

M. & W. Good afternoon.   2

S.W. I'm glad you could both get along this afternoon . . . we   3
felt it would be an idea if you could both get here this after-   4
noon so that we could discuss things a little bit further.   5
Basically the impression I have is that you both realise some-   6
thing is wrong and that you would hope to be able to over-   7
come this and not let the marriage end at this stage. You've   8
obviously discussed the things we talked about – I gather you   9
do find it fairly easy to discuss these things. What do you   10
feel we can do about it?   11

W. It's difficult to say really, because as I say if anybody can say   12
if something can be done about it then we should be able to.   13
I think half the worry is the fact that we can't resolve this our-   14
selves.   15

M. Yes, it's just, you know, we've talked this over time and time   16
again, and we come to the intelligent solution, or we know   17
what the matter is and see that the fault lies on both sides, and   18
yet it still happens. It's something that's purely emotional   19
which we don't seem to have any control over.   20

S.W. Do you feel it's your own emotions that you can't control,   21
or your partner's?   22

M. It's probably both – I know that, I mean, I can't control my   23
emotions when I've had one too many to drink but I don't   24
think anybody can – this is one of the effects of drinking, and   25
that normally when, I mean, I generally only drink socially   26
and when everybody's knocking them back a bit and you sit   27
back and you're enjoying yourself then there's no problem, but   28
I find that my happiness can very quickly be shifted to the com-   29
plete opposite by something that's said to me . . . I mean for   30
the same reason that makes people get into fights when they've   31
had . . . you know in a pub, this sort of thing, you know, a   32

few drinks, it just needs somebody to say something which 33
under normal circumstances they would probably ignore . . . 34
S.W. H'm. 35
M. . . . and they leap to their feet and lay into somebody. I mean 36
this is exactly the same thing that happens with us . . . er . . . 37
normally, you know, I think of myself as an easygoing 38
sort of bloke, who, you know, perhaps a bit of an emotional 39
' punchbag ' . . . er . . . take all sorts of things in my stride 40
without getting too worried about them – obviously though 41
they do affect me deeper and when I feel the valve starts escap- 42
ing and when I've had a few drinks then of course I let go of 43
it. There just doesn't seem to be anything I can do about it 44
except obviously not to drink. I must say I don't do it delib- 45
erately, I don't just go out with the intention of getting drunk, 46
and I don't in fact often get drunk. I don't know exactly what 47
my wife has been telling you about this, but you know I hope 48
she hasn't given you the impression that I'm a drunkard, be- 49
cause this is not the case at all . . . um . . . I can hold my 50
beer pretty well and I never drink anything but beer. 51
S.W. H'm. 52
M. It's just the odd occasion when I get niggled. 53
S.W. H'm. It seems that generally you control your feelings. 54
M. Oh yes! Yes. 55
S.W. And this is really what creates the build-up of emotion 56
which tends to come out when you do. 57
M. I think – I think that's what it is, yes. Do you agree with this? 58
W. Yes, I'm not so worried so much about the cause of it or the 59
actual thing that happens, I'm just scared of ending up wind- 60
ing up dead. I don't really think this is a satisfactory way to 61
end up any under circumstances, and this is what I'm trying to 62
{ avoid. 63
{ *M.* I agree . . . I'm not – I'm not trying to justify my actions 64
because we're on the . . . Again this is not something that 65
{ happens often, you know. I don't come home every Friday . . . 66
{ *W.* This is only going to happen once, isn't it? 67
M. . . . and Saturday nights and beat my wife up like one reads 68
about in certain cases, but I feel terrible on the odd occasions 69
that I *have* done it, you know, although at the time I feel 70
quite justified in my actions, the morning after I really do feel 71
terribly remorseful about them 72
S.W. H'm. 73
M. And I wish that it just didn't have to happen. 74
S.W. If it didn't come out – if you didn't have a drink and these 75

tensions didn't come out, what would happen then? 76
M. Well, who can tell? 77
S.W. H'm. 78
M. I don't know, I mean things would just go on as normal . . . 79
er, unless I was triggered off by something else, you know, but 80
under normal circumstances I would be the same sort of placid 81
character that I always am . . . I suppose. 82
W. In a way this annoys me though. Because there are some 83
things I would like you to get worked up about and you don't. 84
S.W. You provoke your husband? 85
W. Well I – probably I do, I don't really mean to provoke him to 86
do actual physical violence, but there are occasions when I will 87
say things that might be slightly outrageous just to get some 88
reaction. 89
S.W. H'm. 90
M. Well I think the reason is that I, you know, I think that 91
I've got a very liberal attitude to things. I can take a lot of 92
different types of people, different attitudes, different points of 93
view, without getting too steamed up about them – about 94
people, you know. Whereas you tend to expect people to fall 95
into line with you and you are very intolerant about people who 96
think in different ways from your own. 97
W. I'll tolerate anything except being beaten up. 98
M. No, this isn't true! Obviously nobody wants to tolerate being 99
beaten up, but what makes me beat you up, if we've to use this 100
crude expression, is the very fact that you are intolerant. 101
W. H'm. 102
M. You're intolerant of my attitude to a lot of things and people 103
as well, particularly members of the opposite sex, and the 104
moment you see me in conversation with a woman you come 105
rushing up, you want to know what it's all about, and more 106
often than not you drop some catty remark or other when quite 107
possibly we might just be talking about a film we went to see 108
last week or something. 109
S.W. You feel you are able to talk this over? When you're talk- 110
ing this over on your own is this the sort of barrier you always 111
come up against? You're more accusing than reconciling? 112
M. Yes, it usually gets that way. 113
W. No, it's a question of : no – it's a question of us seeing, each 114
seeing the other's point of view, but not feeling capable of do- 115
ing anything about it. I understand what motivates you doing 116
this and you understand why I can't tolerate it, but at the same 117
time nothing, it won't stop it, we don't agree to sort of suit 118

each other on these occasions. We both know exactly what's 119
wrong, but it's just a question of . . . as I say all I'm worried 120
about is ending up with a knife in my back, and I do believe 121
that if we were in the kitchen and this sort of thing occurred, 122
that hands would be laid on whatever was available. 123
M. Quite, well yes, all this . . . 124
W. And this is really what's frightening me, not the lack of being 125
    able to talk it over but the . . . 126
S.W. You feel . . . 127
M. But you've got to get to the root cause, you can't, I mean if 128
    this situatioñ occurs and is likely to arise then I mean what 129
    are we doing here if we're not trying to get to the bottom of 130
    it? 131
S.W. You feel that your . . . 132
M. I think this is a typical . . . sorry . . . as I say this is a 133
    typical attitude of my wife's in that she's not interested really in 134
    motivation here, all she's interested about is not getting a knife 135
    in her back. 136
S.W. H'm. 137
M. And she's not going any further than this, you know, this is 138
{   the end of the problem, isn't it? 139
    W. It's far enough. 140
M. Whereas to me I mean, I don't want to put a knife in her 141
    back either, but I want to know *why* I want to put a knife in 142
    her back. 143
S.W. H'm, and you've no idea why? 144
M. Well, yes, I, I, I've, I think we've already had this out, I, I, I 145
{ . . . provoked. 146
    S.W. Yes, I think we have. You wife knows she provokes 147
    you. Do you in fact know why you provoke him? 148
W. Only that, no I don't, it's not, I don't know it, it's just I'm 149
    very jealous and I don't want anybody else to get the things 150
    that I think are due to me . . . um . . . it's not, I don't really 151
    don't know whether it is in fact deliberate provocation, or 152
    whether it's just purely self-survival and worried about what 153
    I'm going to lose out by just somebody else getting him off 154
    me. 155
M. But this isn't likely to happen, you see we are basically very 156
    happily married and we have a satisfactory home life, and I'm 157
    very happy with you, you know, as a wife and the things you 158
    do for me and certainly wouldn't dream of changing you for 159
    anybody else. 160
W. Yes, but none of these things are worth it on occasions like 161

this.   162

M. But you know you still sort of sometimes seem to be doing   163
your best to get rid of me.   164

S.W. You give a very insecure ; . . do you feel that you are as   165
good as the other woman?   166

W. Yes, I feel, I have become, I have begun feeling a lot more   167
insecure lately because I've seen a great many other married   168
couples around our age group going very much on the rocks   169
. . . and I sort of . . .   170

S.W. H'm.   171

W. ; . . all for differing reasons, but marriages that obviously   172
aren't going to work, and I feel, I then feel insecure just about   173
the whole state of marriage . . . I think and yet for some reason   174
I've got . . . a very traditional view of marriage and what it   175
means and I want to hang on to this, and then sometimes I   176
wonder whether it is the right thing, whether it is the right   177
sort of view and I can't reconcile the different aspects of it.   178

M. Well, we do – we do differ in that my wife tends to be a tradi-   179
tionalist and I tend to be a progressive on this sort of . . .   180

S.W. H'm.   181

M. . . . I am not saying which is right or wrong . . .   182

S.W. H'm.   183

M. . . . but, um, I mean I don't for instance, I have . . . I'm not   184
trying to hold on to a marriage, I'm trying to hold on to a   185
woman . . .   186

S.W. H'm.   187

M. . . . you know, a different thing.   188

S.W. H'm.   189

M. It's not the marriage I'm trying to protect at all, the marriage   190
itself as an institution doesn't mean anything to me.   191

S.W. H'm.   192

M. This is, my wife is just a woman that I've chosen to live with.   193

S.W. You tend to feel . . . er . . . on occasions you feel that you   194
want children, that this arises from time to time.   195

W. Yes.   196

S.W. Is this connected with anything . . .   197

W. I've never thought of it as anything other than a natural   198
maternal instinct common to most women . . . um . . . but I am   199
divided, from a purely selfish point of view because I feel I   200
won't be able to go out and enjoy myself quite so much, and if   201
I do go down even deeper I might even feel that I won't be   202
able to go out and keep my eye on him quite so much.   203

S.W. H'm. You don't feel then that a child would cement things   204 together? This isn't very . . . 205

W. No, I've been against this sort of attitude, I don't really 206
think this is . . . it's complementary rather than . . . um . . . 207

M. Well this is one thing that we disagree on actually, because I 208
think a child would be the best possible thing. 209

S.W. H'm. 210

M. We still have talked about it and we just don't seem to be 211
able to come to any conclusions. I'm quite happy to wait for a 212
couple of years, but I don't want it to drift on for ever. 213

S.W. H'm. 214

W. No, nor do I, as I, sort of, say, it's a deliberate postponement, 215
not a deliberate . . . 216

M. And in fact I would in fact be very pleased if one came along 217
now although it's not planned. 218

S.W. So you could . . . 219

M. But you see, I think you've got to be, you've got to be emo- 220
tional about this sort of thing, and a child is something that 221
you just have to accept when it comes and do your best with, 222
and when we started when we were talking about some months 223
back about having a child, the first thing that she did was to 224
get a piece of paper and pencil out and see if we could afford 225
it. 226

S.W. H'm. 227

M. You know, which, all right, this may be an admirable attitude, 228
but it's . . . um . . . you know, it's not surely the first thing one 229
thinks of when . . . er . . . 230

S.W. H'm. It depends really on the approach to having a child, 231
doesn't it? 232

M. I think so, yes. 233

W. I certainly don't think it should be done to cement a relation- 234
ship. 235

S.W. H'm. What do you think are the reasons for having 236
children? 237

W. . . . It's just a sort of natural manifestation of married life, 238
a sort of family life, it's something that . . . um . . . 239

M. No, I don't agree again. 240

W. Oh, well, I think so . . . 241

S.W. You feel this is something . . . 242

    M. I want to see . . . it's not a question of should . . . I want 243
    to see my own children growing up . . . my own creation. 244
    W. It's a selfish attitude, I don't take this one at all . . . I 245
    don't regard . . . 246

M. It's not entirely selfish because I want to bring them up and 247

bring them into the world and help them to grow up and this   248
is what it's all about.   249

S.W. You feel that it's a woman's place to be a mother?   250

W. Yes I do, not necessarily her first place, it would be very good   251
if she could combine everything.   252

S.W. H'm.   253

W. But, er . . . I think . . .   254

M. Anyway, I think we're getting off the point really, because I   255
don't think this is the main – the main problem.   256

S.W. This certainly seems to have some connection with some   257
of the other things that go wrong . . . er . . .   258

W. H'm.   259

S.W. Your wife admits to being a little possessive, um . . . also   260
there is this feeling of ' What should I do?' ' What should a   261
woman do? um . . . does this apply with the cleaning that you   262
do which some people might consider excessive?   263

W. Yes, I haven't tried to reconcile being a housewife and being   264
a working sort of business woman sort of thing, I can't quite,   265
but perhaps I do over the necessary amount of housework to   266
compensate for the fact that I might feel guilty about going out   267
to work and not being in my proper place and being at home.   268

S.W. H'm.   269

W. I do find it difficult, but these things have come about with   270
the emancipation of women, I think, sort of conflict about   271
whether to be a wife and mother or whether to go out and   272
earn some money and be able to have a better standard of   273
living.   274

S.W. This is a conflict you haven't resolved for yourself yet, isn't   275
it?   276

W. No, I haven't, I haven't sorted it out properly yet.   277

M. I don't think there is a conflict.   278

S.W. I think your wife finds a conflict and everyone finds   279
their own solution.   280

   M. Yes, but this is again because she can't break away from   281
   the traditional standpoint of what a woman is, or what a   282
woman should be.   283

W. Well my idea is there, I can't move it can I, if I've got this   284
idea?   285

S.W. You haven't really though, got a formed idea, you've got   286
two ideas.   287

W. Yes, and I'm not reconciled, this is it. There must be a com-   288
bination somewhere, but I can't really bring them together.   289

S.W. Do you feel that you ought to be a mother, but don't want   290 to? 291

W. This could . . . I don't want to purely for selfish reasons, I, I, 292
on the whole I mean I enjoy myself at the moment, and I feel I 293
might have to give some of this up and become rather house- 294
bound, which in itself I don't really mind the idea, but I also 295
like going out a bit, and I don't really think this, this would 296
be . . . 297

M. But it's not that I'm trying to persuade you all the time to 298
have a . . . to have a child and that you won't. 299

W. No, I haven't said it was 300

M. No, but this is the way its leading which isn't, which isn't the 301
case. 302

W. No . . . 303

M. This is something that we in fact don't talk about from week 304
to week. 305

S.W. No. I agree this is something which isn't talked about, it 306
isn't resolved. There are other things we have been concen- 307
trating on, I feel, what sort of things are contributing to your 308
wife's feelings of insecurity . . . um . . . there's also the other 309
side – the side which is creating the difficulty as to how you're 310
dealing with your wife's insecurities . . . um . . . she is worried 311
about things, she transfers her anxieties to you, and the way 312
you cope with them seems to be to let them build up com- 313
pletely to the stage where some sort of safety valve . . . and you 314
find you can achieve this by having too much to drink which 315
then makes it more acceptable to you . . . lets this go, and the 316
tension can then start all over again. 317

W. H'm. Yes. Perhaps this is something that should be dealt with 318
sort of as it occurs to us, quite quickly. 319

   S.W. That's something, the one things lead to the other, 320
    and what is the more basic thing . . . 321

   M. H'm, you see normally I dislike . . . er trouble. You know 322
I don't like to be continually shouting and screaming all the 323
time. I would much rather just be sitting down quietly in a 324
chair reading a book or something, and so when for instance 325
I'm sitting in this chair and my wife comes along with a carpet 326
sweeper and tries to get all round me I may feel terribly 327
annoyed about it but I just sort of lift my feet up and carry 328
on reading the book, purely because if I do say ' For Christ's 329
sake wait until I've finished ' . . . um . . . she will immediately 330
hit back at me and a row will ensue there and then. 331

S.W. H'm. 332

M. Er . . . and so I've learnt through experience more than . . . I 333

mean a few years ago this was happening all the time.　334
S.W. H'm.　335
M. And we were always having little arguments, just little petty　336
tiffs about this sort of thing, and I just decided in the end it　337
wasn't worth it, so I just keep my mouth shut about it. Perhaps　338
this is wrong because what happens is that this builds up in-　339
side me, this sort of resentment builds up over weeks or　340
months and then suddenly explodes in violent outburst.　341
S.W. Yes, your wife does say that she realises a lot of this is to　342
provoke some reaction. The reaction you seem to be looking　343
for is a reaction similar to the one you would expect from your　344
father.　345
W. Yes, could be. H'm, yes, it could well be in fact that I was —　346
I could go in with stories about school achievements and I　347
wouldn't get any reaction at all so perhaps I'm trying to get it　348
from somebody else now.　349
M. The other thing that I find is that er, you know, I dislike　350
scenes, particularly in public, and although probably nobody　351
even notices little things that happen, I feel very self-conscious,　352
when for instance just a little thing like ' Right, we'll cross the　353
road here,' and if I say 'We'll cross the road here' her im-　354
mediate reaction is ' No we won't, we'll get up there before we　355
cross the road.'　356
S.W. H'm . . . h'm.　357
M. And so, you know, we could have a stand-up row about this　358
in the middle of the road if I was determined to hold my　359
ground and say 'No, you just cross here,' but she wouldn't　360
have this, you see, there would be this great thing about it so　361
I would say ' all right, go on then,' you see, just to avoid any. . .　362
S.W. H'm.　363
M. . . . so you see she always gets her own way in an argument　364
like, purely because I don't . . . you know she considers it im-　365
portant enough to stick up for and I don't.　366
S.W. H'm.　367
M. . . . and I obviously I resent this, I must do, anybody would,　368
and anybody with a stronger will than I have would sort it out　369
there and then and probably, you know, in the end win.　370
S.W. H'm.　371
M. . . . but at a cost which I consider excessive . . .　372
M. . . . so I would rather just sort of shut up about it and go　373
home. This happens all the time . . . er, er . . . everything.　374
S.W. In every marriage there is this adjustment which takes　375
place either on one side or the other, or a modification on　376

both, and this is something you haven't resolved as yet. 377
W. H'm. 378
S.W. You can deal with this in any one of a number of ways, but 379
 isn't this what's got to be dealt with? 380
  W. Yes. 381
  M. This is the basic problem, I think. She tries to be the 382
   dominant, the dominant partner, and most of the time she 383
   succeeds. 384
  W. . . . it probably can be dealt with if I don't have the fear 385
hanging over me that one night you are going to have a bit too 386
much to drink and that will be the end of it, that will finish it 387
once and for all. 388
M. Yes, but the reason that I get nasty when I have had a bit too 389
 much to drink is for this very thing. 390
W. Yes. 391
M. Normally I don't, normally, when I've had a bit too much to 392
 drink I'm as happy as anybody . . . 393
S.W. H'm. 394
M. . . . as you will testify, sometimes I'm just dead happy, par- 395
 ticularly when you've had a few to drink as well, and then 396
 we're fine . . . 397
S.W. H'm. 398
M. . . . and when she can forget her little niggles then it's won- 399
 derful . . . 400
S.W. H'm. 401
M. . . . but when I've had more than she has and she says like 402
 something like . . . well, you know, this same thing about cross- 403
 ing the road or whatever it may be, this is exactly the sort of 404
 thing that's just about the last straw, you see. 405
S.W. Yes, but we do come back to this point, really, I think the 406
 reason why you're provoking your husband. 407
W. Yes. 408
S.W. . . . and the way he reacts is a different thing. We have 409
 talked now about both things, you know, there is a problem for 410
 for both . . . er . . . what can we do about them? 411
W. Well, isn't it a question of my trying to stop nagging, or try- 412
 ing to stop being . . . exerting myself quite so much? 413
S.W. Would it be easier if you knew why you were doing it? 414
W. Yes, it might well be. 415
S.W. H'm. Have you any idea why it might be – in the light of 416
 what we talked about? 417
W. Er . . . well it could be to do with my home background in as 418
 much as my mother was a mother and a housewife and wasn't 419

really interested in doing that and my father was working hard   420
and wasn't . . . and anything I did, it still happens now, if I   421
do anything I tell my parents about it they say ' Oh yes, that's   422
nice, dear,' and that's all I ever get out, whereas he can tell his   423
parents things and a month later they will say ' You told us   424
you were going to so-and-so, did you enjoy it?' – this sort of   425
thing, whereas my parents will have competely forgotten we   426
were ever going to do it anyway.   427

S.W. You tend to rebel a bit against your parents . . . er . . . to   428
what extent are you taking this out on your husband?   429

W. Probably quite a lot, because I've given up trying to take it   430
out on my parents.   431

S.W. H'm.   432

W. I can see now there's absolutely no point in my saying ' For   433
goodness' sake why don't you take any notice ' because they just   434
laugh and say ' Oh well you know you're sort of married and   435
leading your own life ' and so perhaps I do it to get some sort   436
of interest shown in me, that's probably why I don't like you   437
looking at other women because I think it's about time some-   438
body showed some interest in me.   439

M. But I tend to show a lot more interest in you than most hus-   440
⎧   bands that I know when we consider a lot of our   441
⎪   friends . . .   442
⎩   *W.* I don't think . . .   443

M. . . . well, when we consider, when we think, a lot of our   444
friends who treat their wives abysmally . . .   445

W. Yes.   446

M. I reckon you get a pretty good ride.   447
⎧   *S.W.* I think people who do feel insecure and who are in-   448
⎪   terested in . . .   449
⎪   *W.* They keep needing re-assurance . . .   450
⎨   *S.W.* . . . marriages at the moment are much more demand-   451
⎪   ing. This is something, of course, that's difficult by any   452
⎩   standards.   453

M. This is how, what makes me feel a bit, you know, why I feel a   454
little bit sore about it, is that . . .   455

S.W. H'm.   456

M. . . . why do I have to be mistrusted?   457

S.W. H'm.   458

M. . . . You know it's as if you feel a sort of compulsion, to, to   459
not to trust me when I'm sort of even just talking   460
quite happily with a, another, with a woman . . . if it was a   461
man, and we were talking about the same thing,   462

you wouldn't, you wouldn't give a tuppenny cuss about it, 463
but I could be with a woman, and you know, talk about 464
anything, and immediately you know, this sort of automatic 465
distrust comes on. 466
W. Yes, I haven't noticed you talking to any men recently 467
M. This is a typical reaction. 468
S.W. H'm. I think it embarrasses you to talk about this. 469
W. Yes, because I recognise it as a failing in myself. I don't, I 470
don't enjoy it at all. 471
S.W. H'm. You said something in our first meeting . . . you felt 472
that no man virtually could be trusted given an opportunity. 473
Do you think all wives feel that? 474
W. No, I don't. I know they don't, there's plenty of wives I've 475
seen who trust their husbands completely, yet I've seen their 476
husbands in action when their wives haven't been with them. 477
S.W. H'm. 478
   W. And, er, I don't know whether it's better to be like those 479
     wives and be sort of . . . ignorance is bliss. 480
   M. You can't adopt an attitude on this, you can't say ' I'll be 481
     like this wife, or like that wife ' . . . 482
W. I'm not saying that . . . 483
M. Well, you have an attitude . . . 484
W. Yes, of course you have an attitude, so I say I don't, I don't, 485
I think some women don't in fact think that their husbands 486
would ever be capable of doing anything that would upset 487
them, and I suppose really it would be quite nice to be like 488
that. 489
S.W. H'm. 490
W. But at the same time, I don't think, I don't think that men 491
can be trusted. 492
S.W. And yet you constantly say that your husband can be trusted 493
– now is this something else you want to be real but don't feel 494
it is? 495
W. Yes, probably. I would like, it would be ideal I think, in that 496
way, few people would have marriage problems. 497
S.W. H'm, because other women aren't the only things that break 498
up marriages. 499
W. I suppose not, but I can't visualise anything at all that could 500
be as serious as that to me – anything else I feel I could over- 501
come. 502
M. This again is a point where we differ, because to me the 503
physical relationship between man and wife isn't the important 504
thing in marriage and doesn't mean in fact that much to me, 505

and all right, it is obviously not desirable for men, for hus-   506
bands or wives to be unfaithful to their partners.   507

S.W. H'm.   508

M. But if this does happen, and let's face it, it happens all the   509
time, this is not to me sufficient reason for a marriage to disin-   510
tegrate. There are far worse things, like this continual nagging   511
which . . .   512

S.W. H'm.   513

M. . . . could break up a marriage, I think, but if my wife ad-   514
mitted to me that she'd been unfaithful, although I wouldn't   515
be particularly pleased about it, I, it certainly would not make   516
me want to get rid of her . . .   517

S.W. H'm.   518

M. . . . in fact, if anything it could bring us closer together, I   519
think.   520

S.W. H'm.   521

M. But I feel that if I were ever unfaithful to her that   522
immediately she would cease all relationships with me, and that   523
would be the end of it, which is to me not a very adult atti-   524
tude.   525

S.W. H'm. Obviously a marriage has got to be based on far more   526
than that, and a sound, secure marriage one would expect   527
to be able to surmount that sort of thing. But this marriage   528
isn't secure – for what reasons – why does your wife feel in-   529
secure? She is very demanding . . . er . . . have you coped with   530
it in the right way?   531

M. I, I think perhaps the proper way to, you know, if one talks   532
about coping with her, I don't particularly want to cope with   533
her . . . if I have to cope with her, then the only way to do it   534
would be to be really hard, really firm, and to stand no non-   535
sense, but I'm, perhaps you know, I haven't got the guts to do   536
this. It would be too much of an effort, quite honestly, because   537
she never, at least, to start with, takes anything from me, so   538
I've just . . .   539

    {   *S.W.* This isn't . . .   540
    {   *M.* I retire from the, from the race . . .   541

S.W. This is something you have got to work between you,   542
and neither of you as individuals can completely alter the   543
pattern of your marriage overnight.   544

W. H'm.   545

S.W. I don't know how far we have got this afternoon, but what   546
we've really talked about has been your insecurity, and where   547
it stems from. We don't know how far you were able to get   548

into that, and then of course the trouble that that causes be- 549
tween you, and the way in which you deal with it. Um . . . 550
{   *W*. H'm. 551
  S.W. You obviously . . . 552
  M. Sorry . . . 553
S.W. How far you can deal with that now is going to depend on 554
to what extent you can both see some solution. 555
W. Yes, I think it can be dealt with. 556
S.W. H'm. I'm sure it can. 557

Bibliography

Ackerman, N. W. *Exploring the Base for Family Therapy*, Basic Books, 1962

Ackerman, N. W. *Treating the Troubled Family*, Basic Books, 1966

Ackerman, N. W. (ed.) *Family Therapy in Transition*, Little Brown & Co., 1970

Ackerman, N. W. *The Psychodynamics of Family Life*, Basic Books, 1958

Ackerman, N. W. *Family Process*, Basic Books, 1970

Aichhorn, August *Wayward Youth*, Putnam, 1936

Alves, Joseph T. *Confidentiality in Social Work*, Catholic University of America, 1959

Amos, W. E. and Grambs, J. D. *Counselling the Disadvantaged Youth*, Prentice Hall, 1968

Atkinson, J. *Handbook for Interviewers*, Central Office of Information, 1967

Bannister, K. and Pincus, L. *Shared Phantasy in Marital Problems*, Codicote Press, 1965

Bannister, K. *Social Casework in Marital Problems*, Family Discussion Bureau, 1955

Banton, M. *Roles*, Tavistock, 1965

Bardill, D. R. and Ryan F. J. *Family Group Casework*, 1964

Bartlett, Harriet M. *The Common Base of Social Work Practice*, National Association of Social Workers (USA), 1970

Beck, Carlton E. *Guidelines for Guidance*, Brown, 1966

Beedell, Christopher *Residential Life with Children*, Routledge & Kegan Paul, 1970

Bettelheim, Bruno *Love is Not Enough*, Free Press, 1950

Biddle, B. J. and Thomas, E. J. *Role Theory: Concepts and Research*, Wiley, 1966

Biestek, Felix *The Casework Relationship*, George Allen and Unwin, 1957

Bion, W. R. *Experiences in Groups*, Tavistock, 1961

Bordin, E. S. *Psychological Counselling*, Appleton-Century Croft, 1968

Borman, Ernest G. *Discussion and Group Methods*, Harper & Row, 1969

Bott, Elizabeth *Family and Social Network*, Tavistock, 1957

Bowers, Swithun *The Nature and Definition of Social Casework*, Journal of Social Casework USA, 1949

Brayfield, A. H. *Readings in Modern Methods of Counselling*, Appleton-Century Croft, 1968

Brown, J. A. C. *Techniques of Persuasion*, Penguin Books, 1963

Caplow, Theodore *Two Against One: Coalitions in Triads*, Prentice Hall, 1968

Cartwright, Darwin and Zander, Alvin *Group Dynamics: Research and Theory*, Tavistock, 1968 (3rd edition)

Coser, L. A. *Makers of Modern Social Science: Georg Simmel*, Prentice Hall, 1965

Davison, Evelyn *Social Casework*, Baillere, Tindall & Cox, 1965

de Berker, Paul, *Interaction of Human Groups in the Community and Institutions*, Faber, 1969

Deeley, Peter *Beyond Breaking Point: Techniques of Interrogation*, Arthur Barker, 1971

de Schweinitz, Karl and Elizabeth *Interviewing in the Social Services*, National Institute for Social Work Training, 1962

Dicks, Henry *Marital Tensions*, Routledge & Kegan Paul, 1967

Dominian, Jack *Marital Breakdown*, Pelican, 1968

Farmer, Mary *The Family*, Longmans, 1970

Fear, Richard A. *The Evaluation Interview*, McGraw-Hill, 1958

Fenlason, Anne F., Ferguson, G. B., Abrahamson, A. C. *Essentials in Interviewing*

Ferguson, E. A. *Social Work: An Introduction*, Lippincott, 1963

Foulkes, S. H. *Therapeutic Group Analysis*, George Allen & Unwin, 1964

Foulkes, S. H. and Anthony, E. J. *Group Psychotherapy*, Pelican 1957

Frank, J. D. and Powdermaker, F. B. *Group Psychotherapy*, Free Press of Glencoe, 1953

Friedlander, Walter A. *Concepts and Methods of Social Work*, Prentice Hall, 1958

Garrett, Annette *Interviewing, Its Principles and Methods*, Family Welfare Association of America, 1942

Geiger, H. *Comparative Perspectives on Marriage and the Family*, Little Brown, 1968

Glover, Elizabeth R. *Probation and Re-Education*, Routledge & Kegan Paul, 1949

Gosling, R., Miller, D.H., Turquet, P. M., Woodhouse, D. *The Use of Small Groups in Training*, Codicote Press, 1967

Guntrip, H. *Personality Structures and Human Interaction*, Hogarth Press, 1961

Hamilton, Gordon *Principles of Social Case-recording*, Columbia University Press, 1940

Hamilton, Gordon *Social Casework*, Columbia U.P., 1951

Handler, Joel *The Coercive Children's Officer*, New Society, 3 Oct., 1968

Harms, E., Schreiber, P. *Handbook of Counselling Techniques*, Pergamon, 1970

Harris, C. C. *The Family*, George Allen & Unwin, 1969

Heasman, K. *Introduction to Pastoral Counselling*, Constable, 1969

Herbert, W. L. and Jarvis, F. V. *Marriage Counselling in the Community*, Pergamon, 1970

Herbert, W. L. and Jarvis, F. V. *Modern Approach to Marriage Counselling*, Marriage Guidance Council, 1969

Heywood, Jean *Introduction to Teaching Casework Skills*, Routledge & Kegan Paul, 1964

Heywood, Jean *Casework and Pastoral Care*, S.P.C.K., 1967

Holden, Alick *Teachers as Counsellors*, Constable, 1969

Hollis, Florence *Casework: A Psycho-social Therapy*, Random House, 1965

Homans, G. C. *The Human Group,* Routledge, 1951

Home Office Prison Department *Group Work in Prisons and Borstals 1962-1966*, H.M.S.O., 1966

Howells, J. G. *Theory and Practice of Family Psychiatry*, Oliver & Boyd, 1968

Jehu, Derek *Learning Theory and Social Work*, Routledge, 1967

Jones, Ernest *Sigmund Freud*, Hogarth Press, 1953-7
Jones, Howard *Reluctant Rebels*, Tavistock Publications, 1960
Jones, Maxwell *The Therapeutic Community*, Basic Books, 1963
Jordan, William *Client-Worker Transactions*, Routledge, 1969
Kadis, A. L. *et al, Practicum of Group Psychotherapy*, Harper & Row, 1963
Kahn, Robert and Cannell, Charles *The Dynamics of Interviewing*, Wiley, 1957
Kasius, Cora (ed.) *Principles and Techniques in Social Casework*, Family Service Association of America, 1950
Kelman, Herbert C. *The Role of the Group in the Induction of Therapeutic Change*, International Journal of Group Psychotherapy XII, No. 4, Oct. 1963
Kent, Bessie *Social Work Supervision in Practice*, Pergamon, 1969
Klein, Josephine *The Study of Groups*, Routledge, 1956
Klein, Josephine *Working with Groups*, Hutchinson, 1961
Koestler, Arthur *Darkness at Noon*, Jonathan Cape, 1940
Kogan, J. M. and Hunt, L. S. *Measuring Results in Social Work*, Family Service Association of America, 1950
Konopka, Gisela *Social Group Work: A Helping Process*, Prentice Hall, 1963
Konopka, Gisela *Group Work in Institutions*, Whiteside & Morris, 1954
Krumboltz, J. D. and Thoresen, C. E. *Behavioural Counseling*, Holt Rinehart & Winston, 1969
Laing, R. D. *Intervention in Social Situations*, Association of Family Caseworkers, 1969
Lifton, Walter M. *Working with Groups*, Wiley, 1961
Lytton, Hugh and Craft, Maurice *Guidance and Counselling in British Schools*, Arnold, 1969
MacCunn, John *Ethics of Social Work*, Constable, 1911
MacGregor, O. R. *Divorce in England*, Heinemann, 1957
MacLennon, Bernyce W. and Felsenfeld, Naomi *Group Counselling and Psychotherapy with Adolescents*, Columbia University Press, 1968
Matthews, Joan E. *Working with Youth Groups*, University of London Press, 1966
Mays, J. B. *Growing Up in the City*, Liverpool U.P., 1954
McCullough, M. K. and Ely, P. J. *Social Work with Groups*, Routledge & Kegan Paul, 1968

Merton, Robert K. *The Focused Interview*, Free Press of Glencoe, 1956

Miller, G. A. *Language and Communication*, McGraw Hill, 1951

Mills, Theodore M. *The Sociology of Small Groups*, Prentice Hall, 1967

Mills, Theodore M. *Group Transformation*, Prentice Hall, 1964

Mills, Theodore M. *Confrontation in Leadership*, Prentice Hall

Moffett, Jonathan *Concepts in Casework Treatment*, Routledge & Kegan Paul, 1968

Moon, Marjorie and Slack, Kathleen *The First Two Years*, Institute of Medical Social Workers, 1965

Nickolds, E. *In-Service Casework Training*, Columbia University Press, 1966

Nokes, Peter *The Professional Task in Welfare Practice*, Routledge & Kegan Paul, 1967

Northen, Helen *Social Work with Groups*, Columbia University Press, 1968

Olnstead, Michael *The Small Group*, Random House, 1959

Orton, J. W. *Readings in Group Work*, 1964

Ottoway, A. K. C. *Learning through Group Experience*, Routledge & Kegan Paul, 1966

Parad, H. J. *Brief and Extended Casework*, Family Service Association of America

Parad, H. J. and Miller, R. R. *Ego-Oriented Casework: Problems and Perspectives*, Family Service Association of America, 1963

Parad, H. J. (ed.) *Crisis Intervention*, Family Service Association of America, 1965

Parsloe, Phyllida *Some Thoughts on Social Groupwork*, British Journal of Psychiatric Social Work Vol. X, No. 1, 1969

Parsons, T. and Bales, R. F. *Family Socialization and Interaction*, Routledge & Kegan Paul, 1956

Perez, Joseph *Counseling: Theory and Practice*, Addison-Wesley, 1965

Perlman, Helen Harris *Social Casework: A Problem-solving Process*, University of Chicago Press, 1957

Pettes, Dorothy *Supervision in Social Work*, George Allen & Unwin, 1967

Phillips, Helen U. *Essentials of Social Group Work Skills*, Association Press, 1965

Pincus, Lily and Bannister, Kathleen *Marriage – Studies in Emotional Conflict and Growth*, Codicote Press, 1960

Pitcairn, L. *Suggestions for Group Discussions*, National Association for Maternal & Child Welfare, 1967

Plant, Raymond *Social and Moral Theory in Casework*, Routledge & Kegan Paul, 1970

Powell, Len S. *Communication and Learning*, Pitman, 1969

Prins, Herschel *Evaluation and Development of Skills by Supervision*, Probation (Journal of the National Association of Probation Officers) Vol. XV, No. 3, Nov. 1969

Racker, H. *Transference and Counter-Transference*, Hogarth Press, 1963

Ragg, N. M. *Personal Philosophy and Social Work*, British Journal of Psychiatric Social Work, Vol. IX, No. 7, 1961

Rank, Otto *Will Therapy*, Alfred A. Knopf, 1936

Reid, W. J. and Shyne, A. W. *Brief and Extended Casework*, Columbia University Press, 1969

Reynolds, B. C. *Learning and Teaching in the Practice of Social Work*, 1965

Rice, A. K. *Learning for Leadership*, Tavistock, 1965

Rich, John *Interviewing Children and Adolescents*, Macmillan & Co., 1968

Richmond, Mary *Social Diagnosis*, Russell Sage Foundation, 1917

Robinson, Virginia P. *Dynamics of Supervision under Functional Controls*, University of Pennsylvania Press, 1949

Rogers, Carl *Counselling and Psychotherapy*, Houghton Mifflin, 1942

Rogers, Carl *On Becoming a Person*, Houghton Mifflin, 1961

Rogers, Carl *Client-centred Therapy*, Houghton Mifflin, 1952

Ruddock, Ralph *Roles and Relationships*, Routledge, 1969

Sainsbury, E. *Social Diagnosis in Casework*, Routledge, 1970

Salzberger-Wittenberg, I. *Psycho-Analytic Insight and Relationships*, Routledge & Kegan Paul, 1970

Sanctuary, G. *Marriage Under Stress*, George Allen & Unwin, 1968

Satir, Virginia *Conjoint Family Therapy*, 1967

Schwartz, W. and Zalba, S. *The Practice of Group Work*, Columbia University Press, 1971
1966

Sidney, E. and Brown, M. *The Skills of Interviewing*, Tavistock,

Simmel, Georg *The Sociology of Georg Simmel*, Free Press of Glencoe, 1950

Slavson, S. R. *An Introduction to Group Therapy*, Commonwealth Fund, 1943

Slavson, S. R. (ed.) *The Fields of Group Psychotherapy*, International Universities Press, 1956

Slavson, S. R. *Analytic Group Psychotherapy*, Columbia University Press, 1950

Smalley, Ruth *Theory for Social Work Practice*, Columbia University Press, 1967

Sommer, R. *Personal Space*

Sullivan, Harry Stack *The Psychiatric Interview*, Tavistock, 1955

Taft, J. J. *The Dynamics of Therapy in a Controlled Relationship*, Macmillan & Co., 1933

Taft, Jessie (ed.) *A Functional Approach to Family Casework*, University of Pennsylvania Press, 1944

Taft, Jessie (ed.) *Family Casework and Counseling*, University of Pennsylvania Press, 1948

Taylor, F. K. *The Analysis of Therapeutic Groups*, Oxford University Press, 1961

Thomas, E. J. and Biddle, B. J. *Role Theory: Concepts and Research*, Wiley, 1966

Thomas, Edwin J. *Learning Theory in Social Work*

Thompson, S. and Kahn, J. H. *The Group Process as a Helping Technique*, Pergamon, 1970

Timms, Noel *Social Casework*, Routledge & Kegan Paul, 1964

Timms, Noel *Language of Social Casework*, Routledge, 1968

Towle, Charlotte *The Learner in Education for the Professions*, University of Chicago Press, 1962

Towle, Charlotte *Common Human Needs*, National Association of Social Workers (USA), 1952

Trecker, H. B. *Social Group Work: Principles and Practice*, Whiteside Inc., 1955

Trist, E. L. and Sofer, C. *Exploration in Group Relations*, Leicester University Press, 1959

Turner, F. J. *Differential Diagnosis and Treatment in Social Work*, Free Press of Glencoe, 1968

Vass, Frank *The Application of Group Techniques in Social Work Practice*, Case Conference, Vol. XVI, No. 6, October 1969

Voiland, A. L. *Family Casework Diagnosis*, Community Research Associates, 1962

Wallis, J. A. *Counselling and Social Welfare*, Routledge, 1969

Wallis, J. H. and Booker, H. S. *Marriage Counselling*, Routledge & Kegan Paul, 1968

Wallis, J. H. *Marriage Observed*, Routledge & Kegan Paul, 1971

Watzlawick, P., Beavin, J. H., Jackson, D. D. *Pragmatics of Human Communication*, Faber & Faber, 1968

Whitaker, D. S. and Lieberman, M. A. *Psychotherapy through the Group Process*, Tavistock Press, 1965

Wildman, M. *Communication in Family Therapy*, British Journal Allen & Unwin, 1959

Willmott, Peter and Young, Michael *Family and Kinship in East London*, Routledge & Kegan Paul, 1957

Wilson, G. and Ryland, G. *Social Groupwork Practice*, Houghton Mifflin, 1949

Woodcock, G. D. C. *A Study of Beginning Supervision*, British Journal of Psychiatric Social Work, Vol. IX, No. 2, Autumn 1967

Woodcock, G. D. C. *Tutor, Supervisor and Student*, British Journal of Psychiatric Social Work, Vol. VIII, No. 3, 1966

Wootton, Barbara *Social Science and Social Pathology*, George Allen & Unwin, 1959

Wynn, Margaret *Family Policy*, Michael Joseph, 1970

Young, Priscilla *The Student and Supervision in Social Work Education*, Routledge & Kegan Paul, 1967

Younghusband, Eileen (ed.) *New Developments in Casework*, George Allen & Unwin, 1966

Younghusband, E. (ed.) *Social Work with Families*, George Allen and Unwin, 1965

Younghusband, E. (ed.) *Social Work and Social Values*, George Allen & Unwin, 1967

Zaleznik, A. and Mount, D. *The Dynamics of Inter-personal Behaviour*, Harvard University Press, 1967

Index

Acceptance, 36-9
Activity Group, 129-30
Adoption, 168-9
Advice-Giving, 29
Agency Function, 31-2, 102-4, 126-7, 149-50, 210-12
Agency Supervision, 214-17
Aichhorn, August, 24-5
Alcoholics Anonymous, 119, 125
Anger, 62
Anxiety, 60-2
Assessment, 216
Avoidance, 60

Barr, Hugh, 116
Behaviourism, 17
Bettelheim, Bruno, 87
Biestek, Felix, 23
Bott, Elizabeth, 168
Bowers, Swithun, 69, 156
Brainwashing, 10

Caplow, Theodore, 133
Catharsis, 24-9, 97-8
Charity, Organisation Society, 7, 92, 155, 182
Chicago, University of, 202
Columbia, University of, 202
Community Work, 8, 134
Confidentiality, 43-9, 170, 194-8
Confrontation, 100
Consultation, 180, 217-20
Counter-Transference, 56-9, 157-8

Defence Mechanisms, 59-64
Denial, 60
Diagnosis, 186-7
Diagnostic Approach, 202
Dicks, Henry, 144
Displacement, 60
Double-Bind, 174-5

Family Group Therapy, 171-5
Fantasy, 63
Fit, 137-40
Fostering, 169
Freud, Sigmund, 40, 114, 154, 203

Front Sheet, 183-6
Functionalism, 40, 111-13, 178, 202-3

Heterogamy, 137-8
Hill, Octavia, 13, 155, 182, 185, 205
Home Visiting, 82-6
Homogamy, 137-8
Human Rights, 47, 221-6
Hunt, J. M., 203

Intake Worker, 70, 77-9
Intellectualisation, 62
Isolation, 60

Jones, Howard, 116

Kelman, Herbert C., 9, 69, 120, 128
Kent, Bessie, 212
Kibbutz, 170
Koestler, Arthur, 11
Kogan, L. S., 203

Laing, Ronald, 171-2
Leadership, 130-2, 158-62
Learning Theory, 17
Letter Writing, 82-4

Mays, J. B., 68
Medical Social Workers, Institute of, 214
Mill, John Stuart, 41

Natural Law, 42

Office Accommodation, 79-82

Pennsylvania, University of, 40, 202
Perception, 55
Perez, Joseph, 21
Perlman, Helen Harris, 202
Personnel Management, 11
Phantasy, 63
Plan of the interview, 88-91
Positive Listening, 18
Preparation, 87-8
Primary Settings, 182
Process Recording, 192-4, 212-14

Projection, 62
Pychoanalysis, 13-14, 92

Rank, Otto, 40, 202-3
Rationalisation, 62
Reassurance, 29
Reception, 70-5
Receptionist, 71-5
Reconciliation, 150-4
Reflective Counselling, 21
Regression, 60
Relationship, 23-9
Repression, 61
Research, 180-1
Richmond, Mary, 13, 155
Rogers, Carl, 21, 204
Role-Playing, 205-9
Roles, 32-4, 159-60
Running Record, 188-92

Satir, Virginia, 172-3
Scapegoat, 65, 131-2, 153, 161-2, 175
School Counselling, 10
Secondary Setting, 181-2
Self-Determination, 39-43
Settlement Movement, 114
Silence, 101-2
Simmel, Georg, 64, 133
Smalley, Ruth, 202
Social Casework, 8

Social Groupwork, 8
Student Supervision, 209-14
Sublimation, 61
Substitution, 61
Sullivan, Harry Stack, 24, 104
Supervision, 180, 209-17
Suppression, 61

T. Group, 66
Taft, Jessie, 202
Tavistock Institute, 144
Telephonist, 71, 74
Therapeutic Communities, 115
Touch, 38, 173
Transference, 56-9, 157-8

Values, 68
Verbalisation, 20

Waiting Room, 75-7
Watson, J. B., 17
Weber, Max, 131
Will Therapy, 40-1
Willmott, Peter, 168
Withdrawal, 60
Women's Royal Voluntary Service, 76
Wootton, Barbara, 91

Young, Michael, 168